Studies in Scandinavian Literature and Culture

# Studies in Scandinavian Literature and Culture

George C. Schoolfield
Managing Editor

*Fin(s) de Siècle* in Scandinavian Perspective

Harald S. Naess, 1992
Photograph
Courtesy of Bo Elbrønd-Bek

# Fin(s) de Siècle in Scandinavian Perspective: Studies in Honor of Harald S. Naess

Edited by

Faith Ingwersen
Mary Kay Norseng

and with the
Collaboration of

Mary Eaton, Niels Ingwersen, and
Kim Nilsson

CAMDEN HOUSE

Published by Camden House, Inc.
Drawer 2025
Columbia, SC 29202 USA

Printed on acid-free paper.
Binding materials are chosen for strength and
durability.

ISBN:1-879751-24-0

**Library of Congress Cataloging-in-Publication Data**

Fin(s) de siècle in Scandinavian perspective : studies in honor of
   Harald S. Naess / edited by Faith Ingwersen, Mary Kay Norseng and
   with the collaboration of Mary Eaton, Niels Ingwersen, and Kim
   Nilsson.
         p.   cm. -- (Studies in Scandinavian literature and culture)
      Includes bibliographical references.
      ISBN 1-879751-24-0
      1. Scandinavian literature--History and criticism.
   2. Scandinavia--Civilization.  3. Scandinavian Americans--History.
   4. Næss, Harald S.--Bibliography.  I. Næss, Harald S.
   II. Ingwersen, Faith.  III. Norseng, Mary Kay.  IV. Series: Studies
   in Scandinavian literature and culture (unnumbered)
   PT7048.F56  1993
   839'.5--dc20                                                93-2049
                                                                  CIP

# Acknowledgements

The editors would like to extend their thanks to the following people and institutions for the textual material and illustrations listed below.

"Broenes skjønnhet," from the collection *Nattåpent* (1985), by the poet Rolf Jacobson's kind permission                    15

"The Nordic Nineties," a translation, thanks to the efforts of Niels Lyhne Jensen, of Jørgen Elbek's article "Halvfemserne i Norden," from *Dansk Udsyn* 70 (1990): 67-80                    55-68

Photograph of Harald S. Naess (1992), by courtesy of Bo Elbrønd-Bek                    Frontispiece

Bertel Thorvaldsen's engraved portrait of C. *Pram*, from Det Kongelige Bibliotek, Copenhagen, Denmark                    Fig. II.1  18

"Tröstlös en Herde på Hafstranden står," excerpt in musical notation, by permission of Svenska litteratursällskapet i Finland, from Allmänna Arkivet, Helsinki, Finland                    Fig. II.2  41

Edvard Munch's two versions of *Mot Skogen* (1897, 1915), in Munch-museet, Kommunes Kunstsamlinger, Oslo, Norway                    Figs. III.1-2  138

Edvard Munch's *Selvportrett med Sigarett* (1895), in Nasjonalgalleriet, Oslo, Norway                    Fig. III.3  139

August Strindberg's self-portrait (1886), in Strindbergmuseet, Stockholm, Sweden                    Fig. III.4  140

# Contents

# Preface

Some of us think of him as Naess, others as Næss, but we all think of Harald, a man whose life's work has been building bridges of communication between countries, cultures, communities, and individuals. In 1991 he retired after nearly forty years of teaching Scandinavian studies in England and the United States, first at King's College, University of Durham, in Newcastle-upon-Tyne and then at the University of Wisconsin in Madison. But his work is yet unfinished, and as professor emeritus he graciously continues in his role. His books, his editions, his articles and reviews, as well as the many papers he has given at academic forums, are an inestimable resource to Scandinavianists, students and colleagues, worldwide. His research, his writings, and his editorial efforts, documented in these pages in his bibliography, have deepened our understanding of the sweep of Norwegian literature and culture, emphasized the special greatness of the author Knut Hamsun, and expanded our view of nineteenth-century Norwegian immigration, its utopian dreams and everyday experiences.

The present volume encompasses those wide-ranging areas of life-long interest to Harald Naess in literature, music, art, and history. It has been written by his colleagues and friends, both from Europe and the United States, to honor him for his dedication to scholarship; to promoting an understanding, specifically, of Norwegian and, generally, of Scandinavian literature and culture on these now less-than-foreign shores; and for his unceasing generosity and helpfulness, as well as his hospitality, in smoothing the way for students, professors, and all others who have desired to work in the same fields.

Fin(s) de Siècle *in Scandinavian Perspective* has as its emphasis the many periods of transition that have so intrigued readers and that the present era commemorates. The work is part of the Camden House series Studies in Scandinavian Literature and Culture, which is edited by one of the present contributors, George Schoolfield. The press has given the editors a free hand and has allowed them to reflect the diversity of their contributors' interests and backgrounds. Thus Harald is literally Naess to some and Næss to others. Each article tries to maintain an inner consistency but may vary from the others with regard to the use of British or American spelling. Contributors have also made some necessary modifications of the MLA style recommended by the editors. Most quotations appear in their original languages. Written specifically for the occasion, in special tribute to Harald, are Lars Huldén's "Epistel" and Rolf Jacobsen's "Til Harald." Niels Lyhne Jensen's English translation of a Danish poem, also done specifically for the occasion, is one of the literary exceptions to the rule. On the whole, the illustrations have been suggested by the contributors in support of the book's thematic sections or their own articles.

The editors owe thanks to those many and patient contributors; to Bo Elbrønd-Bek for his frontispiece photograph; to Lawrence Berge for the illustrations of immigrant life that he has contributed from the area of the Naess residence; to Thomasin Ringler for her pen-and-ink drawing of Harald Naess; to Ann Mari and Petter Naess for their factual help; to Judy Anderson for keeping the financial records. We owe very special thanks, however, to Steven Sondrup, who has presented the camera-ready copy, and to Mary Eaton, without whom the many disks for Steven could not have been made, library research survived, or proofreading endured. She has worked with a dedication that is truly in the Naess spirit.

In addition the editors thank all those fellow scholars and friends who have helped to make this work possible and who appear here in the *Tabula Gratulatoria*. We thank the Department of Scandinavian Studies at the University of Wisconsin and the Scandinavian Section at UCLA. And, most particularly and gratefully, we thank Bjørn Jensen of the Kongelige Utenriksdepartement, Oslo, and John Bjørnebye and the Norwegian Information Service, under whose auspices the seed money for the project was given.

At last we thank Harald Naess for his devotion, his originality, and his ability to make of life an inspiring, all-embracing work of art.

Faith Ingwersen
Mary Kay Norseng

# Tabula Gratulatoria

Samuel Abrahamsen
Finn Afzelius
Gulbrand Alhaug
A. Gerald Anderson
Judy Anderson
Margy Angle
Kathy Saranpa Anstine

Lawrence Berge
Marybeth Berger
Edvard Beyer
Pål Bjørby
John Bjørnebye, Generalkonsul,
    Kgl. Norsk Generalkonsulat,
    New York
Zoe Borovsky
Susan Brantly
Elias Bredsdorff
Paula Brekke
Birgit Jaastad Brokenleg
Delores J. Buttry
Lars Bäckström
Ulla-Britt and Lennart Bäckström

Birgitta and John R. Christianson
Marlene Ciklamini
Ingrid Claréus
Nancy L. Coleman
David Cooperman

Jørgen Elbek
Bo Elbrønd-Bek
Jerker A. Eriksson
Stanley and Barbara Ewanowski

Haskell Fain
Marna Feldt
Jostein Fet
Gunnar Foss

Kari Ellen Gade
Janet Garton
Betsy Geiger
Steinar Gimnes
Carol Gold
Charlotte Schiander Gray
John Greenway

Otto Hageberg
Peggy E. Hager
Peter Hallaråker
Peter Hallberg
Katherine Hanson
Jorunn Hareide
Einar Haugen
Birgitta Holm
Ola Holmgren
Lars Huldén
Lloyd Hustvedt
Julianne Haahr

Silja Ikäheimonen-Lindgren
Tove Ilsaas and Helge Pharo
Lanae Isaacson

Rolf Jacobsen
Raymond Jarvi
Bjørn Jensen, Ekspedisjonssjef,
    Det Kgl. Utenriksdepartement, Oslo
Niels Lyhne Jensen
Glyn and Kirsten Jones
Aage Jørgensen

Marianne E. Kalinke
Martha W. Keister
Catherine Hiebert Kerst
James E. Knirk
Ingeborg Kongslien
Helga Kress
H. Peter Krosby
Karen H. and Robert B. Kvavik

Barbara Lide
Asmund Lien
Odd Lovoll
Torborg Lundell

Amy van Marken
Leonie A. Marx
James Massengale
Marshall N. Matson
Margareta Mattsson
James and Kathleen McFarlane
John McGalliard
Duncan M. Mennie
P. M. Mitchell
Hans Möller

Gerhard B. Naeseth
Petter Naess
Jim Nelson
Stanley and Violet Nielsen
Usha Nilsson
Bertil Nolin
Annika Normark
Lisa Nygaard
Margaret Hayford O'Leary

Rose Marie Oster
Erik Østerud

Sarah Paulson
Knud Pedersen
Robyn G. Peterson
Göran and Ulla Printz-Påhlson
Inga-Britt Persson

Janet Rasmussen
Sue Reindollar
Donald C. Riechel
Karen and Dick Ringler
Thomasin Ringler
Elizabeth Rokkan
Dominika and Sven H. Rossel
Øystein Rottem
Oddveig Røsegg

Karin Sanders
George Schoolfield
Larry E. Scott
Arne Selbyg
Monica Setterwall
Frankie and Jole Shackelford
Orville Shetney
Ross Shideler
Stefanie Rose Shreffler
Leif T. Sjöberg
Steven P. Sondrup
LuAnn Sorenson
Charles G. Spetland
Kate Kulzick Stafford
Birgitta K. Steene
Kathleen M. Stokker
Torbjørn Støverud
Larry E. Syndergaard
Inga Söderblom

Jane Tammany
Martha Taylor
Laurie and Birgitta Thompson
Playford V. Thorson
Seija Tiisala
Dawn Tommerdahl
Egil Törnqvist

*Ingrid Urberg*

*Halldis Moren Vesaas*
*Richard B. Vowles*

*Carla Waal*
*Ingrid A. Weatherhead*
*Arnold Weinstein*
*John Weinstock*
*Marie Wells*
*Olaug and Inge Wettergreen-Jensen*
*Rochelle Wright*

*Solveig Zempel*
*Virpi Zuck*

*Sigurd Aarnes*
*Asbjørn Aarseth*
*Elisabeth Aasen*

Institutions

*American-Scandinavian Foundation*
*The Dept. of Scandinavian Studies,*
    *University of Wisconsin, Madison*
*Norvik Press*
*Norwegian Information Service,*
    *United States*
*The Scandinavian Section, UCLA*
*Swenson Swedish Immigration*
    *Research Center*
*University College London*
*University of Minnesota*
*University of Oslo International*
    *Summer School*

. . . the *fin* has come a little early this *siècle*.

Angela Carter,
"Grace Paley . . . ," 1980

# I. Introduction

# EPISTEL

*Angående Harald Naess hemfärd från*
*Van Hise Hall en vårdag 1991.*
*Sjunges som*
*Solen glimmar blank och trind*
*av Bellman*

Stämmom upp en sång om Harald från norska fjällen.
Man vet om att han är bra
på de flesta ställen.
Nu är han på hemväg stadd
från Van Hise Hall; ingen gadd
lämnar han nånstans. Oskadd
far han hem till kvällen.

Solen glimmar kring hans färd
över hav och länder.
Skålar är den mannen värd;
glädjens eld han tänder
i vart sinne och var själ.
Tack! Men långtifrån farväl.
Hövding lika väl som träl
trycker Haralds händer.

Se hans höbåt simmar fram
lastad till kajutan.
Lärdom tung som makadam
är det tvivelsutan
som han har i sina rum
där han far på fluidum.
Men av sång och gaudium
skakar ändå skutan.

Vilka sitter i hans mäss?
Vilka höjer sången?
Skepparn själv, han Harald Naess
håller alla stången.
Hamsun, Ibsen, Olav Duun,
ingen, knappt en taifun
trotsar Harald med basun,
när han drar i gång'en.

Många städer har han sett
där som kunskap vördas.
Många papper har han gett,
varav ära skördas.
Särskilt om de nämnda tre
har han gett oss vetande.
Kan det sannas värde se
och det oerhördas.

Vimpeln fläktar i hans mast
på hans väg mot dalen,
där sin farkost han gör fast
och tar ut ur svalen
en väl införtjänad läsk;
administrationens träsk
har han sluppit: Låt en bäsk
krydda madrigalen.

Ann Mari Hans egen vän
vallar fårahjorden.
Sakta faller skymningen
i den Nya Norden.
Drag av Shangri La den bär,
dalen där kollegers här
gärna hur som helst och när
bänkar sig kring borden.

*I bästa välmening skrivet*
*av Lars Huldén*

# Harald Naess: The Newcastle Years

## Leif Sjöberg

In the fall of 1953 Harald Naess was appointed "Lektor" in Norwegian at King's College, Newcastle-Upon-Tyne, Northumberland, in northeast England at a salary of six-hundred pounds annually. Among Harald's colleagues were Niels Lyhne Jensen and James Walter McFarlane, both to be eminent Scandinavianists, both known internationally, both handpicked by the chairman of the German and Scandinavian Department, Dr. Duncan Mennie, a Scotsman and great friend and supporter of Scandinavian studies.

McFarlane, who of course was British, had studied at Oxford and contributed unsigned articles and reviews to the *Times Literary Supplement*. By 1956, when I arrived, he had given an important university lecture on Hamsun and would give an inspiring one on Ibsen, (which was later to turn into "The Oxford Ibsen").

Niels Lyhne Jensen, who spoke like a Lord and did his utmost to out-British the British, would bear comparison with V. S. Naipaul in his manner of speaking, while his command of current theatre idiom shone in his articles on new plays for the stage-bills at Newcastle theatres. Harald Naess, who had a British mother and, for all his genuine Norwegianess, was for all practical purposes bilingual, contributed substantial survey essays on various aspects of Norwegian literature to *Modern Languages*.

## Niels Lyhne Jensen on the First Years

Harald came with his family to King's College and soon showed himself to be a many-sided talent. Without learned airs he was extraordinarily knowledgeable in Nordic literature, but he was also very much at his ease in art and music. What is more, when he acquired a house (at 9 Tankerville Terrace), he tirelessly undertook all kinds of repair work, which often took place during late-night hours. He painted the hallway, three stories high, in a lush geranium red and the balusters of the mahogany handrail, maybe a hundred of them, in gray, white, and gold, as in old Norwegian manor houses. The intricate patterns of the stucco ceilings Harald, together with his wife, Ann Mari, painted in even more [varied] colours.

He soon emerged as a serious rival both to me and to Robert Sinclair (a lecturer in German, who rented the ground floor from the Naesses) on the antiques market, where he quickly showed his flair in that field, too.

One summer [Harald] took six or seven grandfather clocks home with him to Norway. In the clock cases he had also placed the family's clothes and linen for the long summer sojourn in Norway. It looked, as a porter remarked, as if he were bringing home his ancestors in coffins.

As a teacher Harald was patience personified, even to students whose diligence and talents could be rather problematic. It goes without saying that he was dearly loved, not only by the matriculated university students, but also by those in evening school. As one of the latter expressed it at Harald's departure for Madison, Wisconsin, "A wos the doonce of the class, but A laaked yew, Mr. Naess."

Even on short notice Harald was able to demonstrate his talent, as when with riskily short rehearsal time we performed scenes from Holberg's comedies. Harald made an unforgettable Jakob in *Erasmus Montanus*, giving the character all his "lystighed og lune."

It is well known that Harald was an incomparable raconteur, thanks to his humour and good-natured irony. One example will have to suffice here. At a conference in Lillehammer a young Norwegian highflier got entangled in such deep thoughts on poetry and the theory of relativity that he had to give up. "Well," said Harald, "it became so complicated that finally he could not understand it himself" (Niels Lyhne Jensen, University of Aarhus; slightly edited letter, dated December 9, 1991).

Attendance at Friday coffee — meetings of the department when Professor Mennie ruled — was mandatory. This led to an easy exchange of information and helped create a team spirit. After departmental business was done, discussion might focus on John Osborne's "angry young man," Colin Wilson's *The Outsider*, Kingsley Amis's *Lucky Jim*, or Iris Murdoch's *The Sandcastle*.

## Murder in the Cathedral and Mr. Olsen

Imagine my surprise, after a production of Eliot's *Murder in the Cathedral* had been cussed and discussed heatedly for an interminable time, and there came a moment of silence, which I thought would mark the end of all discussion, when Harald revived it by quietly telling what seemed to be an irrelevant story (here slightly edited) of Mrs. Olsen's husband as Sherlock Holmes:

When I [Harald recounted] did the Norway section of *The Year's Work in Modern Languages*, I would travel up to London during the Easter vacation and work at the University College Library in Gower Street. I stayed at one Mrs. Olsen's near Hampstead Heath. Mrs. Olsen was a former nurse who ran a little boarding house for students; it was dirt cheap, ten shillings a day for board (two meals) and lodging. Mrs. Olsen was Scottish and had gotten her Norwegian name by nursing and later marrying a sailor from Bergen. She was a marvelously contradictory character who could be bright and to the point, at other times very entertaining, full of stories of what was happening in the neighborhood, sometimes quite fantastic things. We all wondered what Mr. Olsen was like, but we never saw him — I believe he was working the night shift.

I had been interested in cathedrals, and one day I told Mrs. Olsen I would like to visit Canterbury, just to be able to say I had seen the building. After all, it wasn't too far away, and Archbishop Eystein of Norway had stayed there and possibly gotten some of his ideas for the magnificent Nidaros [Trondheim] Cathedral. The next day Mrs. Olsen told me her husband would like to come along, as he was free on Sunday. We took the train. Mr. Olsen turned out to be a quiet gentleman, soft-spoken, in a Bergen dialect of much charm. We talked about his experiences as a sailor during World War II and how he had come to settle in London.

At Canterbury he brought out lunch prepared by Mrs. Olsen, marvellous food, which we enjoyed sitting on a bench outside the cathedral. Suddenly something fell out of his bag and dropped to the ground. It looked like a large magnifying glass, which it was.

Mr. Olsen had come to Canterbury to look for blood, and while I studied the flying buttresses, he stayed mostly in the area around the altar, like an eager Sherlock Holmes, investigating the murder that had taken place there 785 years earlier. I have tried many times to revisualize my impressions of Canterbury, but all I can see is Mr. Olsen kneeling at the alter with his magnifying glass.

Thus Harald concluded his story. Who knows if he was not also thinking of literary historians with or without magnifying glasses.

## The Last Nobleman

Ibsen's Rosmer has a dream of ennobling mankind by making them abstinent noblemen. As it is, it remains a noble or not-so-noble notion. Swedes point out that the idea may have been brought to Ibsen by a real Swedish nobleman, Count Carl Snoilsky (1841-1903), who visited the Ibsens when they were summering at Molde. At any rate, Norway does not have any nobility of its own. Harald apparently got tired of hearing about this, because he presented a true story of how he himself met Norway's last Nobleman:

Yes, it's true, unlike Denmark and Sweden, Norway has no nobility, and I [explained Harald] might say that I have met Norway's last nobleman. There was a telephone call one day from the Immigration Authority. They had a Norwegian there on a ship [that had] arrived that afternoon from Bergen, one Carsten Anker, who said he had come to study at the university. There was apparently something irregular about his papers, and they needed a guarantee of some kind. Would I be prepared to sign one for fifty pounds? Well, that was more money than I had, but considering the name of Carsten Anker — the man who hosted Norway's constitutional assembly at his estate in Eidsvoll in 1814 — I felt I could safely risk that considerable sum. However, could I see the man first? Yes, that was possible, and the following day he came to my office. I had been wondering if he would look like his great-great-great . . . that is, tall, aquiline face, charming, though with a touch of arrogance?

He was a little, old-looking man, face pockmarked, with rounded features, and he had the humble manner of a clerk, not so much Uriah Heep as Dostoevski's Marmeladov. He seemed somewhat simple. He had come here to study, and it was important for him to do well, for he could not bear to disappoint his young wife, a librarian who meant everything to him.

It appeared that he was a descendant not only of Carsten Anker, but on his mother's side also of Count Herman Wedel Jarlsberg, Norway's last nobleman, and with a burst of humour, he said, "There you see what that much nobility adds up to." I signed his papers, of course.

## The Anglo-Scandinavian Society

Dr. Mennie provided leadership, inspiration, ideas, and — not least important — free premises and help with announcements and mailings. Ms. Steele was the secretary. As a committee member Harald addressed the group, as did other members of the Scandinavian Department, such as James Walter McFarlane, Niels Lyhne Jensen, Duncan M. Mennie, and I myself. Other speakers were Carl Hambro, Paul Brandberg, Sven Arne Bergmann, all from London; Irene Scobbie, Glasgow; Gladys Hird, Auckland, New Zealand; and many visiting scholars from Scandinavia.

After my lecture with music illustrations on Franz Berwald, a young, well-dressed lady from Gothenburg, Inger Wallervik, came up to me and said she liked my presentation. I was so surprised that I married her, the choice of my life.

There were many wonderful social and intellectual activities of the Anglo-Scandinavian Society, that is, the excursions to Hadrian's Wall, Bamburgh Castle, the Farne Islands, the Holy Island, the Lake District, the Riveaux Abbey, Durham Castle and Durham Cathedral.

Most of those excursions were arranged by the Honorary Swedish Consul, Stig Nilebrant. Excursions of a different kind were the long walks and talks with my friend W. H. Beck from King's to Henderson Hall.

## White Nightshirts

Before the Lucia, "Queen of Light," tradition had a chance to develop at King's, some cultural gaps had to be gotten over. No one among the students and others at King's admitted to using white nightshirts, and, of course, without nightshirts, no Lucia. Ever resourceful, Professor Mennie advised the Anglo-Scandinavian Society of Tyneside to advertise in the *Evening Chronicle*. Said and done: "Urgently needed: White Nightshirts. All sizes. Rewards. King's College area. Telephone . . ."

They came from Westgate and Newgate, Gallowgate and Grainger, Nun Street and Fun Street, Bigg Groat and Little Queen, Northumberland and Lambton Road, Ponteland and Tynemouth, Cochrane Park and Jesmond Dene; married, unmarried, widowed or withered, but most of them stately, elderly ladies, a horde of them, with red cheeks, storming into Sydenham Terrace 6 and unceremoniously parting with the white nightshirts in their possession for a few shillings [a somewhat poetic expansion of Niels Jensen's dry, yet nostalgic, account, December 9, 1991: "Havde man blot bevaret disse klenodier til idag"]. At any rate, the Lucia was saved!

## Queen of Light, Tyneside Style

To our delight the local papers carried pictures of our Queen of Light (generally chosen by Dr. Mennie from among his students). A young blonde from Gothenburg, Ms. Olsson, with a good singing voice, had been selected, but owing to a misunderstanding she failed to show up for the dress rehearsal arranged for the photographers and journalists. Patiently awaiting her arrival for twenty-five minutes, the photographers stated firmly, but politely, that they would leave unless they could shoot "The Queen of Light" immediately.

Here was a dilemma. We "lektors" represented nothing less than Scandinavia, and here we had to make a delicate instantaneous decision: suddenly picking a brand new Lucia, which we did, with unexpected consequences. Harald and I picked a pretty, dark-haired student, Ms. (Joan) Williamson, who acted the part of the Lucia with finesse and style, after she was made to realize that the symbolism and the rites of Saint Lucy precluded smoking cigarettes and beating time with one's bare feet, as she first did. It must be admitted that if her singing in Swedish was not exactly beyond hope, it turned out original in the extreme. She simply had inadequate training — but as Harald assured me: that won't be visible in the picture! True enough! The photographers were excited to see the new dark-haired Lucia and on December 5, 1957, put a large picture of her in borrowed nightshirt and all into the London *Daily Mirror* (with a run of 1.6 million copies).

## Harald the Organist

When the organist at the Danish Seamen's Church (Eslington Road) in Newcastle, emigrated to Denmark, Harald stepped in and played the hymns, liturgical ornaments, preludes, and toccatas necessary. Even on short notice it was no problem for him, except that the local pastor had a predilection for hymns with a minimum of eight to nine verses. Harald, with much on his mind (from teaching and research), would sometimes continue playing the organ when there were no more verses, or, contrariwise, abruptly stop playing when there were still one or two verses to go. How to solve such a problem?

With permission from the Lutheran Evangelical State Church of Denmark and the blessing of the local Pastor, Harald installed a driver's rearview mirror on the organ and placed his son Petter so that his little hand, upstretched at the end of each verse, was reflected in the mirror. As Petter pointed one more finger into the air for each verse played, Harald literally knew "hur psalmerna gick." No one seemed to think that it was remarkable that the Lecturer in Norwegian at King's could play the Danish organ. We took it for granted: a well-rounded education includes the ability to play more than one instrument!

The Danish Seamen's Church drew us all. The reading room of the church became a natural meeting-place for Tyne-siders interested in things Scandinavian. In the church's upper regions Niels Lyhne Jensen, Lecturer in Danish, presided with all his learning in European humanities and displayed his Danish culinary arts. If the church became one of our bastions, the Scandinavian Department, at 6 Sydenham Terrace, was the other.

\* \* \*

For all of us who served in the Scandinavian Department at the University of Newcastle, those years became an indispensable preparation for our continued university careers — at the Madison campus of the University of Wisconsin, where Harald Naess served until retirement (as Richard B. Vowles discusses in his essay) and where James McFarlane and Niels Lyhne Jensen served as Visiting Professors; at Norwich, University of East Anglia, where McFarlane served until his retirement and Niels Jensen taught for many years; at Aarhus, where Niels Jensen taught until his retirement, and at Columbia University, New York, and at Stony Brook, where I taught until my retirement.

It was all made possible by the work and effort of two Scotsmen, the strong man, Duncan M. Mennie, and his deputy, Robert Sinclair, and their conviction that Scandinavia was almost absurdly underrepresented and that there was a need for Scandinavian experts in Newcastle. Together, they created what was arguably the best training ground for Scandinavianists in Great Britain, and Harald Naess was one of the finest.

A version of this restrospective appeared in *Norway Times* May 17, 1992, Brooklyn, N.Y.

# Harald Naess: The Madison Years

## Richard B. Vowles

"WE HAD A BALL" may seem a hackneyed expression applied to an outmoded institution, but it didn't appear so on the night of 27 April 1991 at Madison's Concourse Hotel. The occasion was a surprise party of more than one hundred (in itself, something of a miracle) for Harald Naess, a tribute marking his retirement from the University of Wisconsin. American institutions were well represented, from UCLA to Harvard, from Texas to British Columbia, and scholars from five foreign countries were on hand. The mix included secretaries, students past and present, colleagues, two university presidents, a geographer of renown, and a musicologist. The spirit was wonderful; the professional became familial as it, at best, should be. And as the evening wore on, Chicagoans were heard to remark, in their native argot, it was not so much a ball as it was a wang dang doodle.

Harald Naess taught 32 of his 38 teaching years at the University of Wisconsin. He and I came here at almost exactly the same time, I both inside and outside the department (a joint appointment with Comparative Literature); so I think I am peculiarly qualified to survey Harald's career. He came on a Fulbright in 1959, as a temporary replacement for Einar Haugen. When Haugen's move to Harvard seemed imminent, he went to unusual lengths — along with Wisconsin's two senators — to get Harald's visa status changed so that he could remain in this country.

So it came to pass that Harald Naess was next in a distinguished lineage that has made this the oldest Scandinavian department in the U.S.: Rasmus B. Anderson (1869-83), Julius E. Olson (1883-1931), and Einar Haugen (1931-64). There was little more than this monolithic continuity, except for the interim aid of a talented housewife or a graduate student. Then came the expansive '60s with the growth of the department to approximately ten, depending on how you count part-time appointments, and with this the development of the program to comprehend undergraduate, graduate, and area studies curricula. All of this happened under the careful guidance of HN, who was chairman from 1962 to 1968, after which he could turn over the reins to the rest of us who, in orderly and harmonious fashion, served three-year stints (Naess was back at the helm from 1983 to 1986). Appropriately, HN became Torger Thompson Professor in 1967, assuming the name-chair mantle from Einar Haugen, who had engineered this major bequest, which also guarantees support for a number of graduate students.

In those first years HN taught just about everything in the book, and then some — frequently exceeding the load limit. He always maintained that his major concern was teaching, before research and administration. It might be said, in passing, that the department has always been united, if only in its healthy disregard for deans, particularly demonstrable during times of campus unrest. HN has been the benign presence behind us all.

As the department grew, HN was able, increasingly, to coordinate his teaching with his research, first on Knut Hamsun and later on Scandinavian immigrants in America. But throughout his teaching career he was responsible for such staples as Ibsen, third-year Norwegian, and "Bibliography and Research" (for graduate students). And he never lost interest in "Life and Civilization," a broadly based survey of what was going on geographically, geologically, historically, and culturally in all of "Norden," an impossible task, of course, but all the more compelling on that account. We experimented with the staff, the approach, and the materials in all kinds of ways. The course, more than any other, was constantly undergoing change, not always for the better. In addition to a certain centrality in the department, it accomplished three things: (1) it brought in for guest appearances Scandinavian specialists from virtually all disciplines on the campus; (2) it necessitated a spirit of team-teaching and self-appraisal that carried over to other courses, chiefly the literary surveys; (3) it revealed the sad paucity of an encompassing text, which manifested itself annually in the scramble for tourist pamphlets (at least they were free) and a confusing flurry of xeroxed handouts (by no means free nor exactly risk-free from copyright laws). In 1981 HN rose to the occasion and launched a series of pamphlets, or fascicles, under the title of *Wisconsin Introductions to Scandinavia* (with the pleasant acronym of WITS), so far devoted to the history, geography, languages, and some of the literature of Scandinavia, each coming from a distinguished specialist. Previously HN had been a strong editorial presence in any number of projects: the Nordic Council Translation Series, *Americana-Norvegica*, and special issues of the *Literary Review* and *Scandinavian Studies*.

Original scholarship has come in a steady and — as it seems — effortless flow. Knut Hamsun dominates, beginning with *Knut Hamsun og Amerika* (1969), which explores in detail Hamsun's four years in the Midwest and their influence on his writing long after his return to Europe. "Well documented . . . an example of careful scholarship . . . impressive for its readability . . . an excellent study," wrote Gerald Thurson in *Scandinavian Studies* (43 [1971]: 205-06). The next major event was the appearance of *Knut*

*Hamsun* (1984), which rises far above the multitudinous and often uneven volumes of the Twayne Series (in the series' favor one should note that finally American publishing gives its due to Scandinavian writing, largely through the careful shepherding of Leif Sjöberg). "A brilliant introduction to a complex and ambiguous body of work," wrote Rolf Nyboe Nettum, himself a major Hamsun authority. "The amount of material may seem oppressive, but Naess combines a sure eye for the development within Hamsun's output with a sensitive feel for the value of individual works. The result is then something more than an introduction: it is a personal interpretation and assessment." "[As for] Hamsun's *message of joy*: Naess deserves particular thanks because he never loses sight of this dimension" (*Scandinavica* 24 [1985]: 233-35). And now, in collaboration with James McFarlane, a selection of Knut Hamsun's letters has appeared, for an English-reading public. This is by way of prelude and appetizer to a full edition of the letters, which HN has been busy rounding up. Ultimately, and well into HN's pensioned years, we can expect the significant biography of that complicated and still embattled man of letters. I am sure there will be no diminution of vitality and understanding.

There are few corners of Norwegian literature that have not been penetrated at some time or other. HN has devoted critical attention to Henrik Ibsen, Olav Duun, Tarjei Vesaas, Aksel Sandemose, Stein Mehren, and Rolf Jacobsen; he is the editor — and writer of parts — of the forthcoming Norwegian volume in the University of Nebraska Press's projected literary history of Scandinavia. Nor has he disdained the routine but vital chores. For years he compiled the annual Scandinavian literary bibliographies for the Modern Language Association of America and for *The Year's Work in Modern Languages*. Writing of the accreted material, *Norwegian Literary Bibliography 1956-1970* (Oslo, 1975), which picked up where Øksnevad left off, Ronald Popperwell observed: "It is good that a scholar of Professor Naess's standing has not thought it beneath his dignity to compile a bibliography, a work which is frequently undervalued, making young scholars wonder whether, career-wise, it is worth doing. The paradoxical thing is that a good bibliography will exceed in usefulness and outlive many (? most) of the items it contains" (*Scandinavica* 17 [1978]: 75).

Increasingly HN's scholarship and teaching, hand in hand, have dealt with ethnicity, beginning with the U.S. Bicentennial and the concomitant Scanpresence conferences in Minneapolis and Duluth and perhaps intensified by the Naesses' "return to the soil," the gradual move from 2110 Chamberlain Avenue to the historically quintessential Norwegian farm community of Springdale, Wisconsin, just east of Mt. Horeb.

In the area of representation, HN has hardly been remiss. I have images of his rehearsing the Bellman singers, presenting programs for the local chapter of the Sons of Norway, giving a brilliant impromptu lecture for the Ygdrasil Literary Society when the scheduled speaker failed to show, and I am told that he has even addressed the male elitist Torskeklubb of Madison.

He has visited practically every Norwegian enclave in the Midwest, not just the academic ones, and in 1970 he was the Lithgow Osborne Lecturer for the American-Scandinavian Foundation. He has been steadily active in the Society for the Advancement of Scandinavian Study, serving as its editor in 1973-77 and its president in 1967-69. His special visitations, on Norwegian business, have been widely dispersed: New Haven, Los Angeles, Winston-Salem, Houston, Palm Beach. In short, he has been, and continues to be, one of Norway's best diplomats. It was entirely appropriate that he be dubbed, in 1986, Knight First Class of the Royal Norwegian Order of St. Olaf.

Conversely, he has entertained a steady stream of Scandinavian luminaries on his country acres, Maridal, as they have recently been named. Visitors will not soon forget those mellow summer evenings on the greensward, with Harald decanting wine and Ann Mari serving a not less than spectacular hickory nut pie. Evenings are not always so mellow in Madison, and others will remember a peculiarly Naessian ritual, namely, the fish boil at Picnic Point on Christmas Eve. Whence what occult Nordic rite nobody knows; this has always been a more private ceremony — and just as well considering risks of weather; but as long as the Naesses and Kim Nilsson remain in Madison, this rite will go on — but only for the stalwarts.

What, then, is the essence of Naessdom? Wide-ranging intelligence, from linguistics to ovinology (sheep culture to you). Accessibility: nothing is so urgent that Harald doesn't have time for you. Modesty, a disappearing, but still very real, scholarly virtue. Geniality, patience, and generosity as the only way to cope with feckless tenants, rude neighbors, unreliable workmen, uncooperative nature, and rigid authority — all those examples of inelasticity that Bergson found at the heart of comedy. So we hear of Ann Mari being butted by a goat, her dog being slapped with a ticket for loitering while she was inside the campus ice cream emporium. Harald falling from a tree, power saw in hand — at full throttle. Harald backing into a campus police car and then immediately signing a statement absolving the copper of any responsibility, he who shouldn't have been there. Innocents abroad. Our hearts go out to them. The genius here lies in self-irony and in the ability to translate life's indignities into a comic scenario. Harald takes great pleasure in doing just that, and it puts us in a community together.

Harald Naess has every right to bask in his knighthood, but I suspect he appreciates just as much the retirement accolade of one of our former students, George Hesselberg, the popular columnist of the *Wisconsin State Journal* (21 May 1991): "Naess is the first person I ever met who really does have a twinkle in his eye. He is proof that a person can be a gentleman, scholar, wit, and farmer, all in one. *Lykke til.*"

*Til Harald Næss*

Det hører med til en dikters jobb å måtte reise rundt
og lese dikt. I mange år av mitt liv har jeg fartet
rundt med boken under armen — men aldri har jeg opplevd
en slik opplesningsaften som ved Madison-universitetet
en påskekveld en gang midt i 1970-årene.

Harald Næss hadde tilkaldt dikteren Robert Bly og vi leste
vekselvis norsk og engelsk. — Det kom dobbelt så mange
som beregnet, det store auditoriet var mere enn overfylt.
Og vi holdt på dobbelt så lenge. Aldri — hverken før
eller senere har jeg hatt et så våkent og engasjert
publikum. Salen formelig kokte av spørsmål. Jeg hadde av
og til inntrykk av at mange av tilhørerne hadde mere greie
på nyere norsk litteratur enn jeg selv. Jeg innså snart at
her var jeg under palmene i en oase.

Tar jeg ikke feil er nettopp Madison-universitetets norske
og nordiske seksjon et slags sentrum for studiene av norsk
og nordisk litteratur i hele USA. Og mannen bak det hele
var professor Harald Næss.

Jeg ble i Madison i flere dager. Det ble både presse og
radio. To ganger var jeg ute på familien Næss' idyll av en
sørlandsfarm vest for byen. Mange små hus, mange dyr og
blomster. Men blåveisen fikk han ikke til. Den ble hvit,
han mente det kom av solen. — Men hør her Harald Næss.
— Hva med å plante dem i skyggen. Og gi dem litt ekstra
med kalk.

Ta imot min hilsen og takk. — Med dette diktet fra
*Nattåpent.*

— — —

*Rolf Jacobsen*

## BROENES SKJØNNHET

Stål eller sten. Der står de
brospennenes strenge buer
meislet inn i landskapet
som porter til fred.

Verrazano Narrow Bridge, Bosporus,
Rheinbrücke, Sotra-
og Sortlandsspennene, Golden Gate
lysende som smykker, blomsterkranser,
kniplinger kastet gjennom luften:
Min hånd i din. Kom over og se.

— — —

Regnbuen sier: Se på meg. Jeg er en bro.
Jeg er et tegn på himlen. Bygg broer.
Bøy dere. Løft armene til en bue.
Bind sammen. Bryt lenker. Bygg.

Se stålsøyler og tårn mot skyene: En bro.
Hør vindfløyten mellom wirene: En bro.
To mennesker møtes. Ansiktene blusser: En bro.
Ord som blir sagt. Hengivelse, fred: En bro.

The social, friendly, honest man,
Whate'er he be,
'Tis he fulfills great Nature's plan,
And none but he!

Robert Burns, "Second Epistle
to J. Lapraik," 1786

II. *Fin de Siècle*: The 1700s

Fig. II.1

Bertel Thorvaldsen, *C. Pram*
Engraved portrait
Det Kongelige Bibliotek, Copenhagen

# C. H. Pram: A Norwegian Writer and Patriot of the Late Eighteenth Century

## Niels Lyhne Jensen

CHRISTEN HENRIKSEN PRAM (1756-1821) is a central figure in the group of Norwegian poets who were so prominent on the Dano-Norwegian literary scene during the last decades of the eighteenth century. One contemporary critic hailed Pram as Ewald's successor, which he certainly was not. Pram was, however, productive in all the genres that the age held in high regard: heroids, Nordic tales, heroic dramas, bourgeois comedies, opera scenarios, landscape poems, congratulatory and obituary poems, and an epic of fifteen cantos, *Stærkodder* (by Pram modestly described as merely a rhymed chronicle). Only part of this output — perhaps mercifully — has been included in the six volumes of *Udvalgte digteriske Arbejder* (or *UDA*, 1824-29) his friend K. L. Rahbek published after his death. Posterity, alas, has had no use for them. Even more than his contemporaries' Pram's is a forgotten name. Who could say that one line of his is today remembered? That holds true of Pram's criticism, though in the 1780s and 1790s he was an important publicist and reviewer. Pram was Rahbek's co-editor of *Minerva*, from 1785 to 1790, and singlehandedly carried on until 1793, when he resigned as he felt that the powers-that-be frowned upon an article of his expressing moderate sympathy for the ideas of the French Revolution. His literary pursuits are all the more impressive since he earned his living as an energetic and efficient civil servant in the economic and commercial office of the Crown and in the eighties even found time to publish a newsletter.

Christen Henriksen Pram was born the son of a parson at Lesje in Gudbrandsdalen on 4 September 1756. When he was eight years of age, his father got a position in Slaglunde in North Zealand. Though Pram was to spend most of his life in Denmark, he considered himself a Norwegian, always stressing his Norwegian ancestry and allegiance. At Slaglunde Pram had his upbringing and education, until he was admitted to the

University in Copenhagen as a private student. He studied jurisprudence, but as his interest in literature, classical and modern, took up most of his time, he left his Alma Mater without a degree. His father, though without means, was well-connected, and Pram himself, after a period as a tutor with a distinguished family and a precarious spell as a free-lance writer, got his own post as a civil servant, in which he remained in various capacities until 1816, when he was rather brusquely retired on a meagre pension. Pram, though impecunious, married early, an equally penniless Bergen girl, a match that turned out rather unharmonious, what with Pram's tempestuous temperament, what with his wife's being ever fretful, disgruntled, and ailing. He still dutifully supported her right on to her demise in 1819 after protracted infirmity. Pram, described as the most virtuous of men, except for the sixth commandment, condoned young Jens Baggesen's worshipping her as his Muse and "Sus-Mamma" and addressing her as Seline in a series of high-flowing love poems.

Pram was immensely active in the intellectual life of his day. In 1789 he made contact with academics at the University of Lund, an initiative that was rather unusual to take in Denmark at that time and one of which he has given an account in the epistle "En Rejse over Sundet," 1825. In 1796 he was a co-founder of a Scandinavian literary society, which made him a forerunner of things to come. Needless to say, Pram was interested in everything concerning his native land of Norway. In 1795 he won a prize for an essay concerning the establishment of a university in Christiania, cogently arguing that a country so different from Denmark needed a seat of learning of its own. Pram's employment in the royal office of economics and commerce sent him to Norway on two missions, one from June 1804 to the spring of 1805, another from June 1806 up to the end of the year. His account of his travels in the dioceses of Trondheim, Aggersborg, and Christiansand — supported with numerous economic-statistical tables, diagrams and drawings — goes to ten handwritten volumes and is a mine of information about the agricultural, economic, demographic, and social state of Norway at the time. Apart from extracts it remains unpublished. The report on the burning of kelp in the coastal regions, with its economic, social, and ecological effects, is eminently readable, showing Pram's thoroughness and investigatory zeal.

Pram hailed Norway's declaration of independence and adoption of a constitution in 1814 with enthusiasm, but he openly expressed his resentment when the Storting adopted the Swedish King as sovereign of Norway. This outspokenness probably foiled Pram's hopes of obtaining a chair at the University of Christiantia, which started up in 1813, or a post in the Norwegian civil service, for which he would have been so eminently qualified. In addition his stance was frowned upon by the Danish absolute monarch, who spotted a revolutionary in his loyal and meritorious servant.

When, much to Pram's chagrin, he was prematurely pensioned off in 1816, he found it impossible to make ends meet. He incurred debts as often before, and as a way out he applied for the post as head of the customs and excise office in the Danish West Indies, the salary and perks of which he hoped would bring his finances on an even keel. In 1819 he got the appointment at last. Before his departure in the spring of 1820 friends arranged a farewell party for him, to which fellow poets, including Rahbek, Oehlenschläger, and Grundtvig, contributed songs.

In the spring of 1820 the aging man sets sail for the Virgin Islands. A hazardous undertaking! He suffers immensely from seasickness during the voyage, as his letters home reveal, and on arriving in Saint Thomas he soon finds the heat unbearable. Utterly debilitated he seeks cure for his ailments and renewed strength in New York, where he arrives on 12 August, remaining on the North American mainland until 20 October. An invalid or not, Pram does not neglect to report on what he observes in the new world. His impressions are printed in Nyerup's *Magazin* (4: 291-310). New York strikes him as most pleasant. He praises its broad streets and neat houses that are without ornament, which is reserved for the few public buildings. Pram, who never fails to point out the ragged misery of the poor wretches he meets on the roads of Norway, claims that in New York there are no beggars or people who look poor. The standard of hygiene, even with the common people, is high. Pram approves of the unassuming style in costumes, men being invariably dressed in black coats and white waistcoats and breeches, while the women wear white or black dresses. In the fashionable street called "Shroudway," which is illuminated at night, one finds great propriety. No brawls or drunkenness. Pram is also pleased to note that with the many carriages in the street there are no footmen or people looking like servants except for a few black people.

Pram also makes observations on cultural life. He is struck with the number of bookshops and the fact that everywhere he goes people are avidly reading. At first Pram is disappointed to find that there is no theatre in New York, public or private, since the only theatre building has been burnt to the ground. He is delighted, however, when he discovers that in a hippodrome a temporary stage has been erected, where he has the good fortune to see performances of *Hamlet*, *Othello*, and *Romeo and Juliet*. All he could ask for!

From New York Pram sails up the Hudson River on a comfortable riverboat to visit the springs at Ballston and Saratoga. On this trip he also pays visits to Albany and Patterson, New Jersey, which he faithfully describes. The sick man even attempts to get to Niagara Falls but gives up halfway because of a storm, consoling himself with the thought that in Norway he has seen no less impressive waterfalls. Pram's account of his visit to New York and environs shows that in spite of advanced years and infirmity he has retained his keen interest in the world around him and the manners of men. And as ever he must record his observations with his pen.

On his return to the West Indies Pram settles in a pleasant house in Saint Thomas. There he survives an epidemic of yellow fever, during which he watches new friends and acquaintances succumb. Pram dies from other causes on 28 November 1821 and lies buried in Saint Thomas, far from the lands he had so patriotically served and loved.

The picture of a highly unusual character that emerges from a sketch of Pram's career is filled out by the testimonies of contemporaries. He commanded a wide circle of friends, including — besides such representatives of an older generation as Luxdorph, Suhm, Tyge Rothe, Edvard Storm — the younger writers Jens Baggesen, Oehlenschläger, and Grundtvig. Baggesen, for a time closely attached to Christen and Marie Magdalene Pram, says about his friend in a letter dating from 1789: "den underlige, rasende, ubegribelige, yderst ulykkelige, i Grunden overordenlig ædle [Pram]" (Arentzen 1: 17). In a letter thirty years later Baggesen finds him unchanged:

> det frommeste, velvilligste, bedste Hjerte, der nogensinde har slaaet i en næsten altid kogende, altid ved mindste Leilighed vildt brusende Barm — det lyseste bedste Hoved, næsten uophørlig omskygget af denne vilde Barms opstigende Taager og Dampe — med eet Ord: det bedste Menneske maaske i Guds, det sletteste i Fandens Øine — (Arentzen 3: 222)

That Pram was a soul ridden by conflict and despair is evident from the confession he made in a letter to Rahbek, dating from 3 February 1800:

> Opdragen af Mennesker, som kiendte intet andet Religionsbegreb end dummeste Fanatisme, indpræntede man mig fra mit tredie Aar af, at hvis jeg ikke troede paa . . . . . . alt hvad man har udpillet af Biblen som ej staare der, . . . . . . saa blev jeg fordømt; . . . . . . men jeg var ærlig nok til ikke at bilde mig selv ind eller lade som jeg troede, hvad jeg ikke troede, saa fulgte deraf den Tilstand, Fanatikerne have kaldt aandelig Anfægtning. Denne var jeg i græsseligste Maade plaget med fra mine spædeste Aar af til langt hen i min modnere Alder. Thi skiøndt jeg ikke troede alt det, Fanatismen foreløp mig, saa syntes mig dog, efter adskilligt af hvad jeg saae om mig i den physiske, politiske, og moralske Verden, at det ikke var saa afgiort, at der jo kunde være et Væsen til, der . . . . . . fandt Fornøielse i at pine Menneskene, og følgelig, at det maaskee blev min Lod at kaages evig eller længe i Svovelpølen. — Dette var Pine, sand, sand, græsselig Elendighed. Tid, Beskiæftigelse og Vellyst svækkede, sløvede hine Ængstelsers Braad. — (Øst 50: 254)

Oehlenschläger, Pram's junior by many years, entertained a long-standing friendship with Pram in spite of differing views on poetry and their personal clashes. He confirms Baggesen's picture of Pram in these words in his autobiography:

> Denne fortræffelige Mand kom mig strax venlig og fortrolig imøde, og jeg maatte ogsaa drikke Du's med ham. Jeg har intet Menneske kiendt, der forbandt en saa høi Grad af Godmodighed og Velvillie med en saa opbrusende Hidsighed. Men han meente intet Ondt dermed; og hvo, der kiendte ham, betragtede hans Larmen som en Mølles Klappren, medens det nærende Korn males deri. Rigtignok kunde den, der stod de susende Vinger for nær, stundom giøre Regning paa et dygtigt aandeligt Ørfigen. Ingen Ven havde han, som han ikke havde viist Døren eller truet med Prygl; og han havde dog

mange Venner, og var hiertelig elsket af enhver, som kiendte ham. (Oehlenschläger 1: 176-79)

The ebullience and passion that are so dominant traits of Pram's character are not immediately in evidence in his writings. As a true exponent of neoclassicism Pram looked upon poetry, not as self-expression, but as an art and craft to be learnt and mastered by energetic study and exercise. No one has more faithfully than he practised the motto of the Norske Selskab: *Vos Exemplaria Graeca*. Whether Pram really attained mastery is another matter. One quality, which he in his above-mentioned confession ascribes to himself, is a dogged determination to write. To a modern reader it lends to his work, rather than spontaneity and grace, a quality of cool energy and forced rhetoric.

Pram first drew attention to his name with "Emilias Kilde" (1782), in which he combines the descriptive landscape poem — so popular with Dano-Norwegian poets at the time — with an elegy for the woman to whom the spring is dedicated and a narrative of a tragic-heroic love story, without really achieving a unity of the three parts. The description of the idyllic locality on the coast north of Copenhagen is done with an ample display of classical mythological apparatus showing Pram's familiarity with the prescribed model for such poetry, Alexander Pope's *Windsor-Forest* (1713).

"Emilias Kilde" is very much an ambitious young poet's demonstration of his talent. The epic *Stærkodder* (1785), in fifteen cantos, is Pram's most impressive bid for securing himself a place on the Danish Parnassus. He found his subject matter in Saxo's *Gesta Danorum* and has narrated the adventures of the six-armed Norse Hercules with a tremendous, grotesque imagination that brings to mind Holberg's *Niels Klim* (in Latin, 1741). The grandiose project is marred, however, by passages of bathos and tedious moralizing digressions. The romantics did not think that Pram's epic had what they considered was a truly Nordic spirit. They ridiculed its rugged dactylian metre and bold anachronisms, and nineteenth-century critics agreed. Francis Bull, however, and critics after him have rehabilitated Pram's poem, attempting to see it in a proper historical and generic perspective.

In the eighties and nineties Pram devoted much of his creative energy to drama, hoping thereby to earn, beside recognition and fame, financial gain. Of the plays Pram submitted for production to the management of the Danish Royal Theatre (often with urgent requests for advances on royalties), Rahbek has included — besides prologues, a ballet scenario, and an opera text — five heroic plays and six comedies in Pram's selected works. Of the heroic plays only *Lagertha* (1787; pub. 1801) has a tragic ending. The others bring about sentimental happy endings after testing the barbarous and warlike heroes for their unselfishness, tolerance, and love of peace by means of all the stock-in-trade of comedy. Pram shows his obedience to the conventions of genre, in this case the *Rührstück* so popular with eighteenth-century audiences, for the view of man's nobility that his theatre figures represent cannot possibly be his own. Pram's outlook on life seems more likely to be reflected in the satirical stories in the manner of Voltaire's *Candide* (1759): "Hans Kruskop" (1786) and "Jørgen. En Dosmers Levnets-beskrivelse" (1786). Here his innocent protagonists face a world teeming with corrupt and perfidious scoundrels.

Pram had more success as a dramatist with his comedies. *Negeren* (perf. 1791; pub. 1824) was performed several times, though it is moderate fun, taking its plot from Terence's *Eunuchus* and modelling its figures on Holberg's. *Brønden* (perf. 1800; pub. 1826), a dramatization of a novel by the popular German author Lafontaine, in spite of too much sentimentality and philanthropy, conveys a colourful picture of the life and manners at the Spa of Pyrmont, both its fashionable follies and its seamier sides of prostitution, gambling, and gulling.

Pram's best play, *Ægteskabsskolen* (perf. 1795; pub. 1825), has love and marriage as its theme. Pram develops it by juxtaposing three relationships: a couple of young lovers who spite parental opposition to their union, a middle-aged pair who are estranged after a love match, and the union of a mature husband and a young wife in a marriage of convenience that has problems.

The chain of events that removes the hindrances set up by the parent generation against the coming together of the young lovers is as usual the mainspring of the action, but it is not what makes the play noteworthy. The resistance to the union of the lovers comes from one Vilhelm Stjernholm. He is a rich man recently returned to his brother's estate in Zealand from sixteen years in the West Indies (there is almost always a returned West Indian in the comedies of those days), where he has lived estranged from his wife. He has just concluded a marriage agreement with the girl's parents on behalf of his son, whom he has not seen since he was an infant, having left him to a friend to bring up. He insists on such a marriage contract of convenience because he is against any love match. He and his wife married for love to their great unhappiness, as he explains:

> Jeg har nu mit Begreb om de Inclinations Givtermaale. Jeg har forsøgt det. Jeg var givt med Deres Tante. Vi var unge unge, hun var smuk, hun var romantisk; jeg fængede. Vi var saa forlibte i hinanden, saa det var en Lyst. Hun havde læst i Pamela og Frøken von Weissensee, hvorledes man skal have det; jeg tog mig hendes Hjernespind til Hjerte. Vi bleve givte i al Elskovens Henrykkelse. Men hvad skede? — Forlibelsen og det hele Romanvæsen gik over. Min Constance kom efter, at jeg ikke var det Ideal, som hun havde i Hovedet, og jeg, at min Amaryllis var en arrig Havgasse, en herskesyg, indbildsk, dum Ting. . . . Vi levede sammen fire Aar; og hadede vi hinanden ikke af Hjertens grund, saa ærgrede, og kjedede, og piinte vi dog hinanden saa umaneerlig, at det omsider ikke var at udholde for nogen af os, og vi maatte skille os ad. (Pram, *UDA* 2: 318-19)

This account of the sad outcome of a love match is an almost Shavian challenge — on the eve of the Roman era — to the notion that mutual attraction is the proper basis of matrimony, something that has been accepted and practiced nearly as a dogma by the middle classes to this day. Pram further explores the ill-fated relationship of Vilhelm and Constance with great dramatic effect when he lets the estranged spouses confront each other again in a scene that has less pathos than humour and irony. After long years they are immediately at it again:

Vilhelm.

— Nu hvorledes har Du levet, og hvorledes lever Du?

Constance.

Ak Mand! hvorledes? Du veed, hvor inderlig jeg elskede Dig! hvorledes kan jeg have levet i de seksten bedrøvelige Aar?

Vilhelm.

Nu. Jeg elskede Dig ogsaa. Det var derfor, jeg tog fra Dig. Jeg saae, Du var ikke lykkelig med mig, eller jeg stod Dig ikke an. Jeg haaber, Du har udholdt mit Savn.

Constance.

Udholdt dit Savn! at Du endnu, efter hele seksten Aar kan begynde i den samme Tone! Jeg udholdt dit Savn! At Du ikke mærkede paa mig, hver Dag i de fire Aar, vi levede sammen, hvor ondskabsfuld og egensindig Du endda var imod mig, hvor lunefuld og halstsarrig og arrig Du førte mig op ved hver mindste Bagatel; Du dog ikke mærkede, og siden har faaet Tid at tænke paa, at jeg elskede Dig saa inderlig, saa jeg intet Øjeblik kunde leve lykkelig uden Dig.

Vilhelm.

Nu, nu, Kone! jeg vilde ikke fornærme......

Constance.

Kan jeg faae tale et par Ord, uden at afbrydes, naar jeg skal svare fornuftigt paa de Bebrejdelser, han behager at begynde med, det allerførste jeg efter seksten Aar seer ham igjen? Jeg skulde udholdt dit Savn! Sorg og Bedrøvelse, maatte Du jo dog see, har gjort mig gammel for Tiden. — Eensomhed og Kiedsomhed har fortæret mine Leveaar og mine Kræfter. Nei det veed vor Herre, jeg har ikke kunnet udholde det, uden paa en jammerlig Maade.

Vilhelm.

Ja, Ja! det gjør mig ondt. Jeg havde haabet......

Constance.

Jeg veed, hvad Du vil sige! Du havde haabet, at jeg havde givet mig tilfreds. Nei! det har Du ikke haabet. Du har haabet, at Sorgen skulde lægge mig i Graven, har Du. Det var dit eneste Haab, saa Du kunde faae Dig en ny Kone, en frisk. Hvem veed, hvor mange Du har havt derovre paa St. Croix. I lever nok et kjønt Liv derovre. (Pram, *UDA* 2: 429-30)

And so on. In this central scene and in the rest of the play Pram unfolds Constance's nagging and unbearable personality with great comic force, at the same time giving an unmitigated insight into the problem of marital incompatibility. One is glad that he has spared us a scene of tear-stained reconciliation at the end of the play, which was otherwise to be expected in this kind of eighteenth-century comedy. Pram's unsentimental exposure of the discord of spouses, unusual in his day, points forward to the discussion of marriage and the relation between the sexes that the dramatists of realism and naturalism take up.

Otherwise the play takes the conventional course of comedy. As the imbroglio of the plot with disguise, mistaken identities, and misunderstandings is unraveled, the young lover turns out to be the very man the parents had agreed to couple with the girl, and the mature husband, who wrongly suspects his young wife of infidelity, is brought to see that he has shown her no love in their marriage of convenience. So with lofty nobility he forgives her the presumed escapade before he is convinced of her innocence. Well-tried elements of a happy ending. It is however thanks to the characters of Vilhelm and Constance, so vividly shown as the products of their unhappy experience in a love match — he: a bibulous cynic and misogynist; she: a scold and a termagant — that the play stands out among the comedies of its day, deserving better than the oblivion into which it has fallen.

## Works Cited/Consulted

Andersen, Vilhelm. *Tider og Typer af dansk Aandsliv*. Vol. 2: *Erasmus III*. Copenhagen: Gyldendal, 1909. 4 vols. 1907-16. 289-302.

Arentzen, K. A. E. *Baggesen og Oehlenschlaeger*. 8 vols. Copenhagen: Wroblewsky, 1870-78. Vol. 1 (1870): 17-18. Vol. 3 (1873): 222.

Baggesen, Jens. Breve. Det kgl. Bibliotek 1234. Copenhagen.

Bull, Francis. "Christen Pram og Norge." *Edda* 5 (1916): 418-49.

Lundgreen-Nielsen, Flemming. *Den nordiske fortælling i det attende århundrede*. Studier fra sprog- og oldtids-forskning 268. Copenhagen: Gad, 1968.

——. "Christen Prams 'Stærkodder.'" 1785. Rpt. *Edda* 3 (1971): 321-30.

Nielsen, Torben. "Prams Rejser i Norge 1804-06." *Fund og Forskning* 10 (1963): 60-98.

Oehlenschläger, Adam. *Erindringer*. 4 vols. 1831. Rpt. Copenhagen, 1850-51. Vol. 1 (1850): 176-79.

Pram, C. H. "Fragmenter af Prams Rejse i Norge. 1804 og 1805, meddelte af Kammerjunker Rawert." *Magazin for Rejseiagttagelser* [ed. R. Nyerup. 4 vols. Copenhagen, 1820-25] 4 (1825): 169-256.

———. "Hans Kruskop." *Minerva* 1 (1786): 48-83. See also *UDA*.

———. "Jørgen. En Dosmers Levnetsbeskrivelse." *Minerva* 4 (1786): 613-71. See also *UDA*.

———. "Prams Breve fra Vestindien og Nordamerika 1820-21." *Magazin for Rejseiagttagelser* [see above] 4 (1825): 266-339.

———. "En Rejse over Sundet 1791." *Magazin for Rejseiagttagelser* [see above] 4 (1825): 358-95.

———. [*UDA*] *Udvalgte digteriske Arbejder*. Ed. K. L. Rahbek. 6 vols. Copenhagen, 1824-29. See the following vols.
Vol. 1 (1824): *Lagertha. Et dramatisk Forsøg* (965-88) and *Lagertha. Et pantomimisk Sorgespil bandet med Sang* (89-102); "Hans Kruskop" (402-34); "Jørgen. En Dosmers Levnetsbeskrivelse" (347-401); and *Negeren* (183-346).
Vol. 2 (1825): "Emilias Kilde. Et Digt" (9-28) and *Ægteskabsskolen. Lystspil i fem Optoge* (309-476).
Vol. 3 (1826): *Brønden. Skuespil i fem Optoge* (265-424).
Vol. 5 (1828): *Stærkodder* (1-278).

Rønning, F. C. *Rationalismens Tidsalder*. 4 vols. Copenhagen: Schønberg, 1886-99. See vol. 2 (1890): 12-16.

Øst, N. C. *Materialier til et dansk biographisk-litterarisk Lexicon indeholdende: Fortsættelser af Tillæg til Rettelser i de indtil 1835 udkomne Lexia, om Danske, Norske og Islændere* [Et leksikalsk ugeblad. Copenhagen, 1835-38.] 50 (1835): 253-57. Letter of 3 Feb. 1800.

# The Note That Was Worth a Ducat: The Search for the Source Melody to Bellman's *Epistel* 81

## James Massengale

WITHOUT PLUNGING INTO an unsolvable discussion about whether we can really regard Carl Michael Bellman as an eighteenth-century *"fin-de-siècle"* poet — or indeed whether the end of the eighteenth-century in Sweden ought to be sublimated into a *fin de siècle* at all — one may still note with satisfaction that Bellman did survive until late in the century, and he did create works of art near or during the 1790s that deserve particular attention. It is commonly known that there was late flowering of Bellman's poetry between 1789 and 1791, when the aging poet finally saw outside interest and financial backing coalescing in a way that would bring about the publication of a representative collection of his best work. The projected collection, which had a working title of "Den svenske Anacreon," soon lost that appellation and was divided into two volumes, one appropriately named *Fredmans epistlar* (1790), and the other, somewhat less appropriately, *Fredmans sånger* (1791).[1] At least in the case of the first of these volumes, Bellman joined in the publication process with enthusiasm. Although dating the list of his final songs in the suite of *Fredmans epistlar* has its inherent difficulties, there is no question that a virtual hiatus after 1781 in the composition of these poems was broken by the end of the decade. In chronological order, the list of *fin-de-siècle* epistles — if we accept that term — is the following:

> *Epistel* 81: probably the end of the 1780s or 1790.
> *Epistel* 77: 1788 or 1789, possibly 1790.
> *Epistel* 70: earliest 1789, no later than 1790.
> *Epistel* 80: probably 1789 or 1790.
> *Epistel* 71: 1790.
> *Epistel* 72: 1772, revised 1790.
> *Epistel* 82: probably 1790.[2]

It is an impressive group, containing several of the popular Bellman favorites of all time, as well as some of his most complex and intriguing works of art. Characteristic of this latter group is that their melodies are largely of unknown provenance, and that is a matter of principal concern in this article. An overview of the melodies shows that only two sources out of the possible seven have been identified in any way. Bellman used the operatic aria "Maudit amour, raison sévère" for "Glimmande Nymph" (*Epistel* 72), a version of which was already done in 1772, and for "Klang, mina Flickor, se skyarna glimma" (*Epistel* 77), he used a more elusive French song, "La Maison est à son maître."[3] Beyond this, a good deal of wild speculation has led a number of Bellman enthusiasts to accept the romantic idea that Bellman was the composer of some of his best tunes: "Hvila vid denna källa," "Charon i luren tutar," "Märk hur' vår skugga," "Ulla, min Ulla," and "Liksom en herdinna."[4] The argument supporting his authorship is that we still lack definitive sources for these tunes after two hundred years of academic interest in Bellman. It is a compelling one, although it is *e silentio*. The counterargument sounds like this: if Bellman had not distinguished himself as a composer from the age of 15 through 48, why should we expect him to have emerged at age 49 on a level with a Duni or Grétry — and yet not to have had any of his contemporaries record the fact? This argument is also powerful, and, as you will notice, equally *e silentio*. The fact is, we are compelled to continue to look for provenance melodies to Bellman's songs, however faint the hope may be after two-hundred years to find any trace of a new source for any of them.

"Märk hur' vår skugga," *Epistel* 81, falls clearly in the *fin-de-siècle* period: it is a product of Bellman's "last flowering"; it is so completely hopeless in message that it has become modern;[5] and it lacks a verified source melody. It is not by coincidence that Bellman places it near the very end of the published cycle, with its graveyard imagery and its despairing contrast to the famous early morbidity of "Full och våt / Står jag i Charons båt" of *Epistel* 3, here reduced to a literally dry reference to the dead wife of "Grälmakar Löfberg":

> Hvem skall nu Flaskan befalla?
> Torstig var hon och uttorstig är jag;
> Vi är torstiga alla.

It is a black poem, starting in darkness — "Märk hur' vår skugga, märk, Movitz, mon frère!, / inom et mörker sig slutar" — and ending in sad musings over the extinction of love, happy times, and drinking bouts, altogether. There is a bitter correspondence between the music and the poetry, as if they had been bonded together like two helpless drunks, trudging along in falling lines to a stop, then trudging forward again to a cadence-fall. Small wonder that a subsequent tradition, beginning with Erik Drake, music editor for the Sondén edition of Bellman's poetry in 1836-37, attributed the staggering melody to Bellman himself. But Drake's tradition includes an additional kernel of information that makes his short commentary worth repeating in full:

> Melodien påstås vara af Bellman sjelf, enligt en tradition, som tillika berättar att, när han sjöng den för Kraus, denne vid tonen F i dess sjette takt utropade: "Detta F är värdt en dukat!" (Sec. 3: 78)

It must be clearly stated from the beginning that all such anecdotal material should be taken with a grain of salt. There have been as many "Bellmanshistorier" in circulation as all the ducats in Sweden. What I propose to do in this article, for the sake of experiment, however, is to assume, hypothetically, that Drake's anecdote contains some element of truth: namely, that element which reproduces verbatim a remark by J. M. Kraus. The assumption cannot be proven through sources independent of Drake, but the quotation does not totally lack plausibility. Bellman's close contact with Kraus probably dates from the time of that composer's return to Sweden in 1788, when he took the post of Royal Conductor after Uttini. At least by early 1790, the poet and composer collaborated on songs, and the relationship continued until the composer's death in 1792.[6] Whether or not Kraus had an active part in the musical formation of *Fredmans epistlar* and *Fredmans sånger*, he certainly spent time with Bellman during that active *fin-de-siècle* period, and it would seem almost unthinkable that Bellman failed to sing those last great epistles for him. Furthermore, the comment Drake attributed to Kraus, apocryphal though it may be, is wholly in character with the harmonically sensitive musician. A glance at the melody will also tell us that the exclamation may well be justified. The plodding, descending melody sets up its pattern in the first two bars:

And the death-march rhythm returns throughout the piece. When the initial phrase is repeated, however, in bars 5-6, there is a change in the melody that underlines the pathos:

And, indeed, the single note of F in bar 6 effects this alteration. This is the "F" that "is worth a ducat," whether or not it was Kraus who initially thought so.

The problem with Drake's anecdote (besides its unprovability) lies not in the idea of anyone placing a nominal monetary value on Bellman's genius, but in the preceding supposition that Bellman was the composer of the melody. When stated in this way, the anecdote quite simply makes no sense. If Bellman were the composer of the whole melody, how was it that Kraus should be so enthralled by the F in the sixth bar? Are we to assume that Kraus was less enthralled by the rest? Or are we supposed to understand that Bellman composed the melody, sang it for Kraus, and then altered the music, causing Kraus to express his enthusiasm? Or — as several Bellman researchers before me have speculated, without supportive evidence — did Bellman's musical creativity in this matter restrict itself to the alteration of a single note?

\* \* \*

This last idea was launched by the music historian Julius Bagge, who took up the problem of Bellman's melodies in his studies in the early 1880s. Bagge belonged to that group of researchers who had abandoned the "orphic" notion of Bellman as a fountain of improvised musical-poetic creations and had retreated to a position that appeared more defensible: that Bellman did not write his own music but rather chose classical melodies from the best operas, chamber music, and symphonies that the latter half of the eighteenth century had to offer. In accordance with that hypothesis, Bagge thought he had solved the problem of *Epistel* 81 when he found a piece of chamber music in which Bellman's melody appeared. He noted that "Melodien förekommer såsom `Rondo moderato' i ett Divertissement för violin och bas af E. L. Zebell" (Bagge 46).

Bagge left no further commentary, nor did he tell anyone where he had seen such a melody by Zebell. The response of other scholars to Bagge's claim was mixed. The music researcher Adolf Lindgren took it on faith (see Lindgren). Patrik Vretblad, the music commentator for the first volume (1921) of Bellmanssällskapets "Standard Edition" of Bellman's *Skrifter,* quoted (1: cclxvi) Bagge's identification but added the remark: "ha dock ej kunnat verifieras."

Sixty-five years after Bagge, the chief librarian at the Royal Library, Nils Afzelius, finally produced both a corroboration and a counterargument:

[Man] måste . . . bestämt bestrida att Bellman skulle ha hämtat musikalisk inspiration ur ett divertissement för fiol och bas av en litet känd svensk musiker vid namn Erik Lorentz Zebell. Bagge har funnit den gripande mollmelodin till [Epistel 81] i Zebells Tois sonates et trois divertissements pour le violon avec accompagnement de basse . . . Œuvre I:er. A Paris, chez Lobry (utan tryckår). Senare musikforskare har förgäves sökt efter nothäftet i Musikaliska akademiens bibliotek. Det finns emellertid i Kungl. Biblioteket, och ovanför Rondo moderato i det andra divertissement har Bagge med egen hand antecknat: "Märk, hur vår skugga." (*Bellmans melodier* 20)

This passage at least clears up the verification problem. Afzelius's skepticism about Zebell's melody as a source for Bellman derives primarily from the chronology involved:

> Granskar man nu det franska nottrycket, så inser man att det måste ha utförts efter att Zebell flyttat till Paris 1805, där han till sin död 1819 verkade som violinist och kapellmästare. Att kompositionerna inte bara har befordrats till trycket utan också tillkommit flera år efter att Fredmans epistlar gavs ut, tycks framgå därav att också ett annat tema är senare än 1790: ... en revolutionsmelodi från 1795, "Le reveil du peuple," används i det första divertissement. Har Zebell lånat från Bellman i stället för tvärtom? Frågan får lämnas obesvarad. För närvarande får det räcka med att slå fast att melodikällan till Epistel 81 *icke* är en violinkomposition. (Afzelius, *Bellmans melodier* 21-22)

I am inclined to support Afzelius's conclusion, although not necessarily his argument. The fact that Zebell wrote one melody after the French revolution does not in and of itself eliminate the possibility that he could have written another one before that. Alternatively, he could have picked up a popular tune that Bellman also had used. There is a different reason, I think, that we shall have to eliminate Zebell's version as a source, a point to which I shall return below. Meanwhile, we should follow the rest of Afzelius's perceptive discourse, which adds several new pieces to the puzzle.

Bellman wrote two additional poems based upon the same melody, but neither of them saw the light of day before 1790.[7] One of them, "Charon, din färja den kom ej försent," is a moving testimony to the shock in Bellman's circle of friends upon the sudden death of Elis Schröderheim's wife, Anne Charlotte, on New Year's day, 1791 (Bellman, *Skrifter* 11: 46). The other, "Klockorna röras med sorgliga slag," was apparently written to, or about, Bellman's father-in-law, Gabriel Grönlund, as the latter lay on his deathbed in late March of 1792 (Bellman, *Skrifter* 11: 111). The sense of doom in this final setting of the melody is intensified by reference to Gustaf III, who lay dying at the same time.

Two matters of interest should be noted with respect to these so-called "secondary settings": one is that their utter seriousness provides a confirmation of the funereal quality of "Märk, hur' vår skugga," which must not be regarded as a tongue-in-cheek satire: Bellman would not have drawn upon a melody with frivolous overtones for two of his most painful and serious experiences. The melody to *Epistel* 81 clearly became the poet's primary funeral march in the period of his "late flowering." The other matter of interest is that *Epistel* 81 did not achieve clear primacy for Bellman as a setting for the melody. Atterbom has related how Anne Charlotte Schröderheim's song — not *Epistel* 81 — was still sung when he was a young man. A young student in Uppsala, Johan Schedvin, wrote a parodic funereal ode concerning the "entombment of the press," as he called it, in late 1793, in terms more reminiscent of Fru Schröderheim's poem than those of "Märk, hur' vår skugga":

> Uplysning! gråt, Du bar mistat en vän,
> hvilken din fortgång beredde!
> Mörker skall hölja den banan igen,
> Hvartil Tryckfriheten ledde.
> Dine Dyrkare bestörte nu se
> Sine ovänner gå segrande,
> Åt oss som slavar förtryckta;
> Träldom och bojor Tyrannerne ge
> Åt dem, som önska vår lycka.[8]

Subsequently, in 1800, Carl Envallsson, that avid recycler of Bellman melodies into fluffy theater pieces, inserted the melody into the first scene of his parody, "Iphigenie den andra," to set up a mock-funereal tone for the beginning of the operetta.[9] In the published text of his libretto, Envallsson refers to "Caron, din färga den kom ej för sent &c" as the source for his song about Iphigenie's nightmare:

> Ögat, fördunkladt och fullt utaf gråt,
> Häpen tilbaka jag vänder,
> Der står en yngling och ropar på båt,
> Vrider blodiga händer. —
> Strax jag ilar öfver Acherons strand,
> Torkar hans tårar och löser hans band . . .
> Men . . . ack, hvad tröst honom räcktes? —
> (Furiöst.)
> Jo, just med dolken lyft i min hand. . . . .
> (Simpelt.)
> Och jag så ur sömnen väcktes. (Envallsson 7)

Even more than *Epistel* 81, the song for Fru Schröderheim had clearly etched itself into the consciousness of the Stockholm's theater-going public within a year or so of its composition. That public consciousness prompted Envallsson to cite the "secondary poem" as a reference in his printed text. Such references in the libretto were designed to call up immediate recognition on the part of the reader. They were not placed there for academic reasons.

* * *

But what about the "ducat note"? Afzelius has perused this matter as well, and he also finds something of interest in it. Drake's anecdote, he says, "styrks på sätt och vis av versionen i Zebells rondo, som avviker i denna enda punkt" (Afzelius, *Bellmans melodier* 59). Here, however, Afzelius has misread the music. At this point, we have three melodies to compare: *Epistel* 81 from 1790, the manuscript score to Envallsson's operetta from 1800, and

Zebell's duo from about 1805. It may be useful to see where — if at all — ducat notes appear in each of them.[10] The result may be tabulated as follows:

|            | bar 2 | bar 6 | bar 16 |
|------------|-------|-------|--------|
| Bellman:   | –     | D     | D      |
| Envallsson:| –     | –     | D      |
| Zebell:    | D     | D     | D      |

By way of explanation: in the particular harmonic configuration that steers the melody of "Märk, hur' vår skugga," there are three possible places in which a ducat note (marked "D" in the table above) might be positioned: in bars 2, 6, and 16. There is clearly no other note in the melody that warrants the designation of ducat note, and there are no other places to insert such a note. The alteration of the last note of the A-minor phrase to F involves the use of a bit of harmonic finesse. It also increases the tension and the dramatic power of the melody. This is unquestionably the meaning of the idea that "Detta F är värdt en dukat!" — whether it was Kraus or Drake or someone else who was first impressed by it.

In the arrangement of *Fredmans epistlar* by Olof Åhlström, however, it will be noticed that the ducat note has actually been used twice: in bar 6 and again in the penultimate phrase, bar 16. Envallsson's variant, by contrast, delays the effect until the end, but also emphasizes it in the score:

Zebell, on the other hand, scatters three ducat notes across the melody, and his inflationary procedure causes them to have a somewhat reduced value, at least in terms of their psychological effect. In his variant, there is no normal phrase ending on E to provide a basis on which to contrast the sudden shift to the subdominant F. Afzelius is not correct, then, in suggesting that the Kraus anecdote is supported by a comparison of Bellman's and Zebell's melodies. The matter of using one or two or three ducat notes is not the point, if we are to believe the anecdote. The problem is to find a plausible source melody without a ducat note.

\* \* \*

The search for a melodic source for "Märk, hur' vår skugga" was continued in 1970: Stellan Mörner reworked the whole problem, including Drake's by now overworked anecdote, in an article called "Några Bellmansmelodiers ursprung 'gripna ur luften'" (67-74). After a correct assessment of the Zebell material, which Mörner dismisses as derived

either from one of the Bellman poems or from some common source, he
turns to — Telemann:

> 1962 hörde jag på en nyutkommen skiva med musik av Georg Philipp
> Telemann en liten gavottsats, som genast förde tankarna till Fredmans
> epistel nr 81 . . . Likheten med epistelmelodin finns redan i Telemanns
> andra takt . . . , och erinrar om Bellmans takt 2, och just det betydelsefulla
> kvartsprånget c-g finns hos Telemann på samtliga analoga ställen, medan
> alltså Bellman vid upprepning använder en stor ters. (Mörner, "Några
> Bellmansmelodier" 71-72)

Telemann's Gavotte begins in the following way:

The remainder of the piece, which continues at some length, has no
connection with Bellman's melody except when the above bars are repeated.
Mörner informs us that the Gavotte, entitled "Die spielenden Najaden," is
the fifth piece in his *Wassermusik*. He also notes correctly that no ducat notes
(or "ducat intervals," to use a more accurate designation) appear in this
dance. True enough: as a matter of fact, very little of the melody to *Epistel*
81 appears at all in the above example. Mörner's information, very like those
other vague reminiscences that a number of Bellman researchers have given
us, seems to show, on the one hand, what a great connoisseur of baroque and
classical music Bellman was and, on the other, what a fine composer he must
have been to have changed the source music so radically. Even the spright-
liness and the title of the piece seem rather far from the sort that Bellman
would choose for his funereal mood, though one could always posit some
sort of Swedish link that reworked the najads and toned them down. The
libraries and music collections of Sweden, at least modern-day Sweden,
have not, to my knowledge, served up any such lost link.[11]

On the other hand, a most interesting melody has recently come to light
in Helsinki, at the collection of Svenska Litteratursällskapet (SLS). The
dance books in this important collection are a remnant of the old Swedish-
Finnish cultural heritage, of that literate and musically educated class of
Swedish-speaking patricians from the southern and western parts of Finland. The dance book in question is "Roswallska notboken" (signum SLS
92). It is not as old as the publication date of *Fredmans epistlar*: from Eero
Nallinmaa's dissertation (from 1969), we can learn that it was probably

compiled around 1801, somewhere in the vicinity of Åbo (Nallinmaa 199ff). It is a "spelmansbok," a book compiled by, or for, a professional violinist who played for private or public dances, and its repertoire is familiar from similar books from the western shores of the Baltic: such contredanse titles as "Hertiginnan," "Gustaf Vasa," "Börs Pikiniken," and others are frequently found in the books reflecting the period 1785-1800.

Number 54 in this book, however, is no contredanse: it is a song called "Tröstlös en Herde på Hafstranden står, etc., Adagio." Its melody is clearly that of "Märk, hur' vår skugga." Its title or first line does not refer directly to *Epistel* 81, but, more remarkably, the tune to "Tröstlös en Herde på Hafstranden står" lacks any trace of the ducat note.

The chronological argument for this melody as a source for *Epistel* 81 is not strong. As noted above, the Roswall Note Book was copied out around 1801, probably using slightly older dance or song books as sources, as well as melodies that may have been transmitted orally. This argument does not tell us that the book's compositions necessarily fall close to the date 1801, but it gives us no proof that otherwise unidentified material in the book was of older vintage either. The text to "Tröstlös en Herde" turns up very close to the date for the compilation of the dance book. It appears as a broadside published in 1801 in Gävle:[12]

> Fem Stycken helt Nya och ganska Wackra Kiärleks-Wisor.
> Den förste: Om en Herde som mistat sin herdinna:
>    Tröstlös en Herde på Hafstranden står, &c.
> Sjunges som: Caron din Färja, &c.
> Tröstlös en Herde på hafstranden står,
> Gråter en bortrest Herdinna,
> Ögat på henne och Fartyget går,
> Men ack de försvinna.
> Fåfängt lyssnar han at höra dess röst,
> Hafwets toma rymd blef Uslingens tröst:
> I som känt wänskapen gråten;
> Kännen den saknad som sårar hans bröst,
> Där han står förlåten.

This quotation may suffice for this occasion: I need not annoy the reader with strophes 2-4, which maintain the teary and maudlin tone. More important to this discussion is the reference above the text that it is to be sung to the tune of "Caron din Färja," that is, to Fru Schröderheim's song. The question is: how could the Finnish variant of the melody show up in 1801 with no ducat note, when Bellman's melody, to which the broadside refers, contains the note in two places? The following possibilities exist:

> 1. Bellman's song, "Charon, din färja den kom ej försent," was sung without the ducat note. The response to this supposition must be that Bellman would have little reason to exclude an innovative musical effect from the music to "Märk, hur' vår skugga" when be wrote "Charon, din

färja." One should also remember that we have Envallsson's melody, derived explicitly from "Charon, din färja," which contains the ducat note.

2. The Finnish melody to "Tröstlös en Herde" contains alterations to Bellman's melody; the ducat notes from bars 6 and 16 have been removed. The response must be that this thesis is possible, but rather doubtful, for the musical-psychological reasons discussed below.

3. The poem "Tröstlös en Herde" derives verbally from "Charon, din färja," but the melodic tradition for it in Finland is separate and unaffected by Bellman's harmonic tinkering. The response must be that this idea represents an interesting possibility, but that there is no way to prove it without further corroboration. What we need — and what we do not have at this time — is a variant of the melody that is as old as, or older than, *Epistel* 81 and that will thus be found detached from the text of "Tröstlös en Herde." The rest, as they say, is *e silentio*.

For the sake of completeness in this rather complex tangle of evidence, I can offer a bit of peripheral information in the case. While published in 1801 as a "new song," "Tröstlös en Herde" was in fact not entirely newly written. It was used in 1799 as a reference for another broadside, "Min tid är lång till att tänka uppå."[13] The latter text, also published in Gävle, was accompanied by a bit of editorial information:

> En alldeles ny och wacker Wisa . . . författad af blinda Drängen
> Ifwar Ifwarsson wid Wallen och Årsunda Socken i Gestrikeland.
> Gefle, tryckt hos Ernst Peter Sundqvist, 1799. Sjunges som:
> Tröstlös en Herde på Hafstranden står, &c.

> > Min Tid är lång till at tänka uppå,
> > At jag i mörkret skall wara,
> > Och hwarken Stjernor ell' Sol skåda få,
> > Uppå Himmelen klara.
> > Ack hur swårt det skulle wara för mig,
> > Om jag ej o Jesu hade dig,
> > I de bedröfliga stunder,
> > Då alla andre få glädje sig,
> > Af grönskande Lunder.

This song has five additional strophes, mercifully omitted here. There was, incidentally, a young blind man named Ifwar Ifwarsson, living in the village of Wallen in Årsunda parish; according to parish catechetical meeting records, he was born in 1778 (see Landsarkivet). We have no way, of course, of knowing if the young man actually composed the poem himself. The reference from this poem to "Tröstlös en Herde," however, changes the chronological picture slightly. The blind farmhand's poem is from 1799. "Tröstlös en Herde" has to be from before that date, even though we would assume from its own reference that it was written after "Charon, din färja" (January 1791).

If the farmhand wrote "Min tid är lång" himself, he had to learn the older song first, write the new one, and get it into print in Gävle, some distance from his isolated farmhouse in Årsunda parish. He (or his ghostwriter in Gävle) did not refer directly to *Epistel* 81 or to Bellman's funeral songs, because they were apparently superseded in the mind of the publisher, Sundqvist, by "Tröstlös en Herde." The sequence of parody texts — from "Märk, hur' vår skugga," to "Charon, din färja," then to "Tröstlös en Herde," and finally to "Min tid är lång" — can be rather firmly established. But establishing their sequence does not resolve the problem of the melody.

* * *

It is at this point that the matter of the ducat note must be reintroduced into the argument, and the discussion under possibility number "2." above must be expanded slightly. If one looks carefully at the Finnish melody of "Tröstlös en Herde," one will see clearly that it is not a copy of Bellman's melody. It cannot have been taken directly from Åhlström's arrangement of "Märk, hur' vår skugga." If it has been transmitted orally, it has lost much of the character of the Bellman piece. Its overall structure, however, is clearly exactly the same as that of *Epistel* 81, and the text of "Tröstlös en Herde" fits the epistle with no difficulty. But the melody lacks Bellman's funereal dotted rhythm, that halting pace referred to earlier in this article. It has a number of little instrumental cadences that are not found in Bellman's variant, but might be typical for a violinist's style. Finally, as noted above, the ducat notes are missing. How much importance should be assigned to this fact? Is this a matter of only academic interest because of Drake's anecdote, or is there really a significant musical difference between a "ducat note" variant and a "straight" variant of the melody?

There may be a significant difference. Bellman's alleged change is an affective distortion. It is emotionally charged and carries with it, in its harmonically subtle way, a pang of sadness clearly recognizable in the musical language of the late eighteenth century. The pang can still be felt today. Not only were such harmonic distortions gripping, they were memorable. Their effectiveness is what is meaningful in Drake's anecdote — not the question of whether it was Kraus or someone else who reacted to them. If my hypothesis is correct, such a distortion of a melody would, if introduced, tend to stick to the melody as if glued. Corroboration of this hypothesis may be seen in Envallsson's variant, in Zebell's variant. Other musicians may not employ the same notion of where to use the ducat note, but they will not exclude it. It has gotten under the skin of the melody, so to speak, and become an integral aspect of it.

The text of "Tröstlös en Herde" is a parody, a poetic reworking of a Bellman text. One may assume that the Bellman text came packaged with its ducat-note melody. There would have to be a compelling reason to alter such a melody, removing its affective ducat notes. Nonchalance or inadequate attention to Bellman's variant is possible, but we have no direct evidence that the copyist of the Roswall Note Book was nonchalant. On the other hand, the existence of a familiar melody in Finland that resembled Bellman's in all structural respects but happened to lack the ducat note might indeed be a compelling reason for the copyist of the Note Book to revert to the straight variant of the melody.

That is where the matter must stand for the time being. Besides the existence of one straight variant in the Roswall Note Book, all we have to tell us that such a melody might have been heard by Bellman before 1790 is Drake's anecdote from 1837. And we must remember that it was Drake who also contradicted himself by citing a tradition that Bellman composed the melody himself! These inconsistencies may serve as examples of the difficulties involved in the exploration of Bellman's *fin-de-siècle* period.

All we can say with confidence is that, by the turn of the century to the 1800s, two versions of the sad melody to "Märk, hur' vår skugga" were in circulation. One was sung in Stockholm, one in Swedish Finland. One was used to perpetuate the memory of Fru Schröderheim and to sing of the shades of Fredman and Movitz; the other supported a sentimental broadside. One contained the ducat note; the other either lost such a note or never had one to start with. Did Bellman learn a Finnish-Swedish melody and mould it in his own, inimitable way? Or did the violinist from Åbo hear a variant that had lost its Bellman text and some of its musical elegance? That is the sixty-four ducat question.

## Notes

[1] A comprehensive discussion of the interaction between Bellman and his redactional team is given by G. Hillbom in Bellman, *Fredmans epistlar* 2: 109-45. The case of *Fredmans sånger*, which lies outside the scope of this article, is treated in the 1992 edition of that work, also edited by Hillbom and Massengale (2: 135-46).

[2] Translated from Bellman, *Fredmans epistlar* 2: 368. *Epistel* 75 and *Epistel* 79, which could ostensibly fall within this group, are excluded from the list because of the uncertainty concerning the dates of their composition. See, however, my reference to the Kraus *epistel* below, note 6.

[3] "Maudit amour, raison sévère" is from "Le Peintre amoureux de son modèle," by Anseaume (text) and Duni (music); "La Maison est à son maître" has been identified by song title only (Bellman, *Fredmans epistlar* 2: 321-23 and 332-33).

[4] See, for example, Nils Afzelius, *Bellmans melodier* 61-64. Yet Afzelius was surely the most careful representative of this type of argument.

[5] Note recent recordings by Cornelis Vreeswijk and the rock group "Imperiet."

[6] See Mörner, "Bellman" 84-88. Bellman dedicated one of the poems of the "last flowering," *Epistel* 75, to Kraus. In spite of what Stellan Mörner says in his footnote on p. 88 of his article, *Epistel* 75 does have specific reference to Kraus's musical genius: the song is embellished — almost overloaded, one might say — with joking instrumental imitations and Italian technical musical terms. Cf. Krogh 24.

[7] This statement and the following paragraphs comprise a paraphrase of Afzelius, *Bellmans melodier* 58-59. I have also added a few morbid thoughts to his argument, with the help of Olof Byström's commentary in Bellman, *Skrifter* 11: 36-39 and 79-80.

[8] Printed with Afzelius's commentary in "Konventvisor" 238 and 244.

[9] Envallsson's work is an adaptation of Favart's parody on Glucks "Iphigenie en Tauride" (1779). Envallsson substituted popular Swedish tunes for the music in the French parody.

[10] The manuscript score to "Iphigenie den andra" (1800) is found in the collection of Kungl. Theaterns Musikalier at Musikaliska Akedemiens Bibliotek (MAB), Stockholm. Zebell's melody was reprinted in Mörner, "Några Bellmansmelodier" 71.

[11] There is a single instance of a dance-book version of the melody to "Märk hur' vår skugga," in an uncataloged manuscript at MAB in Stockholm, signum Ser. I: 3947. The handwriting is relatively late, however — probably from about 1800, and the melody is referred to as "Andante af Bellman." It is undoubtedly a copy of Åhlström's arrangement in *Fredmans epistlar*, and the reference does not necessarily mean that the copyist believed that Bellman was the composer, any more than I do when I speak of "Bellman's melodies."

[12] Signum N 1801m in the broadside ("Skillingtryck") collection at Kungl. Biblioteket, Stockholm.

[13] Not in 1779, as is recorded through a misprint in Margareta Jersild, *Skillingtryck* (Stockholm: Svenskt Visarkiv, 1975), 423. Its signum is MfT 140 R. 83, H 17, at Kungl. Biblioteket, Stockholm.

## Works Cited

Afzelius, Nils. *Bellmans melodier*. Stockholm: Norstedts, 1947.

——. "Konventvisor och andra politiska dikter." *Samlaren* ns 4 (1923): 235-47.

Bagge, Julius. "Bellmaniana. Om Bellmans melodier." *I* and *II*. *Samlaren* 2 (1881): 44-54, 107-10, respectively.

Bellman, C. M. *Fredmans epistlar*. Ed. Hillbom and Massengale. 2 vols. Stockholm: Norstedts, 1990.

——. *Fredmans sånger*. Ed. Hillbom and Massengale. 2 vols. Stockholm: Norstedts, 1992.

——. *Skrifter*. Bellmanssällskapets's "Standard Edition." 13 vols. Stockholm: Bonniers, 1921-80. Vol. 1 (1925): *Fredmans epistlar*. Vol. 11 (1964): *Dikter till enskilda. IV. 1790-1793*.

Drake, Erik, ed. *Musiken till valda skrifter af C. M. Bellman*. Stockholm: Nordström, 1837. 3 sections.

Envallsson, Carl. *Iphigenie den andra*. Stockholm: Kungl. Tryckeriet, 1800.

Jersild, Margareta. *Skillingtryck*. Stockholm: Svenskt Visarkiv, 1975.

Krogh, Torben. *Bellman som musikalsk digter*. Copenhagen: Branner, 1945.

Landsarkivet i Härnosand. "Husförhörsländer A" 1: 5-7.

Lindgren, Adolf. "Bellmansmusiken." *Samlaren* 16 (1895): 53-78.

Mörner, C.-G. Stellan. "Bellman bland gustavianska tonsättare." *Bellmansstudier* 17. Stockholm: Bellmanssällskapet, 1976. 67-103. 18 vols. 1924-85.

——. "Några Bellmansmelodier, 'gripna ur luften.'" *Bellmansstudier* 16. Stockholm: Bellmanssällskapet, 1970. 56-79. See above.

Nallinmaa, Eero. "Erik Ulrik Spoofin nuottikirja." Diss. Tammerfors, 1969.

"Roswallska notboken." [SLS] Svenska Litteratursällskapet. Signum 92. [From Åbo, ca. 1801. See Nallinmaa 199ff.]

Skillingtryck Samling. Stockholm: Kungl. Biblioteket. Signum MfT 140 R. 83, H 17 and Signum N 1801m.

Fig. II.2.

"Trøstløs en Herde på Hafstranden står"
Roswalds notbok. Svenska litteratursällskapet i Finland
Folkkultursarkivet, Allmänna Arkivet, Helsinki
Collection SLS 92

# Denmark Crosses the Great Divide

## P. M. Mitchell

IF ONE COMPARES the literary production and overall culture of Denmark-Norway in the seventeenth and the eighteenth centuries, one senses differences that make it difficult to perceive a literary tradition. The differences are essential and striking. In the first place, the transmutation from a theologically dominated culture to a more secular culture is pervasive. In the second, the primacy of the Latin language for scholarly and belletristic communication was slowly giving way to the use of the vernacular. In the third, the general historical orientation was being redirected toward the indigenous past. In the fourth, there was an expanding interest in the imaginative literature in foreign vernaculars. In the fifth, there was an increase in criticism of a both scholarly and popular nature that was derived from, or related to, the "Spectator" literature of England and secondarily of Germany. Finally, there was a growing interest in the secular theater — again in the vernacular.

As marked as these differences seem if viewed after the interval of one-hundred years, the changes were accomplished neither over a fixed period of time nor with great speed nor at the same time. Many changes are, however, clearly perceptible after the passage of but half a century. This point is made if we contrast merely the last quarter of the seventeenth with the first quarter of the eighteenth century. These fifty years embrace the division between a culture inculcated with ideas nurtured by the Reformation and a culture that arose outside the boundaries of theological authority. Can we give the earlier quarter century the same cognomen as the later quarter century?

Even the long-time standard history of Danish literature by Vilhelm Andersen and Carl S. Petersen (pub. 1924-34) did not adequately depict the transition from the seventeenth to the eighteenth century. Although volume one does include information on Thomas Kingo (1634-1703), Thøger Reenberg (1656-1742), and a few other writers, volume two begins with a monographic treatment of Ludvig Holberg (1684-1754). To examine the respected Danish literary history of the early nineteenth century (1800-08), by Rasmus Nyerup (1759-1829) and Knud L. Rahbek (1760-1830), is to be confronted by many names and poetic passages, but no synthesis. The newest comprehensive Danish literary history (nine volumes, 1983-85), which is more a sociological than an aesthetic presentation, in its volume four (written by Jens Hovgaard and others, 1983), attempts a comprehensive view of the literature between 1620 and 1746 and achieves a broader image through the use of many illustrations and examples of imaginative text indicative of social awareness among the authors discussed. The impression is that of heterogeneity and much literary activity on the part of a large number of writers. Questions arise: which works can be said to have been intrinsically significant, and how much was simply imitative? Our essay tries to answer those questions by an excursion through a three-volume work by Jens Worm (1716-90), *Forsøg til et Lexicon* (1771-84), which provides more nearly contemporary evidence.

Denmark-Norway was slow in adopting the philosophy of the Enlightenment and the prevalent moral philosophy identifiable in England, France, and Germany in the early eighteenth century. If, after examining only cursorily, widely read books from those language areas around 1700, we then look to the North, we identify entrenched elements of a tradition that was being superseded in the larger areas. The philosophy of Leibniz and Wolff, which unmistakably laid an existential basis for thought in the northern and central German states, is not recognizable in Denmark — which had yet to produce its own philosophers. The pragmatic bourgeois culture of Berkeley and Shaftesbury in England, for example, was likewise without parallel and known little, if at all, in Copenhagen and Christiania. The new epicureanism, with its preëminent theater, was but suggested in the Danish capital by traveling French players. Instead of responding to those currents, Denmark-Norway remained infused with Lutheran sobriety. The hereditary monarchy and its appendages of nobility still set the pattern of daily life. The acceptance of worldly pleasures such as were afforded by a theater that entertained as well as edified was a desideratum.

While there were signs of change on all sides, Denmark of the year 1700 was unlike England, France, or Germany of 1700. Much energy was yet to be expended before Denmark-Norway could be said to have passed the dividing line between the political-theocratic autocracy of the seventeenth century and the more enlightened state of affairs that obtained twenty-five years later, when it could be said that Denmark no longer was lagging behind, ensnarled in the archaic principles of two or three previous generations. We seek here to sketch transitional elements and to identify those figures who were responsible for a Danish monarchy more nearly resembling the rest of central and northern Europe after the victory of the philosophy of the Enlightenment, of bourgeois culture, and of a popular theater.

The hypothetical border between the two centuries has a ragged edge. Some disciplines, notably philosophy, were without antecedents, while others, notably philology, had roots that stretched back beyond the mid-seventeenth century. Discernible nevertheless is a break between the two quarter-centuries, as well as motion, if only of the spirit, toward the beginning of modern times, which we are now wont to recognize as dating from the last quarter of the eighteenth century.

Within the limited territory of poetry — that is, verse — change is less apparent than in several other areas, simply because of the vast amount of traditional occasional poetry that continued to be produced throughout the eighteenth century. As little as most occasional poetry from earlier times may hold our attention today, it played no small role in a social order that was hierarchical and even feudalistic. It was customary to write verse for every special occasion and in connection with any undertaking that relied, or hoped to rely, on support from some higher social level, more often than not a member of a royal house or of the nobility. On the whole, such verse had little formal or aesthetic value. What is, however, significant about the nonreligious occasional poetry written around 1700 was the fact that so much of it was in Danish. No longer was it essential to be able to versify in Latin, although any educated individual capable of composing verse was surely able to write in Latin. The outstanding example of the shift from Latin to the vernacular was given by Frederik Rostgaard (1671-1745), a man of many facets, a well-to-do polyhistor and bibliophile who was to hold a series of important governmental posts — but who is remembered today primarily because of a ridiculous skirmish with his contemporary and fellow professor Ludvig Holberg, as a result of Holberg's derogatory remarks in the satire *Peder Paars* (1719-20) about the island of Anholt, of which Rostgaard was overlord. After matriculating at the University of Copenhagen, Rostgaard spent three years at the home of the German professor of theology at the university, Hector Gottfried Masius (1653-1709), who held the young Dane in high regard. In those earlier years Rostgaard wrote some poems in Danish, of which at least two were published, but after launching an academic career in 1690, he wrote mostly in Latin.

It was Rostgaard who, while in Leiden in 1693, published a two-volume anthology of Latin poems by Danes: *Deliciæ quorundam poetarum Danorum*. With regard to it, the young Rostgaard had a double role: he was the roving student absorbing new ideas seriatim in Germany, the Netherlands, England, and France and at the same time using the international medium of Latin to make his creative countrymen known abroad. While in Paris in 1696, Rostgaard translated and published a scene from Corneille's *Le Cid* (1636) — the first translation of Corneille into Danish. Rostgaard continued writing occasional poetry in both Latin and Danish in those early years but concerned himself chiefly with medieval manuscripts and bibliothecal matters. The latter activity generated a projected new method of cataloguing books, which was published in Paris in 1697. Four years after his return to Copenhagen in 1699, Rostgaard anonymously issued a bibliography of the poetry of Anders Bording (1619-77), the one important secular poet writing in Danish in the seventeenth century. Incidentally, Bording was the first Danish poet to live by his pen; most of his career was spent writing occasional poetry for pay; for a few years (1667-70) he was in fact the official Danish court poet. Not until 1725, however, was there to be a collected edition of Bording's poetry, undertaken by the indefatigable Frederik Rostgaard with the assistance of Peter Terpager (1654-1738), a learned historian and theologian who shared Rostgaard's conviction of the desirability of writing in the vernacular. Their edition was provided with an introduction by the younger Hans Gram (1685-1748), later a founder of the Royal Danish Academy of Science, who, like Rostgaard, had been an active member of Denmark's first modern, if short-lived (1705-06), literary society, the "Societas litteraria indagantium," established by Søren Lintrup (1669-1731).

What are the interrelationships of these several men who themselves were forerunners of cultural reform and the rise of a more modern and liberal Danish society in the eighteenth century? Both Lintrup and Rostgaard had lived at the home of Professor H. B. Masius as young men, shortly after Masius had returned from a sojourn in England and France. Subsequently Lintrup served as the rector of the school in Bergen that Ludvig Holberg attended until 1702, when the school burned, after which depredation both Holberg and Lintrup came to Copenhagen. Those five men held many ideas and many goals in common. Viewed together, these men constituted the vanguard of a new literary order; they were aggressive precursors, passing older borders of knowledge and usage in an effort to make the intellectual society of which they were a part correspond to the outside world with which they had made productive acquaintance. Ultimately the most important member of the group was to be Holberg, although his career began slightly later than that of the three others; he may be said to be part effect and part cause of the new currents coming from abroad. There is a parallel between his travels and experiences in the Netherlands, England, France, and Italy with those of Rostgaard. A common bond that includes all five men was an interest in language and especially in the desirability of the use of Danish.

If Holberg is the most important figure historically, Rostgaard must be considered the common denominator of new or developing attitudes with special reference to language. While at Oxford he had devoted himself not only to the study of manuscripts but also to the study of older Germanic dialects: Old English, Old Icelandic, and Middle High German. Elsewhere he also studied Semitic languages. More scholars would later share Rostgaard's linguistic more than his many other interests.

The disposition for the cultivation of the indigenous tongue had radices in the early seventeenth century. In particular, the beginnings of Old Norse-Icelandic philology antedated Rostgaard's generation. Ole Worm (1588-1654) had occupied himself with runes in the 1630s, and in 1638 Peder Claussen Friis (1545-1614) translated Snorri's *Heimskringla* and also issued some annotated Latin translations of skaldic poetry. In this Friis had enjoyed the assistance of several Icelanders (who, at the time, were more aware of their own cultural past than were most Danes and Norwegians of theirs). Despite Rostgaard's early difference with Holberg, Holberg and he, both professors at the University of Copenhagen, shared the vision of a Danish theater. Rostgaard wrote the prologue for the opening in September of 1722 of the Danish stage in "Grønnegade" — a street in central Copenhagen — for which Holberg had started writing the comedies that were to immortalize him and that began to be published in 1723.

In 1725-26, there appeared in Copenhagen an anthology in fourteen parts with the common title *Samling Udaf smukke og udvalde Danske Vers Og Miscellanea Nationen til Ære Og Sproget til Ziir*, a title that enunciated the ambitions held by the advocates and apologists of Danish. The 950-page collection was published by Joachim Wieland (1690-1730), printer to the Danish crown and himself a minor poet. The anthology was necessarily retrospective, although it points to a path from the baroque to the Enlightenment. The hold of the baroque was strong in the anthology; there were only suggestions of a new lyric poetry. Even the most gifted of the poets represented, who aimed beyond their time, as, for example, Vilhelm Helt (d. 1724), were nevertheless oriented toward earlier poetry. In the earlier parts of the anthology, Thomas Kingo dominates. In part one are both his poem on political events of the year 1716 and some admiring lines about the religious poetry of his Norwegian contemporary Dorthe Engelbretsdatter (1634-1716). By virtue of her sex, Dorthe Engelbretsdatter is historically noteworthy, but she must be identified as a static seventeenth-century baroque poet.

Vilhelm Helt occupies a special place on Parnassus around 1700 because of his extensive use of the Dutch poet Jacob Cats (1577-1660) as a basis for much of his work, at a time when reworking older poets was accepted and not considered plagiarism. Much of what Helt wrote can be classed simply as Danish versions of "Vader Cats," but special mention should be made of Helt's lengthy "Rodope" (pub. 1732), the story of the Egyptian courtesan for whose favors seven very different suitors plead at length. Helt's versification and narrative skill represent an advance over his predecessors and models. Newer currents were early represented by Anders Bording and Thøger Reenberg.

Of special note is the short poem by Anders Bording from the year 1671 commenting on the epic *Hexaëmeron* (1661) by the earlier baroque poet Anders Arreboe (1587-1637); Bording commended his predecessor for writing in Danish and, as well, avoiding the use of foreign words. This of course suggests the attempts of the seventeenth-century German "Sprachgesellschaften" to support a puristic trend in languages. Bording, who looked upon Arreboe as the Danish Martin Opitz (1597-1639), bridges the seventeenth and eighteenth century, whereas Kingo's poetry, although it represents the high point of Danish baroque verse, brought with it no fresh poetic attribute. Nonetheless, it was never rejected by a younger generation.

Thøger Reenberg's satirical disquisition, termed a "Samtale imellem Timander og Philemon om at gifte sig" (1725), is in the spirit of Jacob Cats. Among the contributors to Wieland's anthology was, once more, Frederik Rostgaard, whose brief translation of Corneille was reprinted. In addition to his edition of Bording's poetry mentioned above, he published many poems of his own, mostly in Danish, and also three groups of German hymns in Danish translation — as well as a work on the study of Arabic, part of an edition of Thucydides, and some essays on linguistic and poetic matters.

We sense a nice balance between Thomas Kingo and Frederik Rostgaard when we learn that Denmark's great baroque poet, Kingo, composed a poem on the occasion of Rostgaard's marriage in 1703. Although Wieland's anthology would seem to be simply a collection of baroque verse reprinting occasional poems by Thomas Kingo and many poems by other, lesser, authors, the anthology is not without suggestions of different styles, as evidenced by two New Year's poems included in issue number 10 (1726). The one poem is by Kingo, the other by the versifying clergyman Jørgen Pedersen Friis (1684-1740), and each addressed to a reigning Danish monarch (Christian V in 1681 and Frederik VI in 1719). Kingo's verse is the more formal and is but a single stanza; Friis varies meter and includes a poem within a poem. Friis's six stanzas are not so suggestive of burning incense at the monarch's shrine. Both poems incorporate a plea for peace, and both poets conclude their verses deferentially, with the hope that the Danish crown will prosper for unlimited generations.

A more modern note than any sensed in Wieland's anthology is struck in two satirical poems written eleven years apart: "Adelens Oprindelse" by Vilhelm Helt and *Den Daarlige Udenlandske Rejse Og Modige Hiemkomst* by Christian Falster (1690-1752). The first — generally believed to have been written by Frederik Rostgaard — was circulated only in manuscript; it was not published until 1791, whereas Falster's poem was first published, albeit anonymously, in 1721, a year before the establishment of a Danish theater. F. J. Billeskov Jansen has pointed out that some of Falster's satires are to be looked upon as immediate forerunners of Holberg's comedies, specifically Holberg's *Jean de France* (1723) and *Den honette Ambition* (1731). Both satirical poems contain a modicum of social criticism. Helt's anonymous poem was more biting and daring, for it attacked the concept of hereditary rights. No wonder that it could not be printed at the time it was written. Falster's more humorous satire had as its subject the young Dane who traveled abroad, found conditions there to his taste, squandered his inheritance in wild living, and returned to Denmark only to be dissatisfied with homely conditions. Falster was no more radical a critic than his contemporary Holberg. Both writers mocked the acquired snobbishness of the well-to-do young man who enjoyed the pleasures of Paris — and, in Falster's poem, Halle, London, and Amsterdam as well (all of which cities are mentioned). The poems by Helt and Falster exuded a new spirit that was to find eloquent and effective expression in Holberg's comedies and, later, in his essays.

Another early piece of social criticism, which, again, circulated only in manuscript, was the so-called *Grevens og Friherrens Comedie* (written ca. 1678), of uncertain authorship but probably the work of Mogens Skeel (1650-94). In form like the French classical drama in five acts, in substance it ridiculed the new nobility and, as in the French and later in Holberg's Danish comedies, lets the servants dupe the parvenu parents so that the youthful lovers can be united. Mogens Skeel, if indeed he is the author, had already translated Martin Opitz's *Judith* (1635) into a *Dansk talende Judith* (1666), the very title of which emphasizes the utility of the vernacular in imaginative literature. Here were examples of what is called "world literature" making themselves known on the Danish literary scene. Otherwise there is on the whole little that can be identified as "world literature" in Danish dress. One might expect an influx of works of world literature making themselves felt in Denmark at the beginning of the eighteenth century, but that is not the case. The English and French writing that characterized belles-lettres in their respective countries of origin was slow in being translated and published in Copenhagen. For example, the enormously successful *Télémaque* (1699) by François Fénelon (1651-1715) was not translated until 1727-28 (by Søren Olsen Dametius, 1681-1741), and the *Spectator* (1711-12, 1714) had to wait until 1742 before assuming a Danish configuration. Such relatively late translations were at least partially responsible for the delay in Denmark's creating a new literary scene dominated by the vernacular. It was consequentially the more difficult to see beyond the borders of the Danish monarchy, although there was an awareness of literary activity in the vernacular elsewhere. There were, however, other translations that served a double purpose: to continue the dominance of classical Latin literature and to make some of that literature available in translation. Thus Christian Falster published an edition of the elegies of Ovid in translation in 1719. Translations of individual elegies had preceded his — by the Odense precentor Christian Rose (d. 1711) and a single elegy by the jurist, university professor, and historiographer royal Christian Reitzer (1665-1736). Falster published Reitzer's translation in his edition. Incidentally, at his death Rose left additional manuscript translations from Ovid — which bore a dedication to Frederik Rostgaard.

The importance of these and other translations of classical works into Danish is not intrinsic but lies in the fact that such secular, albeit classical, works were done into Danish for the reading public. Moreover, if the sort of secular classical works that were being made available toward the end of the seventeenth century and into the eighteenth century were permissible for the public at large, indigenous secular poetry and prose might also be acceptable. Some works appearing in Danish at the time were borderline cases. Thus two devotional works by Frands Kyhn (d. ca. 1721) enjoyed considerable popularity. The one, *Aldrig vel tilfreds* from the year 1677, was reprinted seven times, while *Altid vel tilfreds* from 1680 was reprinted ten times, through 1740. Kyhn was also the author of a Danish version of the Biblical tale of Esther: *Den poetiske Esther*, 1701.

It is difficult to find a lode vein of a new literature around 1700, but the growth of interest in the study of Danish language is more easily traced and put into focus. There is a line of productive development starting in the first third of the seventeenth century and increasing in strength and volume as the century progressed, so that, by about 1690, philology had taken on new life and may be said to have left Danish imaginative literature behind. The concern with language was not only a more serious endeavor but, unlike occasional poetry, not conducive to imitation. Between 1601 and 1700 some 56 general works on language were published — not including new editions and reprints — in Latin. During that century there were only 15 that dealt with Danish, whereas in the next century (1701-1800) there were issued over 50 works that dealt with Danish as against 65 pertaining to Latin. This rough statistic is evidence of the shifting balance between Latin and Danish in the course of a hundred years.

The earliest champion of Danish, especially in ecclesiastical connections, was Søren Paulsen Judichær (or Gotlander, 1599-1668), who was the forerunner of several later clergymen and scholars who were interested in linguistic matters. Judichær was the author of a Danish prosody, an abbreviated version of which appeared in 1650; the complete version was issued by his widow in 1671. *Nogle Betænkninger om det Cimbriske Sprog* (1663) by Peder Syv (1631-1702) was at the same time a grammar and an introduction to literature and is unique as a precursor of Danish literary studies. In the foreword to his work, Syv wrote courageously,

> Nogle maa skee meene og at der var vel andet i det Latinske og Grædske sprog hvor paa jeg heller buurde at anvende tiden. Men mig bør jo først at vise mit fæderneland og dets sprog nogen ære.

Peder Syv was not writing what others had written before him, although his awareness of the German "Sprachgesellschaften" is apparent; he mentioned specifically the "Fruchtbringende Gesellschaft" by name.

On the whole, philology had an easier path of advancement and more solid ground to tread on than belles-lettres in Denmark, and the history of Danish philology is easier to plot than the irregular course of imaginative literature. The transition from the classical languages to the vernacular was gradual, but regular. Interest in the indigenous tongue evidenced itself in two ways: in attention to the Danish language itself and in a growing awareness of Old Scandinavian literature — meaning basically Iceland's — which the other Scandinavian countries eyed covetously. Old Norse-Icelandic offered a mass of historical evidence that otherwise would not be preserved and to a certain extent seemed also to make up for the medieval literary tradition that Denmark-Norway and Sweden lacked. The esoteric quality of that evidence made runic inscriptions seem a continental complement to the oldest material preserved in Icelandic manuscripts and thus evidence of an earlier culture.

In the second half of the seventeenth century there was considerably more activity in the field of Scandinavian antiquities in Sweden than in

Denmark. One need only to mention the translations of Olof Verelius (1618-82), Jón Rugman (1636-79), and Johan Peringskiöld (1659-1720), as well as the better-known Olaus Rudbeck (1630-1722). Yet Denmark had also its enthusiasts for the monuments of Old Norse antiquities, starting with Ole Worm, who published *Danica litteraturum antiquissima* in 1636. The current of interest reached a high point with the editions that Peder J. Resenius (1625-88) had published: in the year 1665 a trilingual edition (Icelandic, Latin, Danish)[1] of Snorra Edda and a single edition of two of the lays of the Elder Edda, *Völuspá* and *Hávamál*, both with Latin translations.[2] Almost twenty years later and thirty years after Guðmundur's death, Resenius issued Guðmundur Andrésson's *Lexicon Islandicum* (Copenhagen 1683). The credit for making such important material available accrues ultimately to the Icelanders who were responsible for the texts and the translations.

There was now a considerable hiatus in such activity until the Árna Magnæan Commission began actively to support Old Icelandic studies by publishing texts, some four decades after the death of Árni Magnússon in 1730. Resenius may be said to have laid the groundwork for future scholarship in the field of Old Norse-Icelandic studies in Denmark — but of course the Icelander Árni Magnússon to have gathered and salvaged the material on which such scholarship — which was progressively to become more and more important in the course of the nineteenth and twentieth centuries — might flourish. With such a promising background it is difficult to understand that so little was done for nearly a century after Resen's edition of Snorra Edda. The explanation seems simply to have been human lethargy.

For its day, the 600-page *Grammatica danica* (1668) by Erik Eriksen Pontoppidan (1616-78) was monumental. Although the language of presentation was Latin, the examples and citations were in Danish. The book is in two parts: "Observationes etymologicæ" and "Observationes syntacticæ." As could be expected, Danish is explained in terms of Latin grammar and syntax so that any user, whose mother tongue was presumably Danish and who could be expected to be thoroughly grounded in Latin, might readily comprehend the argument. Pontoppidan can be said also to have bridged the two centuries. Although his linguistic orientation was on the past, his subject was of the present — and future. Later Danish grammarians all drew on Pontoppidan as a matter of course. Peder Syv mentioned his debt to Pontoppidan in the foreword to the *Danske Sprog-Kunst* in 1685. Henrik Thomæsen Gerner (1629-1700) acknowledged both Pontoppidan and Syv in his *Orthographia danica* in 1678. Peder Syv planned a Danish-Latin dictionary, of which but two pages were published, first in Copenhagen and then at Oxford in the Sheldon Theater at the suggestion of Frederik Rostgaard — who acquired Syv's literary remains after Syv's death. We may conclude that several forward-looking grammarians were willy-nilly attempting to lift Danish to the level of Latin and to make Danish a worthy subject of scholarly endeavor. At the beginning of Gerner's *Epitome philologicæ danicæ*

(1690) he wrote in the same spirit as had Peder Syv: "At dyrcke sit eget Sprock oc i beste Maade udarbejde det er ét uskatterlyt Gaffn. . . ."

The classical languages were not abandoned; they simply acquired a Danish parallel, and their role changed as emphasis changed. Texts were now to be read to be enjoyed and not simply because of their historical importance. Not all learned Danes shared an appreciation of the rise of the vernacular as a counterbalance to classical philology, however. The rector of the Latin school at Holbæk, Torkil Baden (1668-1732), questioned scholarly efforts on behalf of Danish, but, curiously enough, he himself issued a handbook that was meant to demonstrate the close relationship of Latin and Danish vocabulary and phraseology.

The dynamic lexicographer Matthias Moth (1649-1714), like Gerner and unlike most other scholars we have mentioned who were theologically trained, had begun as a student of medicine. He had visited Leiden and Paris and later held a series of governmental offices, in which he performed efficiently while at the same time spending as much time as possible working on a Danish dictionary. Although the dictionary never was published, it was virtually complete at Moth's death. His 60-volume manuscript, preserved in the Royal Library, has been drawn upon by generations of Danish linguists. Even as a lexicographer Moth was ahead of his time, for he made a point of recording the spoken Danish language of his day. There could be no greater contrast to the neoclassical tradition. The trend perceptible in the early seventeenth century, given strength and direction by Peder Syv in 1685 and advanced by Matthias Moth, was to find clearest expression in 1727 with the publication of *Rhetorica laica et pagana. Det er Læg-Mands Tale-Kunst og Bondens Vel-talenhed* . . . , written by Hans Olafsen Nysted (1664-1740), who called himself one who loved his forefathers' language. With this book, written in Danish, linguistic scholarship is clearly over the great divide. It would advance Danish rhetoric to a position equivalent to that of Latin, while explaining figures of speech in contemporary Danish. We are now well into the time of Ludvig Holberg; Danish had achieved a level of respectability and even warranted attention from abroad.

Once again looking back to the first third of the seventeenth century, we find some limited Danish interest in foreign tongues other than Latin and German, as indicated by the appearance of grammars of French and Italian by Daniel Matras (1598-1689), himself a native of France who taught at the venerable Sorø Akademi and also published a quadrilingual collection of proverbs. His were the first works in Denmark that addressed themselves to modern Romance languages. At the end of the seventeenth century two grammars of English were issued, the one by the much-traveled Norwegian Frederik Bolling (d. 1685), *Fuldkommen engelske Grammatica* (1678), presumably as a teaching aid, the other by Christian Lauridsen Nyborg (1658-1702), who had served as a chaplain to Danish forces in England during a brief span of peace, *Addresse Til Det Engelske Sprogs Læßning* . . . (1698). There were several other French grammars published throughout the eighteenth century, as well as French-Danish dictionaries, but somewhat fewer English grammars and English-Danish dictionaries. Interest in foreign languages other than German (which was the language of the court and of the army) was not widespread.

Of modern drama there was next to nothing available in Denmark even in translation at the turn of the century. The desire to be entertained in theaters was, however, a reality, doubtless furthered by the theatrical experience of the numerous Danes who had sojourned in France and in England. The establishment of a Danish-language theater by René de Montaigu (1661-1737) with the subsequent creation of a body of comedy written in short order by Professor Holberg is well known. The year 1722 meant not only the establishment of a theater but also the beginnings of a dramatic tradition, which, although held in abeyance for economic and religious reasons in the 1740s, could not suppress the lasting success of a new genre in the North. Within a few years after the opening of the Danish stage in 1722, some 60-odd plays had been staged — 40 of them works in translation, but 21 from the pen of Holberg alone.

The new theatrical situation was the most telling evidence of an important literary mutation. Moreover, the introduction of a popular theater could only encourage the growth of other literary genres. Denmark and Danish literature had passed the great divide between the baroque and the Enlightenment.

We may conclude that, in the critical fifty-year period when there was a visible shift from the baroque to the Enlightenment in Danish literature, a very few men were the prime movers of the action and changes that took place. Foremost among them was Frederik Rostgaard, whose name one meets at every level. We can actually narrow the period of transition to about thirty years, if we view Rostgaard as the symbolic central figure from the publication of his Latin anthology in 1693 to his prologue for the Danish theater in 1722. Progressive philology, on the one hand, and the popular theater, on the other, then encouraged the creation of a new critical and imaginative literature. There was no reversal possible.

## Notes

[1] Latin translation by Magnús Ólafsson (1573-1636).

[2] Latin translation of *Völuspá* by Stefán Ólafsson (1620-88).

## Works Cited

Gerner, Henrik Thomæsen. *Epitome philologicæ danicæ*. Copenhagen, 1690.

Nysted, Hans Olafsen. *Rhetorica laica et pagana. Det er Læg-Mands Tale-Kunst og Bondens Vel-talenhed* . . . Copenhagen, 1727.

Syv, Peder. *Nogle Betænkninger om det Cimbriske Sprog*. Copenhagen, 1663.

III. *Fin de Siècle*: The 1800s — In Scandinavia

# DRIPPING EAVES

Between grimy walls, looming red and gray,
In a fog under rain-dripping eaves feeling spring to be
nowhere nigh,
I love nightly vigils (on dozing all day)
When I think of the times with a violet evening sky.

Like a withered vine that is budding anew,
And when greening will garland a marble, a goddess brought
down,
There will grow from my solitude here in a winterly town
The springtime of thoughts darkly twining remembrance of
you.

I remember the twilight of hours we were seated there
I and you:
I as a cherished guest who was treated with loving care
(Hearts will get tender apart and from longing more meekness
ensue),
You with your eyes all alight being happy and moved
in your chair.

And our wood-seat in summer. In winter your inglenook.
Or our evening group that would blush from the glow of
the fire.
Then your love and our vita nuova, a secret and sacred
book:
— We were one as our hands and our eyes let transpire.

We were one. It was comfort, indeed, of a kind!
Though our lives we but managed in middling fashion,
One being tearful, the other resentful of mind,
As we meanly disputed our heavenly passion.

Then all graceful and tall you would light me the way
with the lamp
Up to the guest-room — an ever remembered plight!
Where in the eye-galling smoke from the damp
Sticks in the three-leggéd stove you would linger
to say goodnight.

Sophus Claussen, "Tagdryp," 1899
*Translated by Niels Lyhne Jensen*

# The Nordic Nineties

## Jørgen Elbek

SPEAKING OF THE NINETIES — as well might happen in the decade of their centenary — it will soon emerge that their spiritual current, symbolism so-called, will only admit of epithets equally attributable to other -isms: modernism, expressionism, romanticism.[1] Indeed, naturalism or impressionism cannot be said to be out of range. Instead of asking a straight question — what is symbolism? — it might be meaningful for us to approach the problem in a roundabout way, though still without getting to the heart of it, by studying how individual major writers — one from Denmark, one from Norway, and one from Sweden — developed into symbolists, the term they have had to bear in critical and historical discourse but were hesitant to adopt themselves. When one of those three, Sophus Claussen, in the middle of the nineties went to Paris, he was to hear, in the first instance, how the leading light of French symbolism, Paul Verlaine, jeered at the word — *Cymbalism* — hooting through his hand as through a trumpet. In the second, he had to take exception to the term as applied to his own literary credo — though a friend and intellectual comrade-in-arms, Johannes Jørgensen, had penned the manifesto "Symbolism" (1893), in Danish, the authorized version for all later talk on the subject.

Some ten years earlier in the life of the said Claussen, when he was a young student, he knew nothing about Paul Verlaine, but all the more about Georg Brandes, whose "Moderne Gennembrud" was not yet a spent force. For one thing, it meant to young academics that "free love" was the order of the day. It was best practised with girls who were some rungs lower on the social ladder than the students themselves. Higher up there were too many precautions to be taken, but Claussen contributed to the glorification of the principle as he extolled the eternal merry polygamy of nature, which he called the law of change, and by composing a couplet that was widely applauded: "Hvad er hundrede Kys af *ét* Par Læber / mod at kysse hundrede Piger?" ("Antonius Gynt 6: Nye Piger," 1887; see *SCL*). Whatever they are, these lines are not symbolism. The poet himself talked about a view of life based on love, and that motto he stood by for the rest of his life, although he was soon to ascribe a different meaning to the word "love."

It so happened that Claussen left the big city, with Georg Brandes and all he stood for, to go to the provinces where one is closer to the soil. There he falls in love and gets engaged to a middle-class young woman who is anything but free with her favors. The course of events one can follow through the letters he addressed to Viggo Stuckenberg (see Lasson), and it is surprising how poorly the young man is able to express what is on his mind. At least the engagement takes the reader of the letters completely by surprise, as, on one hand, he has been told that in spite of her excellent mind the girl is tongue-tied, on the other, he has learned that Claussen calls himself (see Lasson 1: 82) too much of a Mr. Lovelace bent on sinking to the very bottom of "Plathedens og Naturlighedens Gadekær" (one way of defining naturalism!) and consequently had better refrain from making advances. The next turning point is the break-up of the engagement after the lapse of a year in which the parties cannot have had many chances of being together. "Og hun vilde aldrig give mig lidt mere end min Ret," it says in a much later poem ("Mennesket og Digteren," 1907) in which Claussen looks back on the affair, making his line rhyme with "og jeg følte, jeg var slet." And another poem ("Tagdryp," 1899; *SCL* 2: 1.24) dating from shortly after the break-up, ends as follows (the situation being that he is on a visit to his provincial fiancée):

> . . . . . . . . . . . . . . . . . . . . . . . . . . . . . . . . . . . . . . . . . . . . . . . . . .
> Vi hørte jo sammen . . . og det var bestandig en Trøst,
> skønt Livet, det ordned vi kun med saa maadeligt Nemme.
> Den ene med Graaden, den anden med Nag i sin Stemme,
> vi førte en mager Proces om vort Himmerigs Lyst.
>
> Saa greb du en Lampe og lyste mig ædel og høj
> til Gæstekamret, jeg husker til Timernes Ende.
> Der gav du mig længe Godnat i den bidende Røg
> fra en trebenet Jærnovn, stoppet med halvfugtigt Brænde.

In the last stanza we note a kind of symbolist imagination in operation. For what happens is that the properties around the lovers — the wood-stove, the acrid smoke and the kerosene lamp, the damp firewood — turn into an image of the painful, bittersweet engagement for the simple reason that the conflict-ridden tangle of their affair cannot possibly be expressed directly. A similar telescoping is at the base of the entire poem — and for many others from the same span of years (ca. 1888 to 1892) — for the love relationship, which could not be realized when it was real, assumes all the more body and colour in remembrance. In other words, the girl turns into a muse, a poetic inspiration of a feminine sort, that has risen from his memory.

Som en udtørret Vinstok, der bryder med Knopper paa ny
og grønnes og favner et Marmor, en styrtet Gudinde,
saa gror af min Ensomhed midt i en vinterlig By
det Foraar af Tanker, hvis Mørke omranker dit Minde.

("Tagdryp")

Teasingly, he compares his two girls, the fiancée and the muse, and the former is told, by way of a sweet goodbye, that she does not compare at all with the latter, who is always with him, never telling him off — and not afraid of getting pregnant: "hun bærer ikke Sorg for det alt for virkelige" ("Afskedsvers," 1912 — rev. of "Foraarsvers," 1897; SCL 4: 28). But the score is nonetheless not one to nil: the Muse, he tells his fiancée, will willingly sit on his lap and look at him with eyes "som efterligner dine en ganske lille Smule" (SCL 4: 28).

Is it truly symbolism into which Claussen has now launched himself? I should say Yes, and in corroboration of my answer might point to the fact that in this very period Claussen discovers Baudelaire, the founding father of symbolism. He translates him, too, a handful of poems from Les Fleurs du Mal (1857), but the motifs he notes in Baudelaire are those that flourish in his own poetry of the period and that are associated with love remembered. The poems in question are "Harmonie du Soir" ("Aftenharmoni," 1892), with Claussen's final line "dit Minde lyser i mig som et helligt Sølverlad," and "Le Flacon" ("Flakonen," 1892), which is about the perfume memory of the lost sweetheart. He appropriates Baudelaire: in "Brumes et Pluies" ("Taage- og Regndage," 1892) the heart that is full of "choses funèbres" the translator involuntarily turns into "et Hjerte, opfyldt af Ting, der længst er døde." I include these examples in order to show how personal is the road Claussen takes to symbolism. There is no question of his arbitrarily adopting a literary fashion or artistically recording the new signals of the age. It is rather a case of an experience that demanded a new style, a pressure of feeling that forced the poet beyond the literary boundaries he had first marked out.

At the same time there moved in Claussen's circles in Copenhagen a Norwegian, Knut Hamsun. He was the literary lion of the season, thanks to a recently published chapter (1888) of the later novel Sult (1890), but as literary debutants go, he was not young — nearly thirty years of age — with a long history behind him. It starts in North Norway, where he allows himself to be born among the common peasantry, then progresses through a number of itinerant years on both sides of the Atlantic, years of his youth filled with a welter of short-lived occupations — as a road-worker, a schoolteacher, a tram-driver, a postal worker — but through all this vagrancy he is guided by an immovable lodestar: he wants to become a writer. For a time he stays in Minneapolis with an emigrant countryman, the Unitarian preacher and writer Kristofer Janson, who gives him the following testimonial:

Jeg har aldrig truffet paa noget Menneske, som har havt den sygelige
Lidenskab for æstetisk Skjønhed som han, hvis hele Aandsretning har været
saa behersket af denne Lidenskap som hans. Saa som han kunde vugge sig
paa Rytmerne i Holger Drachmans Sange, saa som han kunde beruse sig i
Jacobsens minute Farvemaleri, saa som han kunde hoppe af Glæde og
fraadse Dagen lang over et originalt betegnende Adjektiv, han havde fundet
i en Bog eller selv opfundet, saa som han svælgede i tilspidsede, lavede,
farvemættede Udtryk, der efter min Mening forstyrrede og forpestede den
klare Tanke og bare blev den mest topmaalte Affektasjon. Ja, jeg har aldrig
truffet hans Mage i dette. Han kunde ofte gjøre mig rent sint, naar han kom
op og presenterede mig et Digt, som jeg fandt mildest talt meningsløst, bare
en vild Henflyen i en vis Stemning, en Jagen efter Musik og Farve, der blev
forceret ud i det smagløse. Og et Menneske med denne iboende Tørst efter
Kunst, efter raffinert Skjønhed sprunget ud i en norsk Bygd af fattige ulærde
Forældre, et Menneske som har tilbragt hele sit Liv saagodtsom paa Jagt
efter det daglige Brød, og som har maattet sanke sammen sin Dannelse af
brudte Stumper Læsning snart hist snart her af det mest blandede Gods!
Kan nogen raade mig den Gaade? (In *Budstikken* July 17, 1889)

This is not yet symbolism; it rather corresponds to what Sophus Claussen
was like before his breakthrough, when he was not only absorbed in the
ideas of his day — which was never the case with Hamsun — but also
entertained a spontaneous and unmotivated enthusiasm for an older and
unideological poet such as Aarestrup. But at the time when Hamsun stayed
with Janson, something significant happened to him that brought him
beyond mere aestheticism.

He fell ill — tuberculosis of the lungs it was surmised — and he was not
supposed to survive. Then it struck him as a disgrace, a rankling concern,
and unbearable grief that he was to go to his grave without having slept with
a woman. And poorly as he was, he had arranged that he was to be taken
to a bawdy house. For reasons about which he is not explicit, his plan was
squashed, but at the same time it turns out — though he remains reticent —
that he had no need to shop around; a proposition was made him. Not that
he accepted it — what he had desired, he did not want to be offered — but
declining left him in a state of great and peculiar unrest, with the result that
he was seized by "photomania," a carnal desire for flames that made him
set fire to the curtains.

My source is what he relates in a letter written some years later (to Erik
Skram, Dec. 26, 1888), just as he was having his breakthrough with the
chapter from *Sult*. What is odd is that he uses the incident to describe his
present inner state, as if the said experience had triggered a permanent
change in his condition. His photomania, according to the letter, was to be
included in the new chapter of *Sult*. There, the public will think that it is due
to the protagonist being starved, but he himself knows better what is
regrettably true. But if you read this chapter, which is not merely about
someone who goes hungry, but also about one who writes, it becomes clear
that the special relationship with light is tied up with the act of writing.

Delicate ripples of electricity run through him as his writing gets under way or he reads through what he has successfully produced. But does not this mean that Hamsun's verbal aestheticism has been brought down from its raving exaltation to be fastened to something outside words and connected with currents in his psycho-physical system as it is in the here and now?

To make things clear: neither at this stage is Hamsun a symbolist; at least, I for one do not know why he should be called so. He is, however, though without yet knowing him, completely in tune with Nietzsche, who is a worshipper of fire and the sun:

> Ja, Ich weiss, woher ich stamme!
> Ungesättigt gleich der Flamme
> Glühe und verzehr' ich mich.
> Licht wird alles, was ich fasse,
> Kohle Alles was ich lasse:
> Flamme bin ich sicherlich!

Nietzsche gave the title "Ecce Homo" to the poem (1882), the very same he used for his little book of prose that is about his dionysian "Sonnen-Vereinsamung" (1888; pub. 1908). When in more advanced years Hamsun spoke of Nietzsche as one of three writers who had really made an impression on him in his youth — though not really saying how — there is every reason to take the words at their face value.

If Freud had been asked what had taken place in the case of Hamsun and the case of Nietzsche, he would hardly have been in any doubt as to the answer: it is a question of a sexual impulse that has not been released in a sexual act but instead is sublimated and transformed into intellectual energy. Proud four-masters with lust in their sails, that is what the great men of culture are. The explanation cannot be contradicted, certainly not argued against — which does not mean, however, that it is true. Another explanation, which at least from a logical point of view is just as satisfying, presupposes that an archetypal passion or fundamental energy is at work, which may be realized partly in sexual activity, partly in spiritual enterprise, a hypothesis that has the advantage of concurring better with Hamsun's own. In his literary programme essay "Fra det ubevidste Sjæleliv" (1890), he mentions, without referring to himself, the obsession with the sun, so widespread with Nordic people, that tends to break out in the spring, and in this, he claims, there is to be found a "Blodsforvandtskab med Alskabningen . . ." (*Artikler* 43).

This last addition makes Hamsun a symbolist. If man with currents flowing through his soul and body is akin to Nature, then man is like Nature; the process unfolding in any individual is identical with what happens in the Universe, and hence the life of Nature may serve as a figure for human consciousness and function as an image, or to use the key word: as a *symbol*. And that becomes the matrix of *Pan* (1894), the short novel with which Hamsun conquered the great world. It *is* about love but has Nature as its subject, painting a landscape of North Norway, with islands, ocean, fjord, and mountain presented as one vast spiritual phenomenon, a psychic summer enchantment:

> ... det blev Uveir, Sydveststorm, et Skuespil hvortil jeg var Tilskuer. Alt stod i Røk. Jorden og Himlen blandedes sammen, Havet tumlet sig i forvredne Luftdanse, dannet Mænd, Hester og spjærrede Faner. Jeg stod i Ly under en Berghammer og tænkte mig mangehaande Ting, min Sjæl var spændt. Gud vet, tænkte jeg, hvad jeg idag er Vidne til og hvorfor Havet aapner sig for mine Øine? Kanskje skuer jeg i denne Stund det Indre av Jordens Hjærne, hvorledes der arbeides, hvorledes alt syder! (Hamsun, *SV* 1: *Pan* 5)

Several chapters will start with dialogue without a situation being indicated; the reason is that the situation is implied in advance, so to speak, by way of the mood of Nature, and then there is no distance to human beings and their speech.

The later large output from Knut Hamsun's pen may be said more or less to be in continuation of *Pan*. The form of symbolism or neoromanticism he had taken up (to use the words uttered by Nordahl Grieg at the close of the entire body of work) might make him humble in the face of space or death, but not as far as mankind was concerned, its struggle and hopes — in Hamsun's own words it ran: ". . . jeg giver Menneskene Fan med Fedt paa, jeg har nok med mig selv . . ." (letter to Claussen, Aug. 24, 1892. See Lasson 1: 141).

But another kind of art issues from *Sult*, a kind that is more inclined to allow for other people to exist. It left its mark, however, on only one other novel, *Mysterier* (1892), which was written between *Sult* and *Pan*, and perhaps also on one episode in the book of his old age, *Paa gjengrodde stier* (1949).

As may be remembered, there is a scene in *Sult* in which the sovereign first-person protagonist, the dubious and problematic hero of the book, abuses and bedevils a simple and gentle working man whom he meets on a seat in a park. The reason for his explosive behavior is not given, but indirectly it is felt that the one of them carries on as he does because the other is in possession of nothing, nothing whatsoever, of what makes a person of value in the view of the former — intelligence, freedom, imagination — but remains bold enough to be there, having the nerve to exist at all and being free enough to exist as something real, as immovable as the seat he sits on, patiently allowing himself to be bombarded with paradoxes about Happolati's electric hymnal and Ylajali, the dream princess. At this point one might remind oneself that the protagonist of *Sult* has his "centre" in his brain, where it shines and boils and flows. What is in question is what I once called cerebral consciousness, the decline of which we watch right through to the end of the novel.

As we turn to *Mysterier*, young Nagel, as the hero is now named, is clearly of the same *ilk*, but he is never allowed to stand alone. Out of a fascination inexplicable to himself, "the superman" — in quotation marks —

is linked to a prole — in no quotation marks — Minutten so called, a lame middle-aged errand-boy who is the butt of ridicule for the entire small town in which Nagel settles down as a highly sensational visitor. In a letter from the same period as the book, Hamsun calls Minutten Nagel's second ego, Nagel himself being without unity, only a loose fabric of megalomaniacal ideas, but the relationship with his antipode or counterpart — his *shadow* you might say, using Jung's terminology — must be absolutely firm, representing, as it were, cerebral man's defenselessness face-to-face with the humility of an evangelical purity of heart. In other words the author has become a psychological symbolist, letting the elements of the psyche, the poles of tension of the mind, stand forth as independent figures. Psychology is not found *inside* the characters, but *between* them, a relationary psychology (as Mogens Bjerring Hansen has called it in his book on Tom Kristensen: *Person og vision. Hærværk og dens forudsættninger*, 1972). And in order that no doubt remain, the distaff side is structured in the same fashion as the spear side. The women that are of importance to Nagel and his second self are a young radiant beauty and a poor woman with snowy white hair and glowing black eyes — Eros and Agape, Amor and Caritas — sexual love and charity as figures in their own right.

*Mysterier* was not properly understood, and all Hamsun's books to follow are, as has been said, different. But toward the end of his life when he had long been past creative writing, he got started again through his heartrending trial for having been a collaborator with the Germans during their occupation of Norway. In his book of memoirs he placed a sketch for a double portrait of himself and an itinerant lay preacher, as if they were Nagel and Minutten. But now the likeness between the first and the second ego is so great that one may speak of an inner identification, the two of them sharing a motivating experience in their youth (*Paa gjengrodde stier* 22-28, 61-68). About himself — and his lack of talent for creating true poetry — Hamsun writes,

Jeg får så mangen velsignet gave fra det høie, men jeg reflekterer dem sønder og sammen. Det er nok at jeg rører ved dem, fingrer ved blomsterstøvet. (*Paa gjengrodde stier* 71; normalized text)

And about the lay preacher,

da han engang sat i sneen på en fjeldtind og fik et sterkt lys fraoven gjennem sig. Men det var ikke et lys, det kunde ikke forklares, det var en hel himmel som kom ned, det var Gud. (*Paa gjengrodde stier* 67; normalized text)

Of the three writers who Hamsun would admit had been of importance to him, Nietzsche was one, as has been said. Strindberg was the second one (with Dostoyevsky being the third). The grouping is not surprising, for when Nietzsche's reputation spread — it happened long after Strindberg had made a name for himself — the latter could not regard the former as much else than a parallel to himself. Correspondingly, when Hamsun writes about Strindberg, he emphasizes the latter's cerebral consciousness; his talent is "en Hjærne tilhest" (*Artikler* 14). Every spring his head is rife with new ideas; in Scandinavia there never was a brain with such an enormous turnover, and he never expresses an opinion, he blasts it forth, even occasionally doing this with inspiration from "en smærtesøgende Tyskers betændte Hjærne" (*Artikler* 30; Eduard von Hartmann's *Philosophie des Unbewussten,* — 1869; rev. 1904 — is what he has in mind here).

The article by Hamsun that I draw on dates from 1894 and was written to come to Strindberg's aid in a deep crisis, which was financial, but also philosophical and literary, for it marks his transition from naturalism to symbolism. Objectively seen, it brought him to the brink of insanity; subjectively, it seemed to take him through hell, Inferno — his own word for his metamorphosis — the title (1897) of his report of crisis.

What Strindberg meant by naturalism is hardly open to doubt, for he explained it in the preface to *Fröken Julie* (1888), which has the subtitle: *Ett naturalistisk sorgspel.* If his many words were to be boiled down to a few sentences, the statement would be: naturalism means complexity, multiplicity, diversity, the richness of details — all the imperspicuity of the composite, which produces an illusion of reality. When Miss Julie, the young lady of the manor, allows herself to be seduced by Jean, the valet, then it is due not to her disastrous upbringing nor to her problematic engagement nor to her premenstrual condition, abetted by the enchantment of a summer night, the atmosphere in the dance hall, as well as sheer coincidence, but to the combined effect of everything at once. Strindberg is probably right in seeing in this a contrast to the fixed characters of classical-romantic drama — the miser who is nothing but miserly, the jealous husband who is only jealous, and so on — and to the simple plot motivations that go with such plays.

Has the writer now said everything there is to be said about his naturalist writings? Off the cuff the critic Vagn Steen once suggested a division between the writers who theorized in accordance with their creative work and those whose theories were at variance with their practice and were in tension with the works. Is not Strindberg to be classed with the latter group? In spite of all its multiplicity *Fröken Julie* has very much the effect of a single-track play, surely the most compact drama to be found. The multifarious details coalesce in a mood riddled with enchantment. The reason may be that the singleness of motivation Strindberg denies his figures, in return for an entanglement of impulses, turns up in his own obsession with his main character, whom he desires and hates, enjoying dragging her through all stages of degradation, the woman who in the very first staging of the play was acted by Strindberg's wife, herself, like Julie, a noble lady. The poet Jess Ørnsbo once casually compared the author of the piece and his relationship with his figure to that of a cavalry colonel with a recruit, and author Dorrit Willumsen has also orally meted out a similar appreciation of *En dåres försvarstal,* which dates from the same period (in French, 1887; Swedish, 1895) and gives the subject (Strindberg's wife) the same treatment. Faced with the opinion that the book is an arrant piece of male chauvinism, Willumsen replied, "Det ved jeg nu ikke rigtig, for jeg blev faktisk skudt i hende da jeg læste den." "Turned on," yes, that is what Willumsen was.

The objectivity that one must associate with naturalism as a doctrine, Strindberg the naturalist does not possess — and he made his last wife promise that she, who was an actress, would never take the part of Miss Julie nor read *En dåres försvarstal*. The extrovertive aggressiveness in the name of justice, which prompts him to write towards the end of the eighties, becomes his own problem, as it is turned against himself in the way it used to be aimed at others, and it takes him from subjective naturalism into symbolism.

The inherent instability of Strindberg's naturalism is evident from *Fadren* (1887), dating from the year before the punitive raid on *Fröken Julie*. In the latter play it is also "Hjärnornas kamp" (as essay topic, 1887; pub. 1890), the concept of the stronger mind against the weaker one, the valet against the lady, the dominant theme for Strindberg at this juncture. Suffice it to point to the one-act play *Den starkare* (1889). The paradox is that the strong person succumbs to the weaker. The husband with the superior mind fully sees through his hare-brained wife who cannot tell the difference between a spectroscope and a microscope. He still ends up as a defenseless victim to her stupid intrigues. He might be mistaken about her, but as a matter of fact he is not. She is the way we see her on the stage, exactly as she behaves in his imagination and thoughts in general. The balance and impartiality with which a dramatist may be expected to conceive of his figures, our author does not muster in the least. But then he must show solidarity with his hero, one might think. He does nothing of the sort; on the contrary: he has dissociated him from his own self, clearly taking up a distancing position. Hence the flickering or confused light that is shed on the play, its unsustained intensity, is owing to an objectively conceived main character whose subjective ideas we as spectators are being strongly forced into sharing.

*Fadren* — or the character of its title — is a product of Strindberg's ability to stand beside himself, turning his vision 180 degrees to record what he sees. At any given moment he may take out all his viscera as they have developed to date — all thoughts, suspicions, wishes, and anxieties — to transfer them into another person by a kind of over-all transplantation, and then finish off saying, This is not I. In a sense it is the same mechanism we the spectators are drawn into by witnessing these unfortunate marital quarrels — and *Fadren* is indeed a marriage drama: you build up an incendiary totality of irrefutable arguments, a complete verbal armour, which you cannot but give your backing, and then your real stance is elsewhere, for your fundamental dependence on the other or the other sex cannot be accommodated in the unassailable chain of arguments. As for *Fadren* it seemed to me a weakness in a recent television production of the play that the husband's burning desire for his beautiful wife did not come through as the all-clarifying undertone it ought to be.

The reason why Strindberg can get away from, or outside, himself — his self being understood as his ego at any given time — may be that he anticipates his future ego, that is, that the pressure of his development makes him see himself as he is from the viewpoint of the one he is to become; in a sense he more or less allows his symbolist ego to keep the naturalist under observation. At first his development leads him away from creative writing to take up a kind of study of nature — "Skönlitteraturen äcklar mig och jag går småningom öfver till vetenskap. Det är en fröjd utan like att öfva," it says in a letter to Ola Hansson from 1889 (*ASB* 7: 348). But his idea of science was something different from established natural science, which otherwise set a norm for the way of thinking of educated people at the time. His method, as described to Bengt Lidforss, is initially to get rid of all preconceived ideas — while the ordinary scientist has the results of others as his starting-point — and when his mind is a *tabula rasa*, he maintains that,

> jag [låter] min hjärna arbeta fritt, utan hänsyn på resultat, bifall, och så växer där fram något, som jag tror på . . . (*ASB* 8: 240)

— whereupon he supports his ideas through experiments that astoundingly enough achieve the expected results. The kind of reputation these experiments earned him need not be said. At the same time they caused his family life to go to pieces. Yet for a number of years he continued to make them, never abandoning them in his mind. Still in 1901 he showed his future third wife some gold he had made, which as she describes it must have looked like something else of his own making.

What did he get from his "science" that writing had not been able to provide? At first glance, nothing, for it was generated in the same way as his creative writing, "väkser fritt i hans huvud som druvor eller mögel," as he once said in a letter (to Ola Hansson, Oct. 1, 1890; *ASB* 8: 96-97). He knew nothing about its meaning. On reflection, however, one may assume that the centre of his being, his sovereign brain, has needed and sought an answer, a confirmation from outside, that casual concatenations of words could not give — to find the answer and the confirmation in the signs of a hidden world order that was identical with his own mental make-up and consequently accessible to his insight. This hypothesis takes support in the fact that Strindberg did indeed reside on the top floor of himself: if he went for a walk with his little daughter, he claims that his brain soon got fatigued from lowering itself to the standpoint of a child.

When he made gold from sulphur and lead or whatever, his aim was to show how all elements really are one, thanks to a secret unity running through the universe. The idea of universal unity makes Strindberg a romantic — as well as an occultist, astrologer, alchemist, and a lot more — but since the fundamental universal always shows itself to him as relationships between elements or in tangible coincidences, it may be just as appropriate, by virtue of the very concreteness of his mysticism, to call him a symbolist. The many symbols he observes, all reflections of a hidden order, might make him a writer anew, but an intermediate link is missing, a painful one, that has to do with him and his responsibility.

It may be studied in *Inferno* (1897), which covers his life in the middle of the nineties. Left to himself and his science in a foreign city — Paris — and surrounded by a sea of unsolved money and family problems, the strain of work takes him to the point at which he feels a kind of electricity stirring within him. Undoubtedly it is akin to Hamsun's photomania, but in contrast to Hamsun Strindberg believes that it is due to aggressively hostile acts from various people who are his enemies or are believed to be. They must have mounted current generators in his neighbourhood. It smacks of paranoia, but it conceals something. What it is, will be evident from other kinds of happenings that befall him. One day he sees in a split walnut the hands of a praying child; another day he meets the face of his wife on a piece of cardboard in the laboratory. On a third day he sees a hind in the evening sky, holding its head towards Austria where his deserted family resides. What it means is that the traumas of his conscience have been projected onto the world around him; his inner conflicts are experienced in external space. The explanation for his paranoid ideas lies here: he thinks he deserves punishment, which he believes is the reason why he is persecuted. When this simple explanation of his tribulations becomes clear to him, the threat of insanity is turned away as he resigns himself to his sufferings as a just punishment, an atonement imposed upon him — and that brings *Inferno* to a close.

At the same time he gives up his research, returning to writing, albeit departing from a new set of ideas. The distance between past and present may be assessed by comparing *Fadren* with *Dödsdansen* (1900). Both are plays about marriage in a naturalist mode, but one is centred on the lord and master — as we learned — the other shows an infernal balance between the spouses. From where did Strindberg draw the liberty required for placing the parties on an even footing? There is no source for it, but my guess is: his recently gained vision of the world as a prison, a universal penal colony in which human beings must atone for crimes committed in this or an earlier life.[2] If the death-dancing couple in their marital hell are not exactly symbolic in spite of the symbolism of the setting — the fortress keep — they are at least representative: their suffering is the suffering of all.

When Strindberg in *Inferno* and after saw the conflicts of his soul in the surrounding world, it represents the experience with which we are all familiar from dreams: what takes place in our minds, seems to be enacted outside. His dramatized version of *Inferno*, the conversion play with the Pauline title, *Till Damaskus* (1898-1901), he may suitably describe as a dreamplay: his conversation in the manner of a dream is visualized as a journey out and back, with the stations of life passed through in a forward movement and then in reverse. The characters, which the traveller encounters, are all of Minutten's ilk, appearing as reminders of neglected and mismanaged opportunities. Uncertain reminders, however, for the play remains obscure, relying on the obscurity that Strindberg retains from now on as a privilege to the very end of his writing days, probably working on the assumption that existence holds a divine meaning, but it has not been God's wish to reveal it, and what chance is there then for the writer to do so?

Speaking of Strindberg you have to bring up *Ett Drömspel* (1901), the *clou* in his career as a writer. What has been said so far still holds good, but with the rider that the anguish underlying Strindberg's resignation, his revolt against piously submitting to the terms of his punishment, is of equal importance. Life and happiness have tempted him once again, embodied in a fair maiden who to the aging writer is youth and love, combining the desire for rejuvenescence with that of falling in love. The ambivalence reveals itself in the fact that she is the daughter of the god Indra but is placed with, or lowered to, representatives of the male sex, whom she passes by like the trees of a country drive, until about the middle of the play she is caught in a lethally closed marriage. The inconsistency represented by the female figure — the daughter, man's natural token of the possibility of rebirth, who is seen as the Beloved, his potential of integrity and union — is keenly illuminated by the fact that the existence on earth of the Heavenly One is a protracted progress through suffering and compassion. The torments that Strindberg heaps on her are equal to Miss Julie's, which are inescapable.

In the second part of the play she is released from her terrestrial chains as she returns to Heaven, and here the poet fares less well, for he simply does not want to let her go.

All the same she disappears from the play and the author's life ... removing his symbolism as well, since in the next play about marriage, from 1907 — the highly evocative *Oväder* — he is back where he was in *Fadren* from his naturalist period. It is again the passionately one-sided pleading, the stubborn holding-at-bay, now centred on an old gentleman's right to live in peace from the inroads of youth, which still remains all the life that he has left.

Translated by Niels Lyhne Jensen, 1992

## Notes

[1] The present author is in the debt of Gunnar Brandell, Aage Henriksen — and Harald Næss.

The article, now slightly revised and translated, was first published as "Halvfemserne i Norden," in *Dansk Udsyn* 70 (1990): 67-82.

[2] These sentiments may be found in "På kyrkogården" (orig. in French, 1896; see *SS* 27: 593-605) and in a letter to T. Hadlund, Oct. 31, 1896 (see *ASB* 11: 375-77).

## Works Cited

Claussen, Sophus. "Mennesket og Digteren." 1907. Rev. in *Tilskueren* (1917): 223-27. See verses 13 and 17. See also *SCL* 5: 39.

——. "Afskedsvers." *Danske Vers.* Copenhagen/Kristiania [Oslo]: Gyldendalske Boghandel, 1912. 30-31. See *SCL* 4.

——. "Aftenharmonie." [Trans. of Baudelaire's "Harmonie du Soir."] *København* [Copenhagen daily newspaper] Feb. 14, 1892: 2. Rpt. *See SCL* 5.

——. "Flakonen." [Trans. of Baudelaire's "Le Flacon."] In "Nogle Vers af Charles Baudelaire. Oversatte af Sophus Claussen." *Tilskueren* 9.1 (1892): 82. 79-83; see 82. See also *SCL* 5.

——. "Taage- og Regndage." [Trans. of Baudelaire's "Brumes et Pluies."] In "Nogle Vers af Charles Baudelaire. Oversatte af Sophus Claussen." *Tilskueren* 9.1 (1892): 79-83; see 79. See also *SCL* 5.

——. [*SCL*] *Sophus Claussens lyrik.* Ed., with commentary, by Jørgen Hunosøe. 9 vols. Copenhagen: Gyldendal, for Det danske Sprog- og Litteraturselskab, 1982-84. See the following poems:
"Antonius Gynt 6: Nye Piger." From *Naturbørn* (1887). In vol. 1: Naturbørn *og* Mina. 69-72.
"Tagdryp." From *Pilefløjter* (1899). In vol. 2: Pilefløjter *og* Trefoden. Part 1: 24.
"Mennesket og Digteren" (1907; rev. 1917). In vol. 4: *Danske Vers.* 28.
"Afskedsvers" (1912). In vol 5: "Fabler." 39.
"Aftenharmonie." From *København* (1892). "Flakonen," and "Taage- og Regndage." From *Tilskueren* (1892). In vol. 5: "Juvenilia." Respectively 114, 111, 109.

Frandsen, Ernst. *Sophus Claussen.* 2 vols. Copenhagen: Gyldendal, 1950.

Hamsun, Knut. *Artikler 1889-1928.* Comp. by Francis Bull. Oslo: Gyldendal, 1965. Includes "Fra det ubevidste Sjæleliv," 33-44; and "Lidt om Strindberg," 14-32.

——. Letter to Erik Skram. Dec. 26, 1888. In *Knut Hamsun som han var. Et utvalg af hans brev.* Ed. Tore Hamsun. Oslo: Gyldendal, 1956. 51-55.

——. *Paa gjengrodde stier.* Oslo: Gyldendal, 1964.

——. [*SV*] *Samlede Verker.* 2nd ed. Kristiania [Oslo]/Copenhagen: Gyldendal, 1918-20. 12 vols. See vol. 1 (1918): *Sult* and *Pan* (chap. 3) 5. Vol. 2 (1918): *Mysterier.*

Hansen, Mogens Bjerring. *Person og vision. Hærværk og dens forudsætninger.* Grenå: GMT, for Hansen, 1972.

Hartmann, Eduard von. *Philosophie des Unbewussten.* 1869; rev. 1904. 12th ed. Leipzig: Alfred Kröner, 1923. In Swedish, 1878.

Janson, Kristofer. In *Budstikken* [Minneapolis newspaper, 1873-95] July 17, 1889.

Jørgensen, Johannes. "Symbolisme." 1893. Rpt. in *Taarnet. En antologi.* Ed. Carl Bergstrøm-Nielsen. Copenhagen: Gyldendals Uglebøger, 1966. 54-59.

Lasson, Frans. *Sophus Claussen og hans kreds. En digters liv i Breve.* 2 vols. Copenhagen: Gyldendal, 1984. Letter from Claussen to Viggo Stuckenberg, July 1, 1886, in 1: 80-82. Letter from Knut Hamsun to Claussen, Aug. 24, 1892, in 1: 141-42.

Nietzsche, Friedrich. "Ecce Homo." In *Die fröhliche Wissenschaft.* 1882. Leipzig: C. G. Naumann, 1908. 30.

Strindberg, August. [ASB] *August Strindbergs brev*. Ed. Thorsten Eklund. Strindbergs-sällskapets Skrifter. 15 vols. Stockholm: Bonniers, 1948-76. Letter to Ola Hansson, July 6, 1889, no. 1867 in vol. 7 (*Februar 1888-december 1889*): 348. Letters to Ola Hansson, Oct. 1, 1890, no. 2034, and to Bengt Lidforss, Apr. 1, 1891, no. 2173 in vol. 8 (*Januari 1890-december 1891*): 96-97 and 235-41, respectively. Letter to T. Hadlund, Oct. 31, 1896, no. 3414 in vol. 11 (*Maj 1895-november 1896*): 375-77.

———. [SS] *Samlade Skrifter*. Ed. John Landqvist. 55 vols. Stockholm: Bonniers, 1912-20. See the following:
Vol. 22: "Hjärnornas kamp." In *Vivisektioner* 123-57.
Vol. 23: *Fadren; Fröken Julie*.
Vol. 25: *Den Starkare*.
Vol. 26: *En dåres försvarstal*.
Vol. 27: "På Kyrkogården." 593-605.
Vol. 28: *Inferno*.
Vol. 29: *Till Damaskus*.
Vol. 34: *Dödsdansen*.
Vol. 36: *Ett drömspel*.
Vol. 45: *Oväder*.

# Heidenstam's *Karolinerna* and the *Fin de Siècle*

Susan Brantly

*Om du också uppsöker det förflutna,*
*skall lika fullt din samtids blod fylla*
*ditt hjärta.*

Heidenstam, *Hans Alienus*

When Verner von Heidenstam's novel *Karolinerna* (1897-98) first appeared, it was a political as well as an artistic event. In the book *Heidenstam och sekelskiftets Sverige* (1946), Staffan Björck describes *Karolinerna*'s emergence in a changing Sweden, in which conservative patriotism and a growing democratic movement struggled against each other. "Patriotism" was such a watchword that critics could not fail to cast themselves over a novel treating one of Sweden's most controversial monarchs, Charles XII. Björck describes Heidenstam's particular brand of patriotism as

> politiskt radikal, historiskt inställd, men med sikte på folket och individen, antirojalistisk, amoralisk, hänsynslöst estetisk och hednisk eller själv en religion. (10)

Like Björck, Fredrik Böök, in his two-volume study of Verner von Heidenstam, places special emphasis on the nationalistic qualities of *Karolinerna*, carefully examining the historical sources for Heidenstam's artistic construction. The rubric for Alrik Gustafson's treatment of Heidenstam's historical novels is similarly "Nationalism Reinterpreted" (1940). Subsequent studies of *Karolinerna* concentrated on the artistry of the work. In 1954, Gunnar Axberger explored the fire imagery in *Karolinerna*, and in 1961, Erland Lagerroth executed a careful study of the structural features of *Karolinerna*, in which he describes the tragedy of Charles XII as it plays in counterpoint to the story of the Swedish people.

The focus of concentration upon the nationalistic and artistic aspects of *Karolinerna* has prevented critics from considering the typically *fin de siècle* elements of the work. Heidenstam himself might have protested against such treatment, but as Björck observes,

Med all sin ofta tillspetsade opposition mot den dekadenta riktningen i Europa, har Heidenstam mycket gemensamt med denna, vilket också den borgerliga samtidskritiken underströk. (31)

Contemporary critics of *Karolinerna*, above all, drew parallels between Charles XII and the Nietzschean superman or Ibsen's Brand (-pt- 26 May 1897; T. H. 6 June 1898; Jacqueline 7 May 1898; K. W-g. 1 June 1898; Hammarskjöld 316). Such comparisons flatter the figure of Charles XII; however, the "hero king" was such a cultural icon, it would have occurred to few to compare him to a Baudelairian dandy. In many ways, however, *Karolinerna* was a typical *fin de siècle* product and contains numerous Decadent topoi. It is not necessary to assume any direct literary influences from Baudelaire and his like, but rather, one might say that Heidenstam had breathed in deeply the air of the *fin de siècle* and that, as an aristocrat and aesthete, he could not help but share its interest in Decadence.

We can begin by examining the striking form of the work. Heidenstam subtitles it "berättelser," and certain authoritative sources, like the Natur och Kultur's *Litteraturlexikon*, take him at his word. Several critics, however, have felt the need to appeal to other genres for metaphors that would do *Karolinerna* justice. Gunnar Axberger refers to *Karolinerna* as "en följd av tavlor, sedda och komponerade av en målare" (194). Erland Lagerroth finds in *Karolinerna* the intertwining strands of "en klassisk tragedi" as pertains to the fate of Charles XII and a "berättelsecykel" about the Swedish people (131, 98). Frederik Böök calls *Karolinerna* "en hjältedikt" and "ett modernt epos" composed of "dikter på prosa" (82-85). In *Romanens formvärld* (1953), Staffan Björck tacitly considers *Karolinerna* to be a novel when he compares it to other cyclical prose works (259), such as Selma Lagerlöf's *Gösta Berlings saga* (1891) and Harry Martinson's *Vägen till Klockrike* (1948). When *Karolinerna* first appeared, its form caused just as much confusion as it has in subsequent years. Critics invoked terms like "rhapsodier på prosa," "en tragisk hjältedikt," "en historisk roman," "en mängd anekdoter, trots en viss inre enhet," "det stora krigiska epos," and "stridsmålningar" (Jacqueline 1 June 1897; Jacqueline 7 May 1898; K. W-g. 1 June 1898; T. H. 6 June 1898; Didrik 22 May 1897; L. Hennings 12 June 1897). Several critics, however, found Heidenstam's formal innovations in *Karolinerna* to be wanting in comparison to the standard features of established genres and condemned his attempt at originality.

Even though Heidenstam's generic hybrid did not find favor with his Swedish contemporaries, it might have struck a chord with one fictional critic, Joris Karl Huysmans's Des Esseintes from *À Rebours* (1884). Des Esseintes, a paragon of Decadence, is a great bibliophile, and we learn a good deal about his literary tastes. Des Esseintes seems to favor the mixing of generic attributes, and his favorite literary genre is one such hybrid: the prose poem as practiced by Baudelaire and Mallarmé. Furthermore, Des Esseintes himself combines elements of fragrance, music, and poetry into a new art form, which allows him to refer to "l'odorante orchestration du poème" (Huysmans 156). Moreover, *À Rebours* contains a lengthy verbal evocation of the painting *Salomé dansant devant Hérode* (1876) by Gustave Moreau. In a similar vein, it has been noted (Böök 45, 89) that the pictoral quality of certain moments in *Karolinerna* suggests famous Swedish paintings, such as Johan Fredrik Höckert's *Stockholms slottsbrand den 7 maj 1697* (1862-66) and Gustaf Cederström's *Karl XII:s likfärd* (1884). Heidenstam shared Des Esseintes's interest in mixing art forms. Heidenstam was a man who did not care to have his imagination fettered by the demands of genre, and his earliest works, in particular *Hans Alienus* (1892), are marked by innovation and generic mixes. However, precisely the desire to mix artistic media into new configurations was considered by Max Nordau, the great critic of Decadence, to be one of the symptoms of society's "Entartung." Nordau noted that the public sought out exhibitions "in welchen verschiedene Kunstarten in neuen Verknüpfungen auf alle Sinne zugleich zu wirken bestrebt sind" (1: 23).

The term most frequently invoked by Heidenstam's contemporaries to assess *Karolinerna* was "epos." Runeberg's *Fänrik Ståls sägner* (1848, 1860), which celebrates Finnish bravery at all social levels during the war of 1808-09, was seen as the most immediate literary ancestor to Heidenstam's cycle of prose poems. It may be said of *Fänrik Ståls sägner* that Runeberg's cycle of poems played a considerable role in shaping the Finnish national self-image, over and against years of Swedish and Russian dominance. It was not an uncommon trait of even older epics, from Virgil's *Aeneid* in 19 BC to Milton's *Paradise Lost* in 1667, that the hero founds or saves a nation. The critics who looked to *Karolinerna* for an epic of national glorification and cohesion were disappointed. Narva, the greatest victory of Sweden's "hero king," was passed over in silence: "Narva nämnes ej en gång, men Pultava är en huvudskildring" (Henning 12 June 97). Instead, the hero of Heidenstam's epic, Charles XII, is the instrument of the decline of the once-great Swedish Empire. His is an epic of destruction rather than formation.

The theme of the declining Roman Empire beset by barbarians from the East is central to the phenomenon of Decadence. Max Nordau traced the heritage of "Decadence" to this source in 1892, and subsequent scholars, such as Jens Malte Fischer and Walther Rehm concur (Nordau 2: 91; Fischer 78). The connection between the declining Swedish Empire and that of Rome is made explicit in *Karolinerna* when Cronstedt cries toward the end of the novel, "Det är Nordens romare . . . som i natt stupa för sina sista provinser!" (*Samlade verk* [*SV*] 8: 141). Erik Dahlberg in the fortress at Riga has etchings of Roman ruins on his wall. The night before Poltava, Lewenhaupt recites Roman verses, and the king dreams of a czar who warns him: "På detta samma rum nedhöggo för tre hundra år sedan Tamerlans horder Västerns samlade härskaror" (*SV* 7: 181). The allusion to Tamerlane, the fourteenth-century Mongol warrior, invokes images of his kinsman Genghis Khan and of Attila the Hun, two of the barbarians who have periodically plagued the Western world. Moreover it implies that the Russians assaulting the crumbling Swedish Empire have inherited the role of the barbarians.

Finding beauty in destruction is an old theme with Heidenstam. In *Hans Alienus*, Sardanapal's exotic kingdom is destroyed in a spectacular fashion, and Sardanapal remarks before the prospect,

> Min ande drunknar i vällust vid åsynen av undergångens förfärande vidd. Det kallar jag livets stoltaste sällhet att gå så under, att ett jubel från saliga läppar överröstar murarnas fall och genljuder genom tusen och åter tusen år. (2: 125)

Hans Alienus also describes how pleased Napoleon was to have become a tragic figure, "och med hvilket halfdoldt nöje han ser hän över sin egen undergångs stora linjer" (1: 227). Hans Alienus's words about Napoleon echo Heidenstam's judgement of Charles XII in his essay "Karl XII och det tragiska" (1898): "En hjälte, som ligger utarmad, övergiven och dräpt, först honom vill jag kalla en sann hjälte inför både fiende och vän" (*SV* 9: 32). Citing this passage, Lagerroth discusses the aesthetics of Charles XII's tragedy (118). Heidenstam provides Charles XII with an aesthetic justification for an otherwise questionable political career. The defeat of Charles XII and the Swedish nation is tragic and sublime, therefore beautiful. Further, Lagerroth suggests that this aesthetics of tragedy lies behind Feuerhausen's assessment of Charles XII's strangely light-hearted reaction to the young ensign who has frozen to death at his post: "Das ist nur die Freude eines Helden den schönen Tod eines Helden zu sehen" (119). Heidenstam was drawn to the material of Charles XII not because of his military victories, but because of his spectacular fall. In keeping with the mood of the *fin de siècle*, Heidenstam has written an epic of decline.

Thus, the hybrid genre of *Karolinerna* and the focus upon the beauty of decline might both be described as Decadent traits. Our Decadent literary critic Des Esseintes tells us that an interest in the past is yet another:

> En effet, lorsque l'époque où un homme de talent est obligé de vivre, est plate et bête, l'artiste est, à son insu même, hanté par la nostalgie d'un autre siècle. (Huysmans 224)

Hans Alienus's disaffection with his own time prompts him to seek the past in the form of the grave of Sardanapal's kingdom in the underworld. Heidenstam's dissatisfaction with his own time in large part prompted the writing of *Karolinerna*. In "Om svenskarnas lynne" (1896), Heidenstam complains,

> Sverige har hemfallit åt en materialism, som, blottad på allt idéinnehåll och på varje annan känsla än egennyttan, undergrävt vår auktoritet och vår sista återstod av självkänsla. (*SV* 9: 22)

Sweden's struggle for modernity has caused it to neglect its past, so that a visitor to Sweden might think that it was "ett nytt land utan historia" (*SV* 9: 16). Heidenstam's choice of a historical theme was a direct response to the flaws he saw in his own day.

The Decadent protagonist is in many ways the cornerstone of Decadent prose. Although the Decadent protagonist is almost always aristocratic, he is only rarely royal. Still, Decadents exhibited a fascination with the figure of the insane Ludwig II of Bavaria, who built his fairy castles. The young Rilke wrote poems about Charles XII, directly inspired by Heidenstam's *Karolinerna*.[1] Stefan George's *Algabal* (1892) is a decadent Roman emperor, who smothers his guests in a mountain of rose petals. Alfred Kubin's peculiar novel *Die andere Seite* (1909) boasts a nonroyal Decadent protagonist who has nevertheless managed to purchase for himself a small country in Asia. These examples betray a fascination with Decadent figures who possess unlimited power over others. Charles XII, an absolute monarch, was also such a figure.

Further, Charles XII is a member of a declining noble family and, as such, represents his declining people and empire. Erik Dahlberg declaims:

> Ack, vi svenske, vi blodsförvanter till Vasakungarna, som på sin ålderdom endast kunde anklaga och banna och till sist sutto mörkrädda i sina egna rum ... vi äga i vår själen svart frö, ur vilket med åren reser sig ett grenigt träd, fullt av bittraste galläpplen! (*SV* 7: 76)

Both the king and his man Höök are said to be afraid of the dark, a sign of the weakening of the race. The future prognosis for the Swedish people is not good. At the council table, Falkenberg remarks, "Sedan våra män stupat i fält, leva bara käringsjälarna kvar, och det är de, som nu börja fortplanta det svenska folket" (*SV* 7: 206). The implication is that the bravery of the "Charles men" is a final flourish in a declining populace.

The dandy of Decadence, especially as he is described by Baudelaire, is one who adheres to a stringent code of behavior. The ascetic discipline of Charles XII is one characteristic that qualifies him for the label. Baudelaire tells us that,

> Le dandysm n'est même pas, comme beaucoup de personnes peu réfléchies paraissent le croire, un goût immodéré de la toilette et de l'élégance matérielle. (1178)

Rather, with regards to dress, the dandy finds perfection in absolute simplicity. It is Mazepa who recognizes this strain in Charles XII: "Tror du inte, att han sprättar lika mycket med sina nedsotade paltor som någon fransysk luktvattenprins med sina silkestrumpor!" (*SV* 7: 118). Further, Baudelaire describes the dandy as someone habituated from early youth to being obeyed by others, surely an apt description of the young Charles XII. The dandy is generally wealthy, although "le dandy n'aspire pas à l'argent comme à une chose essentielle; un crédit indéfini pourrait lui suffire" (Baudelaire 1178). The lack of resources becomes so painful to Charles XII, that he allows Görtz to print some money, thereby achieving his "limitless bank credit."

A key character trait of the dandy rests in

> le plaisir d'étonner et la satisfaction orgueilleuse de ne jamais être étonné. Un dandy peut être un homme blasé, peut être un homme souffrant; mais, dans ce dernier cas, il sourira comme le Lacédémonien sous la morsure du renard. (Baudelaire 1178)

Charles XII is always surprising his people and not always positively. Maz-epa also remarks about "det där underliga nordiska lättsinnet" possessed by the king, which causes him to greet setbacks with "Strunt, det här är ingent-ing! Schadet nichts!" (*SV* 7: 119). Nowhere is the king's penchant for surprise and stoicism more clear than in the novella titled "Det befästa huset" (*SV* 7: 148-65). The king risks his own life on a whim, undertaking an escapade that needlessly results in the death of a young ensign. As the king approaches Feuerhausen and the young ensign in the house, he is described as follows:

> De smärtor i huvudet, av vilka han börjat lida, hade ökats av ritten i blåsten och gjorde blicken tung. Ansiktet bar spår av ensamhetens själsstrider, men allt eftersom han närmade sig, återtog munnen det vanliga förlägna leendet. (*SV* 7: 161)

Smiling in the face of pain, stiffly smiling at coarse stories, and laughing at misfortune are all traits of Charles XII that come forth in this episode. Elsewhere there is a reference to the king's "kall fast ännu småleende mask" (*SV* 8: 74). Charles XII summons the smile of the dandy on most occasions.

Finally, Baudelaire characterizes dandyism as "le dernier éclat d'héroïsme dans le décadences" (1179). Thus, Charles XII as "hero king" takes on a different aspect in the light of the *fin de siècle*. He is not the hero of Narva, winning against overwhelming odds, as he was in Esaias Tegnér's famous poem. Charles is a hero because he remains true to his personal code in the face of great adversity and even until his death. It is his misfortunes, Heiden-stam would argue, that makes Charles XII a hero, not his successes.

Jens Malte Fischer notes another quality of the dandy: "Der Dandy betrachtet sein Leben als seine eigentliche Künstlerische Schöpfung" (70). The king's fascination with stories of Greek and Roman heroes, the viking sagas, and the life of Alexander the Great have inspired him to create a saga of his life:

> Allt från bardomsårens upptåg fången i sin egen forntidsaktiga inbillningsvärld, satt han döv för de skärande nödropen kring vägen, och han blev misstrogen mot var och en, som visade en känsligare hörsel. (*SV* 7: 153)

He rejoices in French Mons's story of battle "som ett barn åt en underlig saga" (*SV* 7: 96). Heidenstam offers the epitaph for Charles XII: "Han längta-de att bli ekot av en sjungen saga" (*SV* 8: 234). When he is not able at Poltava to become Hercules on his pyre, he must orchestrate at Fredrikshall another suitable end to his tale. Erland Lagerroth considers this privileging of art over reality to be an influence from Oscar Wilde (134).

Other Decadent attributes that may be assigned to Charles XII include the curse of boredom. "Vad där var tråkigt!" is the exclamation that charac-terizes Charles's life at court before the wars begin (*SV* 7: 39). It is the call to war that pulls him out of his tedium, but it is a remedy that becomes more and more costly. Before Poltava, it is noted, "Han hade tömt krigsäventyrens bägare i botten, och drycken behövde dagligen kryddas allt starkare för att smaka" (*SV* 7: 174). At this point, one might think of Des Esseintes whose tastes have become so jaded he seeks "des parfums nouveaux, des fleurs plus larges, des plaisirs inéprouvés" (Huysmans 145). Or, one might recall Stig Høgh who, stirred to potency only by a brawl and the breaking of a bone, may finally possess Marie in J. P. Jacobsen's novel *Marie Grubbe* (1876). Charles XII mobilizes the entire Swedish army to keep himself from boredom, and he longs for the ultimate experience, death.

Charles XII's attitude towards sexuality is also a familiar topos in the literature of Decadence. Catulle Mendès wrote of *Le Roi Vierge* (1881). Jens Malte Fischer claimes that Heliogabulus is a true dandy because he is always "Herr seiner Sinnlichkeit" (70). Charles XII is a virgin king, who never allows his bodyguards to marry. The king's one brush with sensuality in his youth has pathological overtones. When Rhoda d'Elleville tries to seduce the young king, he finds her scent and touch repulsive:

> Parfymerna, lukten av hennes hår, av kvinna kväljde honom så häftigt, att han var nära att få uppkastningar. Beröringen, känslan av hennes varma hand äcklade honom som snuddandet vid en råtta eller ett lik. (*SV* 7: 56)

After Charles XII rejects Rhoda, he overcomes his discomfort by slicing the head off a calf in a room set aside for this purpose. He savours the feel of blood beneath his fingernails and throws the calf's head out the window upon the passers-by. This type of sadistic sensuality is a Decadent symptom, which Max Nordau (2: 324) finds most strongly expressed in the writings of Nietzsche.

Poltava is an important turning point for Charles XII. Up until then, the only trouble the king had had with his will was that he had had too much of it: "Viljan är för mig en fjättra, en kring bröstet hårt åtdragen kedja, ur vilken jag inte kan vrida mig lös" (*SV* 7: 41). At Poltava, after he is shamed by Rehnskiöld, Charles XII sinks into a state of lassitude, which afflicts him throughout his stay in Bender. This temporary bout of abulia is one of the common Decadent maladies identified by Nordau (1: 34). Until Poltava, Charles XII had gained the respect of his men by being able to "sova på snödrivan och dricka vatten ur träskålar" (*SV* 8: 61). During his stay in Bender, the king demonstrates an interest in his physical surroundings, and the opulent Carlopolis is raised near the river. Charles XII follows in the tradition of Des Esseintes, who painstakingly remodels and decorates his villa to suit his exacting tastes, and even more in that of Ludwig II of Bavaria, who created the exotic retreats of Neuschwanstein and Linderhof. Carlopolis is an artificial paradise in which the king takes temporary refuge. In the long run, however, such opulence does not suit Charles XII's quest for honor.

The *fin de siècle* is also characterized by symbolism and "un certain goût du merveilleux" (Huysmans 113). An inclination toward the mystical is, according to Max Nordau, "ein Hauptstigma des Degenerirten" (1: 37). Both symbolism and the supernatural are present in *Karolinerna*, though they were generally judged to be an unfit intrusion into Heidenstam's topic. Georg Brandes generally approved of Heidenstam's "historisk rekonstruktion" but disapproved of "det symboliske framställningssättet" in the story of Mazepa (Brandes 11 May 97). In that story, Mazepa's ambassador possesses the physical characteristics of the Grim Reaper. Evidently, in Brandes's view, the use of symbolism in the execution of a historical work is not allowed, since it threatens credulity. Other occult references are only obliquely referred to by contemporary critics as "de Heidenstamska bizarrerierna." (-pt- 11 May 1898; Wirsén 6 May 1898; Hammarskjöld 324). This epithet is likely to encompass the episode in which French Mons spends the night in the house of an eccentric recluse in the company of the insane twin daughters of an abducted nun and attended by a dead lackey named Jonathan who plays tricks on anyone who is not an aristocrat. Agathon Hammarskjöld compared this episode to "en febersjuks groteska fantasier" (324). Other supernatural undercurrents include the suggestion made by Mazepa that Charles XII died at Narva, and his shadow continues to lead the troups (SV 7: 119) and "den Svarta bataljonen," which is made up of the ghosts of the troups fallen in battle, who try to keep up with their comrades. In an often-cited anecdote, Heidenstam claimed that Charles XII himself appeared to him while he was composing Karolinerna (Brev 138-40). Heidenstam's typically fin de siècle fascination with ghosts did not mesh with the expectations of nineteenth-century historicism and the fast encroaching modern technological age.

"Jag [är] ju egentligen just den ende, som . . . bestämt avsvurit alla dekadentprogram," claimed Verner von Heidenstam with offended dignity in a letter to Ellen Key (Brev 128). Unlike the average Decadent, Heidenstam took an active interest in the contemporary political life of his country and perhaps therefore resented being easily dismissed with the epithet "Decadent." Heidenstam perceived the tales in Karolinerna to be not an aesthetic escape into the past, but "det mest levande uttryck för den tid då de blivit skrivna" (Brev 125). Heidenstam's perception was even more accurate than he realized. Karolinerna is both a political and an aesthetic manifestation of the 1890s. Although Karolinerna did strike a resounding chord in the political life of Sweden, the instrument was crafted in the Decadent workshop of Heidenstam's artistic imagination.

## Notes

[1] See George Schoolfield, "Charles XII Rides in Worpswede," *Modern Language Quarterly* 16 (1955): 258-67. It seems only fair to mention at this point the great extent to which I am indebted to George Schoolfield for countless observations about the topoi of Decadence and numerous bibliographical references. I attended Prof. Schoolfield's class on Scandinavian Decadence given at Harvard in the spring of 1980 and his seminar on German Decadence given at Yale in the fall of 1983. Prof. Schoolfield allowed me to teach Heidenstam's *Karolinerna* in the Scandinavian Decadence course he gave at Yale in 1986, and many of the insights I had then are being used in this article.

## Works Cited

Axberger, Gunnar. *Diktaren och elden*. Stockholm: Bonniers, 1954.

Baudelaire, Charles. "Le Dandy." *Oeuvres complètes*. Ed. Claude Pichois. Paris: Éditions Gallemard, 1961. 1177-180.

Björck, Staffan. *Heidenstam och sekelskiftets Sverige*. Stockholm: Natur och Kultur, 1946.

———. *Romanens formvärld*. Stockholm: Natur och Kultur, 1953.

Brandes, Georg. "Verner von Heidenstam: *Karolinerna I.*" *Svenska Dagbladet* 11 May 1897.

Böök, Fredrik. *Verner von Heidenstam*. Vol. 2. Stockholm: Bonniers, 1946. 2 vols. 1946.

Didrik. "Ny svensk litteratur." Rev. of *Karolinerna* I, by V. von Heidenstam. *Arbetet* 22 May 1897.

Fischer, Jens Malte. *Fin de Siècle. Kommentar zu einer Epoche*. Munich: Winkler Verlag, 1978.

Gustafson, Alrik. *Six Scandinavian Novelists*. Minneapolis: U of Minnesota P, 1940.

Hammarskjöld, Agathon. "Karl XII och *Karolinerna*." *Nordisk Tidskrift för Vetenskap, Konst och Industri*. Stockholm: Norstedt, 1897. 305-25.

Heidenstam, Verner von. *Brev*. Eds. Kate Bang and Fredrik Böök. Stockholm: Bonniers, 1949.

———. *Hans Alienus*. 2 vols. Stockholm: Bonniers, 1892.

———. [*SV*] *Samlade verk*. Eds. Kate Bang and Fredrik Böök. Vols. 7-8: *Karolinerna*; vol. 9: *Tankar och Teckningar*. Stockholm: Bonniers, 1944. 23 vols. 1943-44.

Hennings, L. "Böcker." Rev. of *Karolinerna* I, by V. von Heidenstam. *Upsala Nya Tidning* 12 June 1897.

Huysmans, Joris Karl. *À Rebours*. Paris: Fasquelle Éditeur, 1961.

Jacqueline. "En svensk rhapsod." Rev. of *Karolinerna* I, by V. von Heidenstam. *Nya Dagligt Allehanda* 1 June 1897.

———. "*Karolinernas* andra del." *Nya Dagligt Allehanda* 7 May 1898.

K. W-g. "Bokvärlden." Rev. of *Karolinerna* II, by V. von Heidenstam. *Göteborgs Handels- och Sjöfarts Tidning* 1 June 1898.

Lagerroth, Erland. *Svensk berättarkonst*. Vetenskapsocieteten i Lund 61. Lund: Gleerup, 1968.

*Litteraturlexikon*. Entry on "Heidenstam, Verner von." Eds. Bo Engman et al. Stockholm: Natur och Kultur, 1974.

-pt-. "Literatur." Rev. of *Karolinerna* I, by V. von Heidenstam. *Sydsvenska Dagbladet Snällposten* 26 May 1897.

———. "Literatur." Rev. of *Karolinerna* II, by V. von Heidenstam. *Sydsvenska Dagbladet Snällposten* 11 May 1898.

Nordau, Max. *Entartung*. 2 vols. Berlin: Carl Duncker Verlag, 1892.

Rehm, Walther. *Der Untergang Roms im abendländischen Denken. Ein Beitrag zur Geschichtsschreibung und zum Dekadenzproblem*. Das Erbe der Alten 18. Leipzig: Dieterich'sche Verlagsbuchhandlung, 1930.

Schoolfield, George. "Charles XII Rides in Worpswede." *Modern Language Quarterly* 16 (1955): 258-67.

T. H. "Literatur." Rev. of *Karolinerna* II, by V. von Heidenstam. *Svenska Morgonbladet* 6 June 1898.

Wirsén, Carl David af. "Literatur." Rev. of *Karolinerna* II, by V. von Heidenstam. *Vårt Land* 6 May 1898.

# The Patriarchal Prison in *Hedda Gabler* and *Dödsdansen*

## Ross Shideler

Both Henrik Ibsen (1828-1906) and August Strindberg (1849-1912) reflect the nineteenth-century's questioning of the father, a development directly related to the Woman's Movement, but one that reached its epitome in, and took part of its form from, Charles Darwin's undermining of the Divine Father. Although other political and social phenomena are part of this transition, such as the French Revolution of 1789, the Age of Industrialism, and so on, once Darwin began what Margot Norris calls "biocentrism," by collapsing "the cardinal distinctions between animal and human" (Norris 3), the patriarchal structures that had been privileged by a supposedly divine authorization became suspect. Nineteenth-century literary representations by men, such as Ibsen and Strindberg, of the weakening of the supposedly traditional, but in fact newly created, "nuclear family" offer a unique insight into this change in family structure. Obviously, much of this questioning of the husband's and father's authority came from women in search of their freedom and their identity.

In brief, through the expression of that questioning in the plays of Ibsen and Strindberg, I believe the Woman's Movement provided a strong impetus for the transition from nineteenth-century realistic drama to twentieth-century ironic and absurdist drama, a transition clarified to us by twentieth-century feminism.[1] This impetus came about because Ibsen and Strindberg experienced and dramatized in very different ways the battle over women's rights and the role of women in the home. Yet, in spite of these differences, Ibsen's *Hedda Gabler* (1890) and Strindberg's *Dödsdansen* (1900) explore families in crisis through imagery of the home as a prison.

Although Henrik Ibsen and August Strindberg have other plays that portray a woman trying to escape from the prison of a patriarchal household, *Hedda Gabler* and *Dödsdansen* present what have by now become familiar twentieth-century family struggles. As if to demonstrate the complexity of the domestic issues involved, both plays confront their audiences with a disturbing or frustrating conclusion. By definition, Hedda's death challenges the norms of the patriarchy and the patriarchal family, defined by Gerda Lerner as:

> the manifestation and institutionalization of male dominance over women and children in the family and the extension of male dominance over women in society in general. (239)

Strindberg also struggled with the patriarchal family by presenting it as a virtual torture chamber for the damned. At the conclusion of the vitriolic *Dödsdansen*, however, Strindberg tries to reinstate a patriarchal order that the play has already undermined. Each of these dramas is representative of other works by their authors.

Through such works, Ibsen and Strindberg wrenched the drama as a genre into the relativism of our century by examining the ambiguous moral framework that underlies the notion of the home and the nuclear family. In many of their dramas both men often used the imprisoned woman trying to break free of the family as the lever that tilts the patriarchal home off balance. But the premise of the family itself was much less clearly defined than we usually admit. As Mark Poster (xii-xiii) and Edward Shorter (23-26) have pointed out, the nuclear or bourgeois family developed in the late eighteenth and early nineteenth century, and it began to be challenged even as it was coming into being. Ironically then, as the notion of this supposedly ideal family was being created, it began to fall apart. Ibsen's and Strindberg's dramas reflect, therefore, the painful and often conflict-ridden reality of the nineteenth-century family trying to become some sort of idyllic patriarchal structure, while the premises of that family were collapsing.

In 1859 Darwin undermined the notion of a divine father who had supposedly authored or authorized the traditional family structure; with the publication of Darwin's work the foundations of the Christian patriarchy itself trembled.[2] Related to those tremors beneath the patriarchal floors, political and social revolutions, such as the Woman's Movement, challenged the stability of the nuclear family.[3] In terms of the family structure, Steven Mintz in *A Prison of Expectations* (1983) has analyzed some well-known Victorian families, and his insights add, I believe, to our understanding of Ibsen and Strindberg.[4] Although he reminds us that there is no single Victorian family type (xi), Mintz looks at the lives of Harriet Beecher Stowe, Robert Louis Stevenson, George Eliot, Catharine Sedgwick, and Samuel Butler. Not surprisingly, in these families, as well as others, he discovers the father's "embodiment of moral and intellectual authority" (50), while "the recurrent image of the mother is one of selflessness" (51).[5]

Ibsen and Strindberg offer penetrating studies of the Scandinavian "Victorian" family and, specifically, of the roles of the "moral and intellectual" father and the problematic "selfless" mother. Many of the women created by these two authors, contrary to the tradition identified by Mintz, resist the "selflessness," the self-effacing and subservient role that their era had cast upon them. In Ibsen, these women tend to be heroes or victims; in Strindberg, they tend to be villains or penitents returning to the fold. Ibsen's Hedda is one of the most famous examples; however, unlike her predecessor Nora, she has been, perhaps because of her cruelty, somewhat difficult to absorb into the feminist canon.

Yet in the hundreds of readings of *Hedda Gabler*, many recognize its relevance to Feminism. For instance, Gail Finney deals with Hedda in terms of maternity, hysteria, and Freudian symbolism (149-65). Evert Sprinchorn ("Ibsen, Strindberg" 61-63) makes a comparison between Strindberg and Ibsen with an emphasis on Hedda's "unmotherliness," and Sandra Saari (31-32) has commented on Hedda's rejection of the role of the ideal wife and mother. I propose that Ibsen and Strindberg wrote about women trying to escape the prison of the patriarchal household, but that each author evaluated the women's attempts differently.

To begin, let me expand upon such a liberal, but still traditional, reading as James McFarlane's, in which he begins from the premise of Hedda's desire to control another's life and relates this to the fact that,

> Woman was often unnaturally deprived by social convention of an adequate opportunity to realize herself; the most she could hope to do, very often, was to make her achievements through the intermediacy, or in the company, of some man. (289)[6]

However, before I pursue the "unnatural deprivations" suffered by Hedda, let me digress to a few of the ways in which Ibsen establishes the play's realism through the use of household paraphernalia. This digression will eventually clarify the nature of the prison I am discussing. Recall Ibsen's blend of realism and symbolism in the stage setting: the detailed description of the interior of a large house with its drawing room, hallways, windows and curtains, the sofa and flowers, the famous portrait of General Gabler. In essence, the opening scene, played out between self-effacing Aunt Tesman and the maid, Berta, suggests the patriarchal nature of the household, which constitutes — and here is where Ibsen surprises us — Hedda's prison.

In *The Madwoman in the Attic* (1979), Gilbert and Gubar have extensively discussed "dramatizations of prison and escape . . . in nineteenth-century literature by women" (85). In a related fashion, Pil Dahlerup's two-volume study of Danish women writers during the 1880s tends to analyze women's writing in terms of their struggle with, or relation to, patriarchal norms, usually as defined by Georg Brandes (Dahlerup 126-27). But while Gilbert and Gubar and Dahlerup focus on women writers, I am arguing that even male writers, such as Ibsen and Strindberg, perceived and wrote — often despite their own political attitudes and desires — about the breakdown of the nuclear family. As an intrinsic part of their portrayals, the patriarchal home often turned out to be a prison for women.

As Ibsen's earlier drama *Et Dukkehjem* (1879) demonstrates — and Joan Templeton (37-38) has now clearly established how conscious Ibsen was of his own feminism — he perceived the nineteenth-century woman's angry sense of imprisonment and helplessness. But Hedda may present a more realistic portrayal. Unlike Nora who escapes — though to what future remains a question — Hedda, no matter how violently or viciously she struggles, cannot escape the household trap.

On the surface, Ibsen's treatment of the family in this play appears to correspond to Steven Mintz's analysis of Victorian families. But even as *Hedda Gabler* ironically unfolds the domestic details, which constitute the happy home and family that so appeal to Jørgen Tesman, the play critiques that image. On one hand, through the patriarchal assumptions of the entire Tesman family, as well of course as through Hedda's own father, Ibsen portrays the pretense that the nuclear family is a longstanding, permanent, and in essence divinely authorized social structure. On the other hand, he dramatizes that same family on the verge, *not* of harmoniously adding a new baby to the patriarchy, but of exploding.

Hedda, imprisoned in the image of a happy home and in a patriarchal heritage that defines her primary functions as a wife, a mother, and, in modern Beverly Hills fashion, a consumer — remember her need for the expensive honeymoon, the house, the butler, horse, and so on — still challenges the premises of the patriarchy. She persecutes both men and women, from Tesman and Løvborg to Aunt Tesman and Thea Elvsted, who, although she has deserted her husband, still seems committed to the patriarchy.[7] Note that all of the men in the play try to live up to, or attain the goals set for them by, the patriarchal society, and they expect women to assist them in their efforts. But Hedda experiences this world as a prison, very much as do the women described by Gilbert and Gubar:

> Interestingly, though works in this tradition generally begin by using houses as primary symbols of female imprisonment, they also use much of the other paraphernalia of "woman's place" to enact their central symbolic drama of enclosure and escape. (85)

It is precisely this "woman's place" and the related household paraphernalia that to a very real extent create the realism of *Hedda Gabler*. As for many women, past and present, no escape opens for the rebellious Hedda trapped in this patriarchal prison-kingdom. However, Hedda and her prison, created by Ibsen's trademark domestic details, are much too complex to be simplistically reduced.

In a discussion of power and authority in nineteenth-century British novels, D. A. Miller suggests a parallel to the aspect of Hedda's imprisonment that is so galling to her. Analyzing Trollope's *Barchester Towers* (1857), Miller comments that strong women and weak men might interfere with the harmonious functioning of patriarchal society, a notion that clearly applies to *Hedda Gabler*.[8] Miller then adds, however, that a merging or mixture of traditional gender roles does not in fact indicate the breakdown of those roles.

The gentleman-woman and the lady-man in Trollope are not symptoms of a patriarchy in disarray; nor do they imply a critique of the established gender code or an invitation to transsexual experimentation. Rather, they are the raw material for that massive stereotyping which, turning them into reminders of the gender norms they seem to transgress, makes radical transgression impossible. (140-41)

Instead of, or in addition to, representing a challenge to the patriarchy, as most of us would tend to argue, Hedda seen from D. A. Miller's perspective reinforces the gender stereotype: this is what happens to women who violate the rules of the divinely authorized patriarchal social order. In other words, even as he was trying to dramatize the idea that, as Sprinchorn says, all women "are not made to be mothers" ("Ibsen, Strindberg" 61), Ibsen may have unintentionally strengthened the narrow categories in which women were placed. In any case, Miller's point that the "gentleman-woman" can be used as a means of reinforcing gender stereotypes adds to our appreciation of Hedda's complexity as a character.

Miller continues with a suggestion that helps to illuminate Hedda's supposed rejection of her femininity. In discussing how the nature of the feminine is psychologically embedded in several of Trollope's female characters, Miller says,

Yet perhaps these characters submit most deeply to patriarchy not when they acknowledge their latent femininity, but when they succeed in repressing it. For their only alternative to a femininity thoroughly circumscribed by its patriarchal determination seems to be a perverse identification with an oppressive masculinity equally and likewise circumscribed. (142)

The most obvious symbols of Hedda's "perverse identification" with the patriarchy are her father's infamous pistols, and it is with them that she ends her life. Thus, Hedda's eventual paralysis — Brian Johnston describes it as a "Hell" (111) — her recognition of being in both a physical and a psychological prison, seems inevitable: she cannot live within the patriarchal parameters set for women, and she cannot join those set for men. This complexity — the desire for all the trappings of a bourgeois housewife on the one hand and the anger against those people who seem to thrive in their restrictive patriarchally defined roles, such as Aunt Tesman or Thea, on the other hand — makes Hedda difficult to empathize with as a character and contributes to the ambivalent or negative response that she often receives.

Miller's vision of the power of gender norms and transgressions of them, which can invoke an almost dialectical response, differs from Declan Kiberd's position. Kiberd suggestively argues that:

Every major play by Ibsen foretells the death of the family as an institution based on false specialization of roles, man for work, woman for the home. (65-66)

But for Kiberd,

> . . . Ibsen developed this basic formula of an unequal encounter between a
> masterful woman and a timid, conscience-stricken man. (73)

For Miller, such a strong woman cannot survive because she represents
an impediment to patriarchal organization (see note 8). But even without
Miller's perspective, Kiberd's claim would appear to be oversimplified.
While this "strong woman" and "weak man" theme is sometimes present
in Ibsen and may apply to Hedda and Tesman, Hedda does not struggle
with just Tesman, but with the patriarchy, which includes Aunt Tesman,
Judge Brack, and indeed her dead father. Yet, as strong as she is, her
sometimes vicious behavior toward other women in the play makes her
much too complicated a role-model to lead a feminist revolution. *What
Hedda does do, however, is personify the problematizing of "femininity" in a
patriarchy.*

Unquestionably, Hedda violates most of the primary roles and codes
established for women by the patriarchy and by its assumptions about
female biology. She hates the pregnancy that Aunt Tesman loves, and she
refuses to be anybody's sweet little wife. She even goes so far as to reject
Judge Brack as a lover when it becomes apparent that her weakling husband
will spend his life giving re-birth to the manuscript, the "child" of Thea
Elvsted and Eilert Løvborg, that Hedda herself had burned — that is,
aborted — just as she will destroy her own child. In her drive for independence and/or dominance, Hedda, inclined toward Greek rather than Christian
mythology, rejects the Christian patriarchal house and family that imprisoned her.

But her final suicide leaves an almost exemplary post-structural conclusion: the "family" (and implicitly, I think, this means the patriarchal family)
remains intact, only this time the offspring is *textual*, not biological. Through
Jørgen and Thea's parental love the manuscript of the future will be reborn;
unfortunately, one suspects that this textual child will reinforce the patriarchy that drove the "unmotherly" Hedda to murder (one could argue that
she induced Løvborg's death) and suicide.

In sum, then, Ibsen's *Hedda Gabler* portrays a woman imprisoned within
a patriarchal heritage, surrounded by the household paraphernalia that
defines her identity, and opposed to the motherhood that will supposedly
fulfill her personal and biological needs. As Finney says,

> Hedda's resistance to the female roles of muse and mother is characteristic
> of her consistent rebellion against the conventional turn-of-the-century
> view of woman's place. (155)

The play leads us from realism into the modern tangled values of relativism
and the problematizing of gender,[9] love, and family. August Strindberg
struggled with the same patriarchal nuclear family, and he remains relevant
to us precisely because he did so. Interestingly enough, even though he tried

to sustain the image and structure of the family, Strindberg still presented it as a prison, sometimes for women, sometimes for men and women.

One may easily demonstrate that Strindberg's writings present the dilemma of the male displaced by a strong woman. Few writers have so effectively captured the war of the sexes as Strindberg has in *Fadren*.[10] In many of his plays Ibsen dramatizes the questioning of the traditional nuclear family from a woman's point of view, or at least with some awareness of her role, but Strindberg's dramas, usually having male protagonists, dramatize the patriarchal family's instability, that is, the family on the verge of collapse. Strindberg found the family to be a tangled, sometimes poisonous web of relationships, in which the fathers usually were threatened with displacement. Perhaps surprisingly, even as he sorrows for the fading traditional family, Strindberg often reveals the imprisoned woman struggling to break free of patriarchal definitions of femininity, namely, those restrictions that limit her to the subservient roles of childbearing and housekeeping.

This ambiguity in Strindberg becomes especially interesting in light of Steven Mintz's analysis of familial loss, (see note 5), for Strindberg's mother died when he was a young boy. Shortly after her death, she was replaced by a stepmother, who was deeply disappointing to him. Since he quarreled with his father a few years later, Strindberg never discovered in his life or drama a satisfactory replacement for the family. He tried several times to create one of his own but always found himself displaced. Eventually, he returned, in his own highly complex fashion, to a variation of the patriarchal structure of his childhood, a Swedenborgian variation of Christianity.

*Dödsdansen*, written relatively late in Strindberg's life, provides an interesting perspective on the combination of the displaced father and the house as prison. The stage setting for *Dödsdansen* is a cell-like round room in a fortress. Although Hedda perceives her dearly bought home as a prison, no one else does. In Strindberg's play, Edgar, the frustrated Army Captain, and Alice, the disappointed ex-actress, experience their home as the confining enclosure it is. The guard that paces outside the door reinforces this image, and the fact that, with the exception of a telegraph key in the room, the couple are cut off from the outside world strengthens the sense of their isolation. Equally important, the larger family unit has already collapsed; because of the parents' fights, the children have been sent away, but they still continue to be used as weapons in the parental war. *Dödsdansen* — like its modern offspring in the portrayal of marital warfare, such as the play *Who's Afraid of Virginia Woolf* (1963) or the film *The War of the Roses* (1989) — attacks home and family from the opening scene.

Within the context of this battle, Alice's attempt to escape seems modest, yet she succeeds, if only briefly, in bringing the patriarchal structure that stifles her to a standstill — something that Hedda may not really succeed in doing even with her suicide. Like Hedda, however, Alice is a strong and willful woman with a "tyranniska och grymma sinnelag" (Strindberg 44: 53), according to her cousin Kurt. Ten years younger than the Captain, her career taken from her, and she herself forced to live in isolation (Strindberg 44: 52) and poverty, Alice consistently criticizes Edgar and resists his control by, for example, secretly learning to use the telegraph to stay in touch with the world around her. D. A. Miller's ideas about strong women apply, I believe, almost as much to Alice as they do to Hedda, and, certainly, the premises of imprisonment in the home identified by Gilbert and Gubar suit her as a character.

When cousin Kurt, the new Quarantine Superintendent, arrives on the island and visits the card-playing Edgar and Alice, they draw him into their dark family game. The couple's attempt to avoid the emptiness of their lives motivates the almost dancelike dialogue in which each of the three characters plays off the other two. In this dance, Alice tries to dominate both men. Like Hedda, Alice's sexual desires have apparently been frustrated; indeed, the prison-homes that both women live in mirror to some extent their repressed eroticism. After all, Alice chooses to fight Edgar with her attempted sexual conquest of Kurt (also a displaced father whose children are referred to as threatening figures), a choice that Hedda could not bring herself to make with Brack. The older, more experienced Alice wants to destroy not herself, but the illusion of the family. Kurt merely offers her a chance to attack the military patriarchy dominating her own home.

As Kurt gradually descends into the corruption and sensuality that characterize Edgar and Alice, the trio find themselves trapped in a game of attack and counterattack. Similar to Albee's *Virginia Woolf*, the games include dominance and submission; kiss the hostess; and, of course, when Kurt is forced to kneel and kiss Alice's foot, humiliate the guest. At this nadir of decadence, Alice has become the strong woman with not one weak man, but two of them. She becomes almost demonic in her desire to destroy Edgar and to seduce Kurt. Like Laura in *Fadren*, Alice makes a grab for power, but perhaps Strindberg, at this point in his career, could not allow a female character, no matter how unpleasant, to triumph.[11] Instead, he reinstates the patriarchal structure that has been so severely strained throughout the play, and, indeed, he extends it. The nearly displaced father-figure regains his position of authority. The play's ending reinstates the supposedly dominant male (the invalid Captain) over a subservient wife (one doubts if Alice will ever fit this role), while the second weak male has departed, returning the married couple to their normal status.

From D. A. Miller's perspective (140; see also my note 8), Alice's brief rebellion represents a threat to the smooth functioning of this patriarchal family, in prison though it may be. But the play also refers to a second form of imprisonment that threatens the patriarchy and is rejected: mortality — in the sense that we are imprisoned in bodies and only through death can we escape them. The acceptance of death's finality in a natural or Darwinian world characterizes the Captain at the beginning of the play.[12] With the references to the Captain's "resurrection" and Alice's prayers to God (Strindberg 44: 131-32), this acceptance is thrown into doubt at the end. In other words, the play's closing reinstatement of a divine father and the rejection of mortality's limitations parallel the reinstatement of the patriarchal family structure.

Traditionally, this play has been seen as a kind of Swedenborgian "conversion" drama in which the couple unite at the end and look forward to a better life. But for me, Edgar's abrupt change, after he discovers the seriousness of his illness, does not satisfactorily resolve the play. The Swedenborgian symbolism discussed by Evert Sprinchorn (*Strindberg as Dramatist* 112-21), with its base in divine patriarchal authority, returns the play to the nineteenth century; yet the irony and near-absurdity of the closing scenes make it a classic twentieth-century work. However, in spite of the play's *Waiting for Godot*-like conclusion, the final scene reverses Alice's rebellion, and Alice and Edgar remain confined within the prison of their home and marriage. But it is only irony, or at best resignation, that sustains the patriarchy. The following dialogue takes place as Kurt announces his departure. It begins with the rebellious Alice being put in her place.

> *Alice*: (*går mot Kurt.*) Nu går jag — med dig!
> *Kurt*: (*stöter henne ifrån sig så att hon faller på knä.*) Gå till avgrunden, värifrån du kommit! — Farväl! för alltid! (*Går.*)
> *Kapten*: Gå inte ifrån mig, Kurt, hon dödar mig!
> *Alice*: Kurt! Övergiv mig icke, övergiv oss icke!
> *Kurt*: Farväl! (*Går.*)
>
>                         * * *
>
> *Alice*: (*sadlar om.*) Vilken usling! Det är en vän för dig!
> *Kapten*: (*milt.*) Förlåt mig, Alice, och kom hit! Kom fort!
> *Alice*: (*till* Kaptenen.) Det var den största usling och hycklare jag i mitt liv har råkat! — Vet du, du är en man i alla fall!
>
>                                 (Strindberg 44: 127-28)

What an amazing reinstatement of the patriarchal male, of the classic father-figure! That the scene has a religious, a Swedenborgian-Christian subtext makes this return to a teetering patriarchal family even more troubling. Should it surprise us that, even though based on Strindberg's much disliked brother-in-law and supposedly representing the portrait of an evil man, the play's husband and father-figure still triumphs?[13] Even Kurt, before he leaves, has more sympathy for Edgar than for Alice (Strindberg 44: 126). In brief, once denied her chance at escape, to leave the prison and go off to a hotel with Kurt, Alice returns to the patriarchy. She gives up her dominant position and admires Edgar's manhood, mercy, and generosity of spirit (Strindberg 44: 129). Her return to the patriarchal fold cannot be seen unequivocally, for the irony at the play's conclusion would seem to deny that. Nevertheless, her attack on Edgar and the patriarchal values he represents has been defeated. Edgar, weakened and humbled though he may be, has regained his position as the household authority, and, significantly, he, too, has returned to the fold of the divine patriarchy. In almost biblical fashion, patriarchy, divine and familial, has been challenged and has triumphed, but in this nineteenth-century version the tyrannical father/husband is now an invalid and the repressed wife his nurse.

The drama, with its use of irony and absurdity, undermines the audience's ability to conceive of true happiness for the couple, but the family structure and the cell that contains it remain intact. Strindberg reveals here the remarkable ambiguity and complexity that characterize so much of his work. He dramatizes as few playwrights have the battle of the sexes; he presents valid arguments for women and for their refusal to accept male-female relationships as they were then defined, and then he promptly resolves the conflict in favor of the divinely privileged — but weak and resigned — male.[14]

To conclude, through Alice's submission and return to the patriarchy, Edgar and Alice reach a bittersweet acceptance of their home and marriage as a prison for the comically insane. Like Ibsen's ironic restoration of the patriarchal family at the conclusion of *Hedda*, Strindberg's closing scene plants us fully in that prison house of the family which would become one of the major battlegrounds of the twentieth century. The insights of twentieth-century feminists have helped us understand those male writers who tried to depict on stage their own patriarchal families struggling to adapt to the new roles of women.

## Notes

[1] Portions of this paper were presented in different papers, at the March 1991 ACLA conference in San Diego, the May 1991 SASS conference at the University of Massachusetts, and the August ICLA conference in Tokyo at Aoyama Gakuin University.

[2] In this post-Darwinian sense, I agree with Charles Lyons's claim that "Ibsen's plays imitate the failure of the Christian myth . . ."(Lyons xix). I differ with him by placing a somewhat greater emphasis on external reality, whereas Lyons emphasizes an internal one.

[3] Finney summarizes part of the relevant background in her introduction (2-20).

[4] Indeed, the domineering and problematic father seems as consistent a figure in Mintz's Victorian England as he is in Ibsen and Strindberg.

[5] The phrases quoted come from the following passage by Mintz. The full quotation provides a suggestive model, particularly in terms of Strindberg, of the family structure discussed in this paper.

In reconstructing these figures' biographies, certain parallels, recurrent themes, and points of similarity have stood out. For example, one of the themes that recurs in their biographies involves the figure of the father, who emerges as the dominant adult influence upon these individuals during their childhood and young adulthood. Again and again, we will see the repeated image of the father as the embodiment of moral and intellectual authority. . . . In contrast to the description of the father as a moral and intellectual authority, the recurrent image of the mother is one of selflessness. For the women, in particular, each of whom lost a mother during childhood or adolescence, the sainted memory of a mother who had selflessly devoted her adult life to the family's good was a powerful image in their home — an image that contrasted sharply, in the case of Stowe and Sedgwick, with their stepmothers, who seemed to be little more than social butterflies, obsessed with the world of society and fashion. For these women, the contrast between their mothers and stepmothers served an important role in leading them to seek a serious and "useful" vocation in life. . . . Still, the association of the mother with selflessness and domestic loyalty and affection was strong even in the cases of Stevenson and Butler. (50-52)

[6] McFarlane places Hedda within the context of a contradictory need to dominate and to be dependent. For him "what used to be thought of as Ibsen's propaganda for Women's Rights now falls into a more meaningful perspective" (289). Although I do not view Ibsen as a propagandist for Women's Rights, I argue that his awareness of the need for a new understanding of women and their rights was and is highly meaningful.

[7] If one accepts Løvborg's manuscript as a child, then Thea's decision to work with Jørgen Tesman to reconstruct the book, to save the child, is a clear indication of her support of the patriarchy. Finney argues for Løvborg's and Thea's joint creation of the manuscript, but she, too, concludes that Thea's "metaphorical maternity is in fact only midwifery" (153).

[8] Miller (140) defines the roles of the strong woman in relation to a patriarchy:

> Patriarchal organization thus incurs two impediments to its own smooth functioning: the "strong" woman (who would be more than the socializing medium in the exchange and transfer of power between men) and the "weak" man (who, falling under the spell of such a woman, would imperil male bonding; or who, alternatively, fixated on male bonding per se, would endanger its social vocation).

[9] I did not even discuss in this paper the lesbian subtext of the play. Finney refers to it in terms of androgynous or bisexual behavior (159). Productions have often used Hedda's love of Thea's hair as a suggestive scene, but one could go even further to analyze Hedda's seemingly masculine characteristics, her guns, etc., as well as the fact that she sends Løvborg forth, once in their youths and later before he dies, in some sense to seduce women for her. Her voyeurism here, usually thought of in terms of simply repressed sensuality, might well be interpreted as an actual desire for the women or, at the very least, a wish to dominate them the way men do. She hungered for excitement and sensuality in life but apparently dared experience it only vicariously through hearing about Løvborg's sexual encounters at the infamous Diana's house.

[10] As Meyer (235) has pointed out, Strindberg himself felt that the "gentleman-woman" (Miller's phrase) Hedda was the unadmitted offspring of two of his characters, Laura and Tekla, in the plays *Fadren* and *Fordringsägare* (1889). Valency (194) draws a series of comparisons between Julie and Hedda.

[11] I have argued that he does not really allow Laura to win in *Fadren* (see Shideler 149).

[12] I refer here to the Captain's description of the end of life. "Det är slut! Bara så mycket som att köra ut på en skottkärra och lägga på trädgårdslandet!" (Strindberg 44, 15).

[13] The biographical sources discussed by Hans Lindström reinforce the "realism" of the play, but my point is that Strindberg's commitment to the patriarchy outweighed his desire to write a negative portrait of a married man (Strindberg 44, 242).

[14] Evert Sprinchorn quotes Strindberg to show that the play's ending, with its potential celebration of the couple's silver anniversary, proclaims "the great resignation without which life is impossible" (119). In a reading that also focuses on Strindberg's religious reading at the time, Susan Brantly connects *Dödsdansen* to Strindberg's study in 1900 of

Paul's letter to the Romans ("Naturalism or Expressionism" 165). Brantly's fine analysis, which I discovered after having written this article, allows her shrewdly to extend the play's sense of imprisonment to human mortality as well as to other religious and psychological levels. Her conclusion, that the meaning of the play lies in the hands of God and the playwright (173), may support my own view of the irony in the play's final scene.

# Works Cited

Brantly, Susan. "Naturalism or Expressionism: A Meaningful Mixture of Styles in *The Dance of Death* (I)." *Strindberg's Dramaturgy*. Ed Göran Stockenström. Minneapolis: U of Minnesota P, 1988.

Dahlerup, Pil. *Det moderne gennembruds kvinder*. 2nd ed. 2 vols. Copenhagen: Gyldendal, 1983.

Finney, Gail. *Women in Modern Drama — Freud, Feminism, and European Theater at the Turn of the Century*. Ithaca: Cornell UP, 1989.

Gilbert, Sandra M., and Susan Gubar. *The Madwoman in the Attic: The Woman Writer and the Nineteenth-Century Literary Imagination*. New Haven: Yale UP, 1979.

Ibsen, Henrik. 9 vols. *Samlede Værker*. Copenhagen: Gyldendal (F. Hegel), 1898-1900. See especially:
Vol. 6 (1899): *Et Dukkehjem*.
Vol. 8 (1900): *Hedda Gabler*.

Johnston, Brian. *The Ibsen Cycle: The Design of the Plays from* Pillars of Society *to* When We Dead Awaken. The Library of Scandinavian Studies 2. Boston: Twayne Publishers, 1975.

Kiberd, Declan. *Men and Feminism in Modern Literature*. London: Macmillan, 1985.

Lerner, Gerda. *The Creation of Patriarchy*. New York: Oxford UP, 1986.

Lyons, Charles. *Henrik Ibsen: The Divided Consciousness*. Carbondale: Southern Illinois UP, 1972.

McFarlane, James. *Ibsen and Meaning: Studies, Essays and Prefaces 1953-87*. Norwich: Norvik P, 1987.

Meyer, Michael. *Strindberg*. New York: Random House, 1985.

Miller, D. A. *The Novel and the Police*. Berkeley: U of California P, 1988.

Mintz, Steven. *A Prison of Expectations: The Family in Victorian Culture*. New York: New York UP, 1983.

Norris, Margot. *Beasts of the Imagination: Darwin, Nietzsche, Kafka, Ernst, and Lawrence*. Baltimore: Johns Hopkins UP, 1985.

Poster, Mark. *Critical Theory of the Family*. New York: Seabury P, 1986.

Saari, Sandra. "'Hun som ikke selv har noe riktig livskall': Women and the Role of the 'Ideal Woman' in Ibsen's Munich Trilogy." *Contemporary Approaches to Ibsen*. Vol. 5. Ed. Daniel

Haakonsen. Oslo: Universitetsforlaget, 1985. 24-38.

Shideler, Ross. "Darwinism, Naturalism and Strindberg." *The Modern Breakthrough in Scandinavian Literature 1870-1905*. Ed. Bertil Nolin and Peter Forsgren. Litteraturvetenskapliga Institutionen 17. Gothenburg: Göteborgs Universitet, 1988. 145-51.

Sprinchorn, Evert. "Ibsen, Strindberg, and the New Woman." *The Play and Its Critic: Essays for Eric Bentley*. Ed. Michael Bertin. New York: UP of America, 1986. 45-66.

——. *Strindberg as Dramatist*. New Haven: Yale UP, 1982.

Strindberg, August. Vols. 27 and 44 in *Samlade verk*. Ed. Lars Dahlbäck et al. Stockholm: Almqvist and Wiksell; Norstedts, 1984, 1988. 25 vols. 1982- .
    Vol. 27 (Ed. Gunnar Ollén. Almqvist and Wiksell, for Strindbergssällskapet, 1984): *Fadren, Fröken Julie, Fordringsägare*.
    Vol. 44 (Ed. Hans Lindström. Norstedts, for Stockholms Universitet, 1988): *Dödsdansen*.

Templeton, Joan. "The *Doll House* Backlash: Criticism, Feminism, and Ibsen." *PMLA* 104.1 (1988): 28-41.

Valency, Maurice. *The Flower and the Castle: An Introduction to Modern Drama*. New York: Macmillan, 1963.

# A Neglected Passage in *Når vi døde vågner*

## George Schoolfield

IN THE SECOND ACT OF *Når vi døde vågner* (1889),[1] the stage directions say,

> *I forgrunden til venstre risler en bæk i delte striber nedover en brat fjældvæg og flyder derfra i jævnt løb over vidden ud til højre. Kratskog, planter og stene langs bækkeløbet. . . . I frastand . . . hinsides bækken leger og danser en flok syngende småbørn. De er dels byklædte dels i folkedrakter. Glad latter høres dæmpet under det følgende* (Ibsen 13: 243)

— a nice contrastive background for the childless couple's uncomfortable dialogue to follow (Ibsen 13: Act 2.243-47). The great sculptor, Arnold Rubek, "*med et plæd over skulderen*" (243), sits on a bench, watching them. It is across the brook that Rubek's young wife, Maja, leaps — in a famous stage pole vault, "*ved hjælp af [spring]staven*" — to inform Rubek that she has spent the day (it is getting on toward sundown) with the vigorous, boisterous, and dirty hunter Squire Ulfhejm (243-44). What is more, she intends to make an evening outing — again with Ulfhejm — to the forests below, where there are bear. Some rather unpleasant conversation ensues, during which Maja hints broadly at the fascination Ulfhejm holds for her; in a supporting strategy, she points out to Rubek that *he*, after all, is constantly followed by "denne blege damen," Madame Satow, Irene, his sometime model, "[e]n, som har klædt sig helt af for dig" (245-46). Such a revelation of Irene's charms, Rubek retorts, "[b]etyder ingenting. Ikke for os kunstnere" (246). Husband and wife agree that they are not getting along very well together and perhaps should go their separate ways, for good and all.

Rubek's particular complaint against Maja is that she has no "rigtig klart begreb om, hvorledes en kunstnernatur sér ud indvendig" (252). When Irene disappeared from his life, she took with her the key to "et bitte lidet dirkefrit skrin" (254) in his breast where his artistic vision lay (like the pope, Rubek has a *scrinium pectoris*);[2] and Maja, who entered Rubek's life later on, has shown that she possesses no key at all. At this point, Irene appears, in

Maja's catty description "skridende — som en marmorstøtte" (255); she stops to talk quietly with the children at the brook, attracted, it may be, by their songs and games (which Maja — herself so noisy — has found irritating), and sends them toward the sanatorium to which the Rubeks have moved from the spa of Act One. Leaping the brook again, the athletic Maja snippily tells Irene that Rubek is waiting for her to come and "hjælpe sig med et skrin, som er gået i baglås for ham" (256);[3] then she goes off in the same direction as the children. Rubek advances to the brook but, briefly, stays on his side, as Irene does on hers.

The conversation (13: 256-68) between this pair is fully as troubled as that between husband and wife has been. After telling Irene, at a distance, that he has waited for her "år efter år," to which Irene makes one of her typically mysterious retorts about not having been able to come ("Lå jo dernede og sov den lange, dybe, drømmefyldte søvn," 256), Rubek picks his way across the stepping stones to her and sits down again on a boulder; directly, she stations herself behind him. In his excitement at seeing her, or in his exhaustion (for Rubek is an aging, tired man), he may have momentarily forgotten what he in fact already knows and what she will bring to his unwilling attention again: that she is deeply disturbed, a mental case — her conversation ranges from the murderous (she plans, she says, to kill her nurse, the deaconess, whom she has momentarily given the slip) to the ecstatic (she calls Rubek her lord, her master). At her persistent questions, Rubek — once more a little foolish, or unforesighted — reveals that he has made considerable changes in the great resurrection statue for which she stood model long ago; he does not know that, behind him, she has half-drawn a knife from her bosom (261), "en tynd, spids kniv." (A careful watcher-and-listener in the audience may perceive the grim irony in the object; Irene has earlier described it as "en fin, spids dolk, som jeg altid har med mig i sengen" [Ibsen Act 1.235], and it is, indeed, a kind of "dirk," a picklock, or could function as such.) As he tells her what he has done (the Irene-statue has been moved to the background, in what has been changed to a group), she toys with her weapon; yet, instead of using it to pry open Rubek's breast, or back, which would have ended the play on the spot, she makes her main and lengthy verbal assault on him, an assault that, simultaneously, has its loving moments. Four times, she calls him a poet, a "digter,"[4] a self-exculpatory dreamer who has been "slap og sløv og fuld af syndsforladelse for alle dit livs gerninger og for alle dine tanker" (Ibsen Act 2.263). (Rubek has just said that he put himself in the foreground of the group, a man sitting on a stone, "foran ved en kilde, ligesom her," dipping his fingers in the stream to cleanse them, "for at skylle dem rene" [263]. It is hard not to think of Pilate, washing his hands in innocence. Earlier, having sent the children away, Irene had let the brook's water run over *her* hands, perhaps as an effort to calm herself — or as her own self-exculpatory gesture toward the children she imagines she has "killed.") Taking revenge for his alterations, Irene — in another of the play's well-known phrases — reminds Rubek that he had called the mutual creation of the original statue, in the wonderful days of the past, "en velsignet episode" (265), and so she finds a word for repetition, or harping, as effective as "digter." (Inadvertently, Rubek has quoted Schnitzler's Anatol in *Episode* [1893]: "nur eine Episode, ein Roman von zwei Stunden" [1: 43].)

Like the preceding passage-at-arms between Rubek and Maja, this "stort optrin" (as Ibsen called it in his notes [13: 290]), has attracted the attention of many Ibsen scholars.[5] What I mean to comment on, though, after my necessarily superficial résumé, is the next and rather relaxed passage, a kind of lyric intermezzo (Ibsen 13: 265-68), following the two great verbal duels of Rubek/Maja and Rubek/Irene and coming before the *coups de théâtre* and foreboding speeches (including the play's title) that make up the finale of the act.

\* \* \*

Told by Rubek that she takes everything too seriously, Irene readily agrees and becomes almost playful. (Ruminating, the sculptor still does not realize that he is in mortal danger.) She says, "Lad os ryste det dybe og det tunge af os," and begins to pluck petals from a "fjeldrose," spreading them in the water (265). The "rock rose" or "Alpine rose" is a *rhododendron lapponicum* or *rhododendron ferrugineum*, the customarily bright red flowers of which, according to Sigurd Almquist in *Nordisk Familiebok* (1875), "bruka tilldraga sig resandes synnerliga uppmärksamhet" (1: 706). Referring to a shared practice of the past, the nature of which will be revealed in a moment, Irene continues (Ibsen 13: 265), "Sé der, Arnold. Der svømmer vore fugle." Rubek asks, "Hvad er det for fugle?" (Is he startled, or does he already have an inkling of what she is driving at?) She answers with what comes as a surprise in the Norwegian-Alpine landscape and is also a *hapax legomenon* in Ibsen: "Kan du ikke sé det? Det er jo flamingoer. For de er rosenrøde." Rubek (and the audience) may well ponder why the flower's red color suggests these tropical birds to Irene. For one thing, in her first marriage, after her disappearance, she had been married to a South American; the flamingo is a bird at home in Central and South America.[6] In her nightclub career or in her two marriages with well-off husbands, Irene has been in other places as well: "Rejst i mange riger og lande" (Act 1.233); Carl Snoilsky, the Swedish poet whose work Ibsen admired (and whose romantic problems he is supposed to have used in *Rosmersholm*, 1886), mentioned flamingos in one of his North African poems, "Kustbild vid Tunis" (1881), to characterize that exotic world:

> Sjöfågel svärmar rundt omkring oss,
> Och skimrande i solens brand
> De rosenfärgade flamingos
> Sig höja flaxande från strand. (2: 114)

(Ibsen himself had no doubt seen plenty of flamingos during his trip to the opening of the Suez Canal.) Further, it is possible that Irene comes up with flamingos as an attention-getter; the color of the Alpine rose and its associated bird are simply striking — the very name means 'flaming'.[7] Finally, Irene is filled with repressed eroticism toward Rubek; she has chided him for not approaching her during their modeling sessions, although — as we know — she has also confessed that she had a long needle in her hair to kill him with if he tried it. Can she be aware of the eroticism that poets, and others, have sensed in the very color of the bird, which she emphasizes?[8] Irene makes a point of the fact that the blossoms and the birds are "rosenrøde," a word Ibsen, in *Kjærlighedens komedie* (1862), applies to love letters and cheeks red for love: "rosenrøde smaa Billetter" (4: 264), and "rosenrøde Kinder" (4: 237), and he makes a less innocently erotic application of the color adjective in *Lille Eyolf* (1894). Rita tells Almers how she prepared for a romantic encounter, which did not take place, upon his return from the mountains; she was in her white dress, her hair let down in a cloud of fragrance, and "Det var rosenrøde skjermer over begge lampene" (12: 222).

Rubek immediately deflates Irene's suggestion, observing curtly, "Flamingoer svømmer ikke. De bare vader" (Ibsen 13: 265). Here, he is the cool professional artist, with an eye for accurate detail, while Irene herself has been the extemporizing poet. But he may also shrink from the erotic overtones of Irene's birds and their color. Acquiescing directly to Rubek's correction (after all, has he not been her sometime lord and master?), she says, "Så er det ikke flamingoer da. Det er måger" (265). At first glance, the gull association seems aesthetically less pleasing and surely less erotic than that with the flamingos — but then, after her bold proposal has fallen flat, Irene may want to withdraw to a safer position with her gulls. Certainly, gulls are not particularly pretty or graceful, and not birds of love, and they make ugly noises as well. The sometime Ibsen translator Christian Morgenstern would seem to cut them off from any poetry at all with his dictum in *Galgenlieder* (1905): "Die Möwen sehen alle aus / als ob sie Emma hiessen" (40). Yet, in Ibsen's case, as can be deduced from the entries in the (admittedly nonexhaustive) *Ibsen-Ordbok* (1958), we know he liked gulls for their strength, if not for their good looks: they stand for daring and sweep. In *Fru Inger til Østråt* (1857), Eline says: "Tanken har mågevinger" (Ibsen 2: 284), thereby inspiring Niels Lykke to expand his vision of political power from Norway to Denmark; and in the poem "Maageskrig" Ibsen expatiates upon the same thought (14: 227-29): gulls, strident gulls, screeching gulls will fly from valiant Norway to soft and Germanized Denmark. (The poem was written before the Dano-Prussian War.) More notably, though, the gulls have appeared in still another love duet, or meeting of the spirits. In the second act of *Fruen fra havet* (1888), Ellida Wangel tells her patient husband how once she had stood beside the sea, in the outer skerries, with her sailor and talked: "om mågerne og ørnerne og alle de andre sjøfuglene, som du véd" (Ibsen 11: 89). She had noticed, fatefully for her, that it seemed: "både sjødyrene og sjøfuglene var i slægt med ham," the sailor, and that they were related to her, too: "Ja, jeg syntes næsten, at jeg også kom i slægt med dem alle sammen." Thus the gull-exchange of *Når vi døde vågner* is actually the third set of gull-words passed between Ibsen's lovers — Eline and Niels Lykke, Ellida and the sailor, Irene and Rubek.

Now, growing less dogmatic and perhaps pleased at Irene's willing retreat from her flamingo statement, Rubek expands upon her substitute proposal, offering a compromise: "Måger med røde næb kan det være, ja" (13: 265).[9] Playing the game with Irene more intently (and remembering, more and more clearly, the game of the past on which Irene's whole present action is based), Rubek plucks some broad green leaves and casts them into the water: "Nu sender jeg mine skibe ud efter dem." The mention of the pursuit, perhaps introduced as a device of clumsy flirtation, inadvertently touches on a very sore spot in Irene, pursued by the deaconess, and, in the last act (3.280), by those forces she thinks of as "[m]ange mænd" (and the deaconess with a straightjacket); the remark is one of several instances of Rubek's thoughtlessness. She stipulates, "Men der skal ikke være fangstmænd ombord" (2.265).[10] Placating her, Rubek agrees there will not: "Nej, der skal ingen fangstmænd være," speaking as though to soothe a child. Rubek grows more sensitive now and more wide-awake: the common experience that lies at the basis of the game becomes fully apparent to him: he asks Irene if she remembers the happiness of the past (as he must know she does): "Kan du huske den sommer vi sad sådan udenfor det lille bondehuset ved Taunitzer See?" (266).[11]

Irene supplements his memories with still more information (266): "Lørdags aftenerne, ja, — når vi var færdige med vort arbejde for ugen —." Rubek takes up where she breaks off: " — og rejste ud med jernbanen. Og blev derude søndagen over —." (We are to assume, to be sure, that there was no overt erotic activity between them in the little peasant house, although Rubek temporarily, for the weekend, was not the consecrated artist nor Irene the untouchable model.) The allusion to the railroad's part in the happy trips of yore (despite what did *not* happen) is a nice touch on Ibsen's part for the reader or spectator able to recall the first act and its account (given antiphonally by Rubek and Maja) of the uncanny railroad trip north to the spa and the sanatorium:

> Ingen rejsende steg ud og ingen kom ind. Og toget, det holdt stille en lang, endeløs stund alligevel. Og ved hver station hørte jeg, at der var to banemænd, som gik på perronen, — den ene havde en lygte i hånden, — og de talte med hinanden, dæmpet og klangløst og intetsigende ud i natten. (Act 1.218)

The detail of the "banemænd," which logically, of course, means railroad workers, also suggests "banemænd," 'slayers,' 'bringers of death.'[12] The parallel and contrast between the two kinds of railroad journeys, those with Irene and the most recent one with Maja, is plain enough. By the end of the play, the audience sees how the northward journey brings Rubek to death in the avalanche. Indeed, the goal of the married couple's northward trip has been a cruise around the North Cape: "lige ind i ishavet" (218).

With another of her frightening glances (*"med et ondt, hadfyldt glimt i
øjet"*), Irene — her mood abruptly turning aggressive — reminds Rubek
again of his unfortunate word, "Det var en episode, Arnold," giving the
noun the air of a passing fling, a quick liaison, quickly forgotten (Act 2.266).
But Rubek, now lost in the full and happy memory, does not seem to hear
her, or intentionally overlooks her spiteful interjection, as he continues to
ransack the past. There, too, she had let bird-flowers swim in the water: "Da
lod du også fugle svømme i bækken. Det var vandliljer, som du — " (266).
His sentence is chopped off by Irene before he completes it; the aposiopesis
is not caused by Rubek's groping memory, but by Irene's violent interrup-
tion. (An actress, playing Irene, would have made her previous replique,
about the episode, insidiously malicious; here, she should be abrupt.) It is
Irene's turn to supply a detail. If Rubek was a realist of art and observation
with his objection to flamingos, Irene is a realist of memory as she hastens
to straighten out a central point about her relationship to the sculptor. Also,
*his* word now, water lilies, not hers, flamingos, seems perilously erotic:
earlier, he has fended the erotic suggestion off, now she does.

"Water lilies," in the mythology of the nineteenth century, are strong
bearers of feminine sexuality. (After all, the nénuphar had been used by the
ancient Egyptians for the production of aphrodisiacs.) The literary evidence
is quite overwhelming: the great Danish eroticist Emil Aarestrup wrote a
ritournelle about naked women, bathing (183):

> Den lysblaa Badevogn var trukket ud paa Sandet,
> Man hørte Fnisen af de unge Skjønne
> Det var, som Lilier blomstred under Vandet.
> (In "Ritorneller," *Efterladte Digte*, 1863)[13]

Every reader of German literature, too, knows the experience of Reinhardt
in Theodor Storm's *Immensee* (1849), when, in his midnight swim, his body
becomes entangled in the "weisse Wasserlilien" — he was

> wie in einem Netz verstrickt, die glatten Stengel *langten* vom Grunde herauf
> und *rankten* [the verbs almost rhyme] um seine nackten Glieder. . . . es
> wurde ihm plötzlich so unheimlich, daß er mit Gewalt das Gestrick der
> Pflanzen zerriß und in atemloser Hast dem Lande zuschwamm. (298-99)[14]

He has been sexually tempted by a reunion with his sometime beloved,
Elisabeth, now married to his friend Erich. In Ibsen's favorite, Snoilsky, we
find the same mysterious and enticing water lily, "en snövit vattenlilja, /
Om djupets hemlighet ett vittnesbörd" (1: 231). But again Ibsen gives evidence
quite as clear as that his contemporaries have. In the poem "Med en
Vandlilje" (1863), the speaker and presenter of the flower attempts to
disarm and domesticize its allure with instructions to the fair and full-
bosomed recipient (Ibsen 14: 330-31):

> Vil du den til hjemmet fæste,
> fæst den til dit bryst, min bedste!

A dangerous mystery clings to it, a nix sleeps in the pond below (hence "näckros," "nøkkerose"), and the speaker, in the poem's last strophe, perceives that merely pinning the sexual flower to the girl's blouse will not tame its allure, or hers. The nix in the depths — his own desire — still lies in wait:[15]

> Barn, din barm er tjernets strømme.
> Farligt, farligt der at drømme; —
> liljer leger ovenover; —
> nøkken lader som han sover.

It is of some associative importance, by the way, that Ibsen, in the little poem's first strophe, characterizes the water lily as a white-winged bird swimming on the water's surface:

> Se, min bedste, hvad jeg bringer;
> blomsten med de hvide vinger.
> På de stille strømme båren
> svam den drømmetung i våren.

Rubek, as it were, has desired and feared the water lily in the past, when (or so he tells Irene in Act One), he had burned to touch her as she stood on the podium all nude: "Som sanseforvildet af al din dejlighed" (13: Act 1.237). (This revelation on *his* part led to *her* revelation about the lethal needle in the piled coils of her coiffure, so different in their meaning from Rita Allmers's loose and inviting hair.) Presently, his boldness, if it is that, is ignored or deflected by the peremptory Irene, who wants to move on without delay to a higher plane of love and to a different, if related, department of the century's mythology. "Hvide svaner var det," she declares, and Rubek agrees less tentatively than in the case of the gulls: "Jeg mente svaner, ja" (Act 2.266). He is quite willing to add details; for him, the game, in its ultimate and authentic form, was vastly flattering: "Og jeg husker at jeg fæsted et stort loddent blad til en af svanerne. Det var endda et skræppeblad — " Translators have struggled to deal with the "endda" of the second sentence;[16] it has an important function, calling attention to the specific botanical detail. The dock leaf is very large, of course, fit to be made into a boat. Yet the Dano-Norwegian reader or theater-goer of Ibsen's time might have had another association for it as well:[17] of domesticity, of the protection afforded by a home, for it is the central plant of H. C. Andersen's tale about *Den lykkelige Familie* (1848),[18] the snails that live under the giant dock leaves in the garden of an apparently abandoned château. In the epilogue to the passage, Rubek will return, quite openly, to the notion of reconstituting, more permanently, the happy and creative domesticity of the weekends at the Taunitzer See.

Now, at the passage's climax, Irene tells what the meaning of the game was, or what the burdock and the water lilies meant to their launchers: "Så blev det til Lohengrins båd — med svanen foran" (266). The aptness of the reference was immediately clear to every member of the audience in the days of the Wagner cult, a reference to the virgin knight[19] Lohengrin, who, after the catastrophic end of his wedding night with Elsa, leaves her (still virginal, even as he) to sail away in the swan-boat, pulled (after the transformation of the swan into Elsa's brother, Gottfried) by the dove of the Holy Grail.

By the operatic allusion, we might suspect that Rubek, that master rhetorician, had once upon a time persuaded Irene of the holiness of his calling and the need for celibacy,[20] thus praising her as the pure inspiration of his art, consoling her for the lack of physical attention she received at the Taunitzer See,[21] and supporting her in her own sexual ambivalence toward him. They both recall the frequency and intensity with which the game was played; Rubek says: "Hvor glad du var i den leg, Irene," and Irene substantiates his memory: "Vi legte den ofte om igen," to which he replies: "Hver eneste lørdag, tror jeg. Hele sommeren udover" (266). Just at this point Irene unhesitatingly remembers how Rubek had called her the swan that pulled his boat: "Du sa', at jeg var svanen, som trak din båd,"[22] and so brings the swan-game wholly into the light. She has called Rubek "digter" repeatedly and mockingly, but here she makes up for the slur; from Pindar and Horace to H. C. Andersen and Baudelaire, the swan has been the bird of Apollo, the bird of inspired poetry.

Nonetheless, Rubek may be a little embarrassed at being reminded of the game of the past (as, indeed, Alfred and Asta Allmers are about theirs): "Sa' jeg det? Ja, det kan godt være" (266). Out of embarrassment, too, he returns to the game in its present form, speaking of gulls once more: "Nej sé bare, hvor mågerne svømmer nedover elven, du." Mindful of the closed casket of inspiration and his confessed lack of creative energy, Irene laughs (and makes a thrust both at him and the inefficacy of his present helpmeet, Maja): "Og alle dine skibe strander." Stung, Rubek boasts, both artistically and, it may be, sexually — does he remember the challenge of Irene's rosy-red flamingos? — "Jeg har skibe nok i behold." (He does not look at Irene as he makes this claim, but continues to put leaves in the water and follow them with his eyes.[23] Is he, again, embarrassed, this time at *his* sudden boldness?) Yet he continues to be bold: "Du Irene, — jeg har købt det lille bondehuset ved Taunitzer See" (266). Unhappily, this move away from the game and into real or hoped-for prospects brings about some suspicious questioning on Irene's part: "Bor du da nu derude — i vort gamle hus?" (267), to which Rubek, who has a weakness for showing off, tells how it has been torn down and replaced by "en stor, prægtig, bekvem villa på tomten, — med park omkring." Thus, he gets himself still deeper into hot water: "Der er det, vi plejer — " (he stops and corrects his words) " — der plejer jeg holde til om sommeren." Controlling herself, Irene hits back at him with an obvious query: "Så du og — og den anden holder til derude nu?" Waxing defiant, Rubek retorts: "Ja. Når min hustru og jeg ikke er på rejser, — som nu iår" (267). Softening a little, Irene calls up memories: "Dejligt, dejligt[24] var livet ved Taunitzer See." (The location-phrase, coming for the third time in close succession, and always placed at the end of a replique, gets the effect of a refrain.)

The conversation drifts toward regret (267), at what has not happened (expressed in Rubek's "Og alligevel" and Irene's completion of his thought: " — alligevel så slap vi to al den livets dejlighed"), and then toward Rubek's attempt to imply that the loss can be recuperated. He speaks softly and urgently, "*indtrængende*": "Kommer angeren for sent nu?" Irene does not answer him directly but calls attention to the sunset and its color: "Sé bare — hvor rødt den skinner på skrå hen over alle lyngtuerne derhenne," by which she may mean to say that it is, in fact, too late — but at the same time she emphasizes the redness of the light, a redness that returns to the reader the implications of the red Alpine rose.[25] To this allusion, Rubek says (probably a negative try at flattering Irene, who has brought him back into contact with the lost world of his emotions): "Det er længe siden jeg har sét en solnedgang på fjeldet." Such, he implies, has never happened in Maja's company. Irene's ensuing question has almost the air of an invitation: "End en solopgang da?" — something which Rubek claims he has never seen. At this, Irene corrects, praises, and chides him all at once; she tells how — the speech is figurative, of course — Rubek lured her into the mountains and promised her that she would see "al verdens herlighed" (268) if she fell down and worshipped him and served him. (Her repliques, with their echoes of scripture and the recollection they summon of what Rubek more recently told Maja [252], are a nice further demonstration of Rubek's techniques of *verbal* seduction, already evinced by the skill with which he planted the Lohengrin-swan notion in Irene's mind.) But, persuasive as he can be on occasion, Rubek presently does not think very well on his feet or consider the consequences of what he says. He may recall that lately (in Act One), Maja had reminded him of his employment of his "all the glories of the world" line (221), something to which he has, very ruefully, been forced to return this very afternoon in Act Two, talking to Maja before Irene appeared; now, wanting to get away from a painful topic (hoist, as it were, on the petard of his own persuasive phrase-making), he blunders into a proposal that is bound to cause exquisite trouble: he proposes what must be taken as a *ménage à trois*:[26] "Kunde du ikke ha' lyst til at rejse med og bo hos os i villaen dernede?" The suggestion reaps a mocking smile and an incredulous query from Irene: "Sammen med dig — og den anden dame?" (268). Ignoring her inference, Rubek grows absolutely passionate (and lets the cat out of the bag that he is still the self-centered artist); as in the case of "Jeg har skibe nok i behold," elements of an artistic and an erotic rebirth are mixed: "Sammen med mig — ligesom i de skabende dage. Lukke op alt det, som er vredet i baglås i mig. Kunde du ikke ville det, Irene?" (268). The locked *scrinium pectoris* returns, but Irene says flatly that she no longer has the key; Rubek insists: "Du har nøglen! Ingen uden du har den!"[27] The stage directions (268) underline his anguish, "*trygler og beder*": "Hjælp mig, — så *jeg* kan komme til at leve livet om igen!" (Italics added: for the third time, Rubek chooses the wrong pronoun — see "*vi* plejer" and "bo hos *os*.")

Implacable, Irene heaps scorn on him: "Tomme drømme. Ørkesløse — døde drømme. Vort samliv har ingen opstandelse efter sig." (Her cuts are cruel indeed, albeit justifiable: "ørkesløs" can mean feeble, impotent; "samliv" shows how aware she is of the erotic component in his pleas; "opstandelse" refers, of course, to the great statuary group, but has physical implications as well.[28]) Humiliated and disappointed, Rubek breaks off the conversation and returns to the game: "Så lad os bli' ved at lege da!" And Irene wistfully and wryly concludes the scene: "Ja, lege, lege, — bare lege" (268).[29] The two sit and continue to strew leaves and petals into the brook.

The second act seems about to conclude in an operatic *stretta*; the entrance of Maja in Ulfhejm's company, singing her (simpleminded) song; her leave-taking amidst Ulfhejm's guffaws and her laughing "Tak, tak, tak, professor!"; the sudden invitation of Irene to have "en sommernat på vidden — med mig?"; and Rubek's ecstatic "Ja, ja — kom!" (270). But the end is not yet: ominous actions occur, ominous phrases are spoken. Irene fumbles at her breast for her knife as she repeats the word "episode"; the deaconness turns up, mute and threatening as ever; Irene insists that Rubek stay put on the bench, not follow her now; as she whispers the last instructions for the assignation, Rubek, anxious ("Og du kommer, Irene?") and still tired, falls into dreams ("Sommernat på vidden. Med dig. Med dig."), and gives renewed expression to his fixed idea — to what has been lost: "Å Irene, — det kunde ha været livet. — Og det har vi forspildt, — vi to" (270-71). Melancholy descends on them both, as Irene declares: "Det uopprettelige sér vi først, når — "; she interrupts herself now, as, to Rubek's "Når — ?", she utters the melodramatic and ambiguous, "Når vi døde vågner" (271). Upon Rubek's last, heavyhearted seeking for specifics, about what they will behold then, Irene has her curtain line, which, among other things, disposes of the game beside the Taunitzer See: "Vi sér at vi aldrig har levet" (271). In the distance, Maja yodels her song about her own quite illusory freedom.

The little lyric interlude, which began with Irene's suggestion that they cast off what is deep and heavy, has been revelatory not only about Ibsen's skill at deploying familiar images of the *fin de siècle* (and of his own work), but also about central problems in the relationship between Rubek and Irene. They are both servants and practitioners of art (Irene, in her way, has turned out to be as much the "digter" as Rubek), and both are human beings who desire one another sexually but do not, or cannot, turn that desire into the deed — for whatever reason or set of reasons: certainly, their devotion to art stands between them.[30] Both are frozen, rather like the statuary they have made together. The interlude in particular lights up an aspect of Irene that Maja in her nastiness and Rubek in his admiration have observed: she has a remarkable and dignified stiffness about her. Much of her appeal for the sculptor has been her stiffly dignified quality — a quality she then debased by standing naked before the eyes of hundreds in variety shows. That she chooses the ungainly, but statuesque, flamingo for her first bird beside the brook is appropriate enough, just as she has readily accepted the swan, ungainly and statuesque, as her bird beside the Taunitzer See. Is she aware of the resemblance between the birds? In his letters from Tunis, Flaubert noticed:

> . . . un de mes compagnons a tiré trois grands flamants sur le lac de Tunis. Ce sont des oiseaux semblables à des cygnes et qui ont les ailes rose et noires. Il y en ici par *millier*, et rien n'est plus joli que de les voir s'envoler au soleil quand on tire un coup de fusil sur eux. (262)

(Later in the play, Irene underscores her beautiful, stiff, and noble swan-role by wearing "en svaneduns hætte" [Ibsen 13: 279] during the night on the fells; while Rubek — unromantically — still has his old man's shawl. In her lineage, she is a descendent of an earlier inspiratrice in Ibsen, Svanhild in *Kjærlighedens komedie*.)[31] Yet she is also a *femme fatale*, a relative of Furia, Hjørdis, Hedda, and Hilde, as commentators from Seip (Ibsen 13: 202) to Haaland (132: "Bleik Hjørdis førti år efter") and Bellquist (365) have observed, and not only in the demises she brings down upon her husbands and Rubek — who, without her invitation, would not have clambered up the mountain with her, to meet the avalanche. She has a gift both for the veiledly alluring statement (or hint)[32] and for castrating innuendo; she stabs Rubek not with her stiletto, but with words — albeit he is not always sufficiently alert to perceive their undertones.

Finally, a concluding nonscientific postscript: some further possible subtexts may lie in the little duet of former lovers remembering a love-game and a love never consummated. The passage is a *cavatina a due* (quite fit for the opera house),[33] properly to be contrasted with Maja's simplistic vocal outburst; but it also resembles a sentimental ditty, a nineteenth-century popular song. Did Ibsen, as he wrote, have some uneasy half-awareness of the Nordic songs of his day, letting them run along beneath the modish surface of his allusion to Lohengrin, the boat, and the swan? Plucking the red Alpine rose to initiate the duet, Irene, as it were, challenges Rubek to do what Kuno, the huntsman of the song "Alprosen," is dared to do by his beloved — to pick the flower "[h]ögt på alpens isbelagda spira." He climbs the peak, falls to his death, and Eveli, the challenger, dies upon finding his mangled body; his blood has turned the white rose red.[34] Also, both Irene and Rubek recall that it was on Saturday evenings they made their country trips and played their game; Ibsen could not have helped knowing another favorite: "Det var en Lørdag Aften, / Jeg sad og vented dig, / Du loved mig at komme vist, / Men kom dog ei til mig."[35] Rubek, however, never came to her, nor she to him, in a physical sense; in Act Three, during Irene's terrible reprise of the game beside the — again thrice mentioned — Taunitzer See, when they "legte med svaner og vandliljer," she tells Rubek she had wanted to stab him even then, because she realized that they were dead: "Død. Død, du som jeg. Vi sad der ved Taunitzer See, vi to klamme lig — og legte med hinanden" (Ibsen 13: 281).[36]

A third popular song of the later century[37] is again about love never to be fulfilled: "O, den som hade vingar, / Som vita svanen bär, / Då skulle jag mig svinga / Till vännen jag har kär." To which may be added, brutally and banally, that the *duettino* about flamingos, gulls, and swans has been a swan song for its singers, who perish on the way to their "bryllupsfest," on the pinnacle, in the ruddy sunrise — which sunrise, if stage directions are followed, neither the couple nor the audience gets to see.

## Notes

[1] All Ibsen quotations are from the "Hundreårsutgave," of the *Samlede verker*. Act Two is in 13: 243-71, and the neglected passage on 265-68. [Although Ibsen is named in the first-cited reference to his work in any new section, the page number for each and every quotation has not been prominently displayed. The changes in page references for any long passage, as well as changes in the play's Acts, are, however, pointed out. A return to volume 13 is noted after the mention of any other Ibsen volume and, of course, after the mention of a work by any other author. — Eds.]

[2] Ibsen would have known the concept of the casket of spiritual secrets kept in the papal breast, secrets to which the popes (for example, Pius IX) alone had access, from the extensive newspaper accounts of the discussion of papal infallibility that raged during the First Vatican Council of 1869-70 and the so-called "Kulturkampf" in Germany; the phrase was used both by the pope's adherents and, satirically, his adversaries: what if the pope lost the key to his *scrinium pectoris*? Its introduction by Ibsen adds measurably to the portrayal of Rubek's self-absorption (as Georg Lukács observed, Rubek represents a turn-of-the-century literary type, the artist as "eccentric egoist" [187]), and is a third example — less obvious than his adaptations of Satan's temptation of Christ (Northam) and the Lohengrin story (see below) — of his ability to dramatize himself, a gift he shares, of course, with Solness and Borkman.

[3] Maja has taken up the word "skrin" immediately after Rubek's first description of it: "Og det er vel sagtens for dette skrinets skyld at hun er kommet" (Ibsen 13: 254). Particularly in Maja's second use of the word, to Irene, there may well lie a nasty irony, i.e., "ligskrin," which would be one of the play's several double entendres. Intentionally or not, most English-language translators capture this ambiguity: Archer: "He wants you to help him open a *casket* which has snapped to" (404), in which he is followed by Meyer (441), Watts (263), McFarlane (271), and Fjelde (1067). However, Forslund obliterates the nuance with "miniature safe" (36, 38), and Rudkin has "treasure casket" (44, 46).

[4] A much more attentive listener than Rubek, Irene has noted Rubek's use of the word in its verb form as he gives his self-exculpatory account of the changes he has made in the great statue (become a statuary group) of "Opstandelsens dag," and turns it against him. Rubek has said: "Den lille runde plint, hvor dit billede stod rankt og ensomt, — den gav ikke længer rum for alt det, jeg nu vilde digte til — ," and Irene, fumbling for her knife, asks, "Hvad digtet du så til?" (Ibsen 13: 262). We may suspect that the verb was a part of Rubek's earlier and seductive adornment of his sculptor's calling for Irene when she was his young model (again, not unlike Solness's dressing-up of his untutored builder's and developer's career into a divine call or Borkman's transfiguration of his embezzlements). In Act One (13: 239), Irene asks, "Hvad har du digtet siden? I marmor mener jeg? Efter den dag, jeg rejste fra dig?" (The remark indicates that Irene, at least at times, sees through Rubek's ability to "digte," to weave alluring and not necessarily factual verbal patterns.) Rubek, taking the word solely in the ennobling sense with which he had obviously applied it to his artistic activity, replies, "Intet har jeg digtet efter den dag. Bare gået og puslet og modelleret."

[5] E.g., Weigand (381-87), Anker (190-95), Arestad (124-27), Ustvedt (282-85), Gvåle (35-36), Holtan (158-68), Hurt (201-04), Northam (*Ibsen's Dramatic Method* 212-14), Lyons (148-49), Durbach (138-46). However, the passage in question has not got much attention, save in Østerud (90-92), Olivarius (204-06), and Beyer (34-35), in which Beyer summarizes the interlude:

> In the course of a few retorts the exotic, wonderful, red flamingoes are turned into modest, homely gulls — white and grey, with red bills only. It illustrates the distance between past and present, dream and reality — and it is, I think, the last glimpse we ever get of Ibsen's humour.

[6] The French-Spanish poet José-Maria Heredia (1842-1905) made the flamingo the bird *par excellence* of the Latin American forest, e.g., in "Les Bois americains" (1860):

> La lagune verdit, morne et silencieuse;
> Juché sur une patte et l'air triste et songeur,
> Comme sondant de l'œil l'onde mystérieuse,
> Le flamant rose dort. (222)

[7] Emily Dickinson uses the word in this way in "How the old Mountains drip with sunset" (210):

> How the old Steeples hand the Scarlet
> Till the Ball is full
> — Have I the lip of the Flamingo
> That I dare to tell?

[8] In *Neue Gedichte* (1907-08), Rilke applied the erethism of the bird's color with startling effect ("Die Flamingos" 1: 629-30):

> In Spiegelbildern wie von Fragonard
> ist doch vom ihrem Weiß und ihrer Röte
> nicht mehr gegeben, als dir einer böte
> wenn er von seiner Freundin sagt: sie war
> noch sanft von Schlaf.

On her first night at Oxford, Max Beerbohm's supreme *femme fatale*, the "tall and lissom" Zuleika Dobson, in the novel of that name (1911), goes to dinner dressed thus: "she was sheathed from the bosom downwards in flamingo silk" (24). Recently, Warren Beatty has reminded us that the nickname the poetic gangster Benjamin "Bugsy" Siegel gave his mistress Virginia Hill was "Flamingo."

[9] Remarkably, R. V. Forslund has expanded the red part of the bird: "They could be sea gulls with red heads" (46).

[10] "[F]angstmænd" has created difficulties for Ibsen's most skillful translators: Archer writes "harpoon-men" (422), McFarlane "bird-catchers" (281), Watts and Fjelde "hunters" (273, 1075). Perhaps there is no adequate way in English fully to express the word's unpleasant air.

[11] The name of this fictitious lake may be taken from the Taunus Range, with its mineral spas and vineyards, an ideal vacation spot. It may also call to mind the once enormously popular series of English-language paperbacks (intended principally for tourists on the Continent, since the books could not be sold in Britain), the Tauchnitz Editions, issued by Bernhard Tauchnitz of Leipzig: founded in 1841, the series had reached 3000 titles by 1894

and could be purchased in every railroad-station bookstall. (A history of the firm notes that they sold better in the "Alpine lands" in summer, in Italy and southern France in winter.) In other words, "Tauchnitz" had a strong association, for the nineteenth-century mind, with travel. Østerud's connection of Taunitz (90) with Tannhäuser, the splendid new villa with the Venusberg, and Maja (perhaps) with Frau Venus should also be mentioned; Østerud observes that Rubek says he has sought happiness in "ørkesløs nydelse" there (Ibsen 13: 253).

[12] Hurt (199) quite correctly notes the "deathly" air of the scene and thus takes a step beyond Seip who wrote in his introduction to the play about Ibsen's feeling of homelessness in his homeland (13: 187-88). However, the translation Hurt employs, Michael Meyer's, simply omits the detail "banemænd" altogether. An awareness of this possible gloomy pun could have supported Hurt's interpretation of the "Beckett-like passage." Ibsen used the word in its Old Norse sense on two occasions (1: 261 and 4: 83): Kjæmpehøien (1854) and Hærmændene på Helgeland (1858), respectively.

[13] Another sensualist, Hjalmar Söderberg, offered much the same image in Hjärtats oro (1909), as, through his spyglass, he watched Danish bathing beauties splashing in the altogether: "dessa kvinnoblommor" (255); Karen Blixen surely remembered Aarestrup in her story about nineteenth-century sexuality, Den gamle vandrende Ridder (in Eng. 1934; in Da. 1935):

Vore Digtere sang jo om, hvordan de unge Skønne, bagved Badevognens Forhæng, hviskede og lo, mens de rødmende "satte Liljer i Vand." (102)

[14] In the short novel Bunte Herzen (1908), Eduard von Keyserling has an episode in which the desperately love-sick Boris almost drowns, "in ein Netz von Wasserrosen und Froschlöffeln verstrickt" (29); here, he is tempted by the thought of death, which he later finds at his own hand.

[15] Peter Olivarius notes that, at the end of Act Two of Lille Eyolf, Asta Almers gives her mourning brother a bunch of water lilies:

Den unge pige ved nemlig, at broderen ikke kender den drift, der drager dem mod hinanden; og hun ved også, at de i virkeligheden ikke er søskende, og at hun bestemt ikke behøver at lade sig nøje med stille søskendekærlighed. Betydningen af vand-liljerne . . . i Når vi døde vågner må derfor være den, at de karakteriserer lidenskaben, der forbandt Irene og Rubek i den herlige skabende tid ved Taunitzer See, som ukendt, mere omfattende og farligere end de selv vidste af. (205)

[16] Archer: "It looked like a burdock-leaf" (422); Meyer: "A dock leaf, wasn't it" (358); Watts: "a dockleaf, it must have been" (273); Fjelde: "A leaf of dock, I suppose" (1076). McFarlane indicates the adverb by an aposiopesis: "It was a dock-leaf . . ." (281), and Forslund simply omits the sentence (46).

[17] Ibsen initially had a much less allusive noun: "Det var bladet af en Tussilago kan jeg huske" (13: 327).

[18] A tale that, as Andersen's diaries report, enjoyed an enormous popularity during Andersen's own life; he was repeatedly asked to read it aloud.

[19] Lohengrin's virginity had considerable fascination for literary artists in the Wagnerian age: see Catulle Mendès's novel about the creator of Neuschwanstein, Ludwig II, Le roi vièrge (1881), and Hjalmar Söderberg's Doktor Glas (1905), with its virginal protagonist and its citations of Lohengrin.

[20] The "virginity" of Rubek at the Taunitzer See is an important point: another of Ibsen's paronomasial usages may lie in the remark of Irene (13: 259): "Jeg haded dig fordi du kunde stå der så *uberørt*" (emphasis added); Rubek immediately takes up the last word, in an anadiplosis, thus calling still more attention to it: "Uberørt? Tror du?" (Cf. "en uberørt pige.")

[21] Ibsen imagined a Taunitzer See containing not just swanlike water lilies but real swans: in a note to himself (13: 342), he gave the following further information: "Hytten ved Taunitzer See. Der ligger den . . . Store, hvide svaner dukker sig i vandene."

[22] Rilke, in his *Lieder der Mädchen* (written in 1898, when the Wagner craze was at its height), has girls sing happily about their inspiratory task: "Schwestern, jetzt sind wir Schwäne, / die am Goldgesträhne / die Märchenmuschel ziehn" (1: 174). Richard Dehmel, in "Landung" (61-62) from *Erlösungen* (1891), does not clearly indicate the sex of his inspiratory swan, but we may suspect that it, too, is feminine:

> Mein weißer Schwan vor mir, noch ziehn wir leise
> auf dunkler Flut durch unser Morgengrauen,
> zur blassen Ferne, wo die Wellenkreise
> dem jungen Tage hoch entgegenschlagen.

Poet and "swan" arrive at "die seligen Inseln," and,

> Da wirst du losgeknüpft von meinen Zügeln,
> der Nachen säumt, wir sind am Heimatlande;
> da dehnst du dich mit ausgespannten Flügeln
> und steigst hinauf mit mir zum hellen Strande.

[23] Earlier in the act, Irene has noticed this habit of a seemingly embarrassed Rubek (Ibsen 13: 257-58); she asks: "Hvorfor sidder du der og vender øjnene fra mig?" Rubek replies: "Tør ikke, — tør ikke sé på dig."

[24] In Helge Rode's play *Sommeræventyr* (1897), to which Ibsen's attention had been called by articles by Georg Brandes in *Politiken*, the affective epizeuxis, "dejligt, dejligt," appears twice (54, 84), both times when Rakel — who is in love with the worn-out *bonvivant* Anders Juul (mockingly characterized by her as "afdød" [55] and old: "De afdøde maa holde sig rolige" [58]) — describes the beauty of the summer night: Rakel and Anders seem to have fallen in love some years before on such a night, when Rakel was linked to Anders's tubercular brother, Knud, now deceased. The revived romance, despite intense yearning on both sides, comes to naught. Ibsen, at work on *Når vi døde vågner*, may have been interested not just by Rode's ability to infuse everyday language with poetic qualities, but by his pervasive use of the death theme elsewhere in the little play. The drunken postadolescent Artur and the clumsy theological candidate Rønneby — both likewise enamored of Rakel — discuss the power of the moon (by moonshine) at the opening of Act Two (64-65). Artur observes, "Ved Fuldmaane, siger man, at de døde staar op af deres Grave og danser i Ligklæderne." After an interjection by the unimaginative Rønneby, Artur continues:

> Blot den skinner paa os, kommer vi at ligne Dødninger . . . Jeg synes, De ligner en Dødning aldeles nu. — Og saa danser vi — saa danser vi Dødningedans for den [i.e., Maanen] . . . Se — kan De ikke se, hvor den ler — for den er jo selv død.

Rønneby agrees, and Artur makes an identification between the dead moon and Rakel (who has laughed at the two unsuccessful suitors): "Og saa elsker vi den alle — ogsaa jeg — vi er nogle Narre alle tilhobe" (65).

[25] Ibsen reworked the sentence, adding the emphasizing dash after "rødt"; also, having started with "Se bare hvor rødt den lyser," he changed the color-word to "varmt," and then returned to "rødt," thus reintroducing one of the two major colors (with "white") of the whole scene. Red, of course, implies (in a simple and common symbolism) passion, and white means purity. Cf. Rilke's poem of 1897-98, "Weißes Glück" (3: 454), with its "Tal der Leidenschaft" and "rote Kraft" opposed to "die leichten Wellen" and "unsre weißen Wünsche," and Edith Södergran's famous statement in *Dikter* (1916), "Den speglande brunnen" (36), about the condition of a tubercular patient in love: "Ödet sade: vit skall du leva eller röd skall du dö!"

[26] Earlier the same afternoon, right after Rubek's recital about the *scrinium pectoris* and its missing key, Maja has suggested a *ménage à trois* to Rubek, but she locates it in their large city house, not in the once creative precinct by the Taunitzer See: ". . . inde i byen, — i hele vort store hus, må der da vel — med lidt god vilje — kunne bli' rum til tre" (Ibsen 13: 255). Weigand, who is so pedantically critical of Ibsen's "faulty" technique in the play, mistakenly thinks the proposal comes from Rubek: "Altogether puzzling is the readiness with which [Maja] accedes to Rubek's suggestion of a *ménage à trois*" (391). Maja cares very little about a preservation of whatever intimacy there may (or may not) exist between her and her husband; in Irene's cutting reaction to the proposal, it is easy to see how much she is still emotionally tied to her lord and master, even though she means to kill him.

[27] In Ibsen's initial version of the concluding pages of the play (13: 336-41), he adduced a comical parallel to the key-motif, which, happily, he jettisoned. In his pocket, Ulfhejm has a key to his hunting hut; with it, he opens the door and serves a picnic to Maja, Rubek, and Irene, during which Maja drinks a toast to freedom, followed by the toasts of her husband and Irene.

[28] The "resurrection" of the (male) lover after the *mors parva* of intercourse is a blasphemous commonplace of Neo-Latin erotic literature. Rilke inserted it into his "Sieben Gedichte" (1915):

> Begreife nur:
> das ist mein Körper, welcher aufersteht.
> Nun hilf ihm leise aus dem heißen Grabe
> in jenen Himmel, den ich in dir habe. (2: 438)

D. H. Lawrence made it the centerpiece of his scandalous story "The Man Who Died" (1929), in which it is applied to a Christ who, surviving the cross, is revived by a priestess of Isis:

> He crouched to her, and he felt the blaze of his manhood and his power to rise up
> in his loins, magnificent: "I am risen!" (444)

In his last play, Ibsen once more displays his well-known taste for the sexually *outré* earlier to be found in the second act of *Peer Gynt* (1867), in the implication that Gregers Werle has a homosexual attraction toward Hjalmar Ekdal, in the location of Ejlert Løvborg's mortal wound, in Rebekka West's incestuous affair with her father, and in the arrangement *à trois* planned by Fanny Wilton. The exchanges in the present play between Maja and Ulfhejm in Act Three are also cases in point; cf. Ulfhejm's "Kan De sé de stakkers hornene, jeg har?" (Ibsen 13: 274), about which Seip primly wrote, "Replikkene om 'hornene' . . . virker nesten 'holbergske' og gjorde virkning på scenen" (13: 204) and the hints passed between Maja: "De med Deres bukkebén, ja!" and Ulfhejm: "Og De med Deres — " (13: 277), at which juncture Ibsen pulls a curtain of decency over what the squire means. Also, Ibsen might be suspected of having toyed with naughty nomenclature in Rubek's case, since he thought of calling him (288-89) both Stubow (cf. D-N. 'stut') and Rambow (cf. German 'rammeln' and D-N. 'ramler'). Accessory evidence in this instance is provided by the merry widow in *De unges forbund* (1869): the original name of Madam *Rund*holmen was the ambiguous Madam *Bag*holmen.

[29] Can the streak of bitter lewdness in Ibsen have betrayed itself ever so slightly in Irene's threefold hovering over the verb, which also means the copulation of animals, birds, and fish? Such an implication would be wryness indeed on Ibsen's (or Irene's) part.

[30] Is Rubek simply one more of Ibsen's impotent or sexually dormant male protagonists? The line is a long one: Bishop Niklas, Rosmer, Solness (whose eroticism may well be first a power play, with Kaja, and then mere talk, with Hilde), Allmers, Borkman (whose resemblance to Wagner's love-renouncing Alberich in *Das Rheingold* is striking). Irene's outburst (cf. note 20) about hating Rubek because he was "kunstner, bare kunstner, — ikke mand," echoes Niklas's remark (Ibsen 5: 79) about himself in *Kongs-emnerne* (1863): "halvmanden"; and her jab about his being "slap og sløv" suggests not merely a moral judgement of him, if the physical import of "slap" (and "slapsvans") is borne in his mind. Haaland suggests that, during the modeling sessions, "For billedhoggeren . . . kommer arbeidet langt på vei til å gi avløp også for hans kjønn," while Irene has been forced to "gjøre pinefull vold på sin natur som kvinne" (138). Thus she takes it as "et slag i ansiktet da Rubek avslutter det lange samarbeidet med å snakke om en velsignet episode" — blessedly productive for him but not for her. However, Irene's case is more complex; her thought that she would have killed Rubek with that "spids nål," as she stood on the podium, if he had dared to touch her, may indicate a lethal frigidity on her part, as do, certainly, her accounts of her two marriages. The story she gives Rubek (Ibsen 13: 234-35) of the Russian Satow's fate is even more sinister than that of the South American's suicide. She implies, in response to Rubek's question, that Satow is "Langt borte i Uralbergene. Mellem alle sine guldminer." Rubek asks, "Der lever han altså?" And Irene, shrugging her shoulders: "Lever? Lever? Egentlig har jeg dræbt ham — " The startled Rubek repeats her verb: "Dræbt —!" And Irene utters her shocking replique: "Dræbt med en fin, spids dolk, som jeg altid har med mig i sengen — " (235). Does Irene mean that she (like Andersen-Nexø's Fru Kongstrup) has castrated Satow in bed? Ibsen's first version of the line, "som jeg havde med mig i sengen," (13: 305), hints at such an intention in Satow's special case, but the revision (as Peter Watts has noted, 300) expands the image of the knife in bed to the whole barrenness of the model's life; straightaway she talks about her children whom she likewise has killed ("dræbt").

[31] In his sketches, Ibsen thought of Irene as being "af rig familie. Forlod hjemmet og rejste bort med ham, den fattige, ubekendte vordende kunstner" (13: 287). As in the marriages of Solness, Allmers, and Borkman, there seems to have been a social and financial disparity between the male and female partners. It can be assumed that Irene has had a proper upbringing, and something ladylike clearly pertains to her — in sharp contrast to Maja's hoydenlike quality. James Joyce (in 1900) was so captivated by the woman of "fine spirituality" and the "intensely spiritual creation" (63) that he — the master punster — overlooked her not-so-occasional barbs, directed below the belt, as well as the putative fate of the South American and Satow. There is, incidentally, some resemblance between Irene's life story and that of the legendary Finnish beauty Aurora Stjernvall-Demidov-Karamzin (1808-1902). As a lady-in-waiting at the court of Nicholas I, she married the fabulously wealthy Paul Demidov, who owned, among other things, gold mines in Siberia. After his insanity and death (1840), she wedded Andrei Karamzin (a son of the historian), who was slaughtered (and his corpse mutilated) by the Turks during the Crimean War. Returning to Finland, she devoted her life and her fortune to charitable deeds, most notable among them the establishment (1867) of Helsingfors' Diakonissanstalt, a hospital and institution for the training of "diakonissor," Ibsen's Norwegian specimen of whom utters the play's last line: "Irene! . . . *Pax vobiscum!*" Aurora Karamzin's fame spread far beyond Finland; in a letter to Peter Nansen of April 10, 1885, from Helsingfors, Herman Bang told how he had met "Fyrstinde Kamrazim [sic] — den skønneste Kvinde, jeg har set."

[32] In the final version, Ibsen reinforced Irene's awareness of her own sexual energy and allure. When, in Act One (13: 235), following Irene's murderous revelations, Rubek (poeticizing as usual) exclaims, "Der er strenge i dig, som er sprunget i stykker," Irene originally retorts, "Det gør det visst altid når *et menneske* dør." The generalizing and colorless noun was then changed to "en ung blodsvulmende kvinde." Similarly, Irene originally says, "Ja, med hele min *sjællivs* varme blod tjente jeg dig!"; that was changed to "med hele min ungdoms bankende blod" (237).

[33] Fritz Paul writes that the play's finale is "beinahe opernhaft" (136), but the same term could surely be applied to the scene just discussed. The sculptor, Rubek, is especially given to musical images: his remark to Irene about the broken strings in her (Ibsen 13: 235) has been mentioned above (note 32); and, as Maja complains to him about the singing, dancing children, he rejoins, "Der er noget harmonisk, — næsten som musik, — i de bevægelser — en gang imellem. Midt i alt det klodsede" (245).

[34] The song was printed in Stockholm in 1871, "blev genast mycket omtyckt och behöll länge stor popularitet" (Dahlberg, n.p.). Its penultimate stanza, of fourteen, goes,

> Och hennes fader äfwen kom till stället,
> Men döden då fören't dem båda två;
> Se'n hela byn med honom tårar fällde;
> *Till brudpar döden gjorde dem ändå.*
> (Italics added)

[35] Coincidentally, a popular Norwegian songbook of 1879, *Den nyeste Visebog for Hvermand*, contains both "Det var en Lørdag Aften," here attributed to Grundtvig, and Falk's song "Vi vandrer med frejdigt mod" from *Kjærlighedens komedie* by Ibsen, and "Solveig's Song."

[36] Ibsen's (and Irene's) formulation, "legte med hinanden," has manifold meanings: that she has seen through the illusory nature of their sometime play; that they used one another to the end of mutual enhancement (she made him a knight in shining armor, he made her an inspiration); and that she was quite aware of the erotic basis of what they did, however platonic it may have seemed. She has just brought up water lilies, with their erotic connotation, once again. Archer's absolutely literal translation: "We played with one another" (432) is somewhat more suggestive than Watts's "we played together" (288); Fjelde's "playing games with each other" (1090) also has considerable ambiguity, as does McFarlane's "playing games together" (295). Forslund avoids the problem: "we played" (59), while Rudnik says too much and too specifically: "playing a children's game with one another" (70).

[37] In connection with *Hedda Gabler*, T. Vogel-Jørgensen notes, "Det blev i sin tid hævdet, at vendingen 'Dø i skønhed' hos Ibsen var affødt af et meget omtalt kærlighedsdrama, hvis personer var cirkusartisten Elvira Madigan og den sv[enske] grev Sparre" (186).

## Works Cited

Aarestrup, Emil. "Ritorneller." *Efterladte Digte.* Ed. Christian Winther and F. L. Liebenberg. Copenhagen: Samfundet til den danske Literaturs Fremme, 1863. 169-86.

Almquist, Sigurd. "Alpros." *Nordisk Familjebok.* Vol. 1. Stockholm: Nordisk Familjebok, 1904.

Anker, Herman. "'Når vi døde vågner.' Ibsens dramatiske epilog." *Edda* 56 (1956): 178-219.

Archer, William. *The Collected Works of Henrik Ibsen.* Vol. 11. New York: Charles Scribner, 1911.

Arestad, Sverre. "*When We Dead Awaken* Reconsidered." *Scandinavian Studies* 30 (1959): 117-30.

Bang, Herman. *Vandreaar. Fortalt i Breve til Peter Nansen.* Copenhagen: Henrik Koppel, 1918. Letter of Apr. 10, 1885.

Beerbohm, Max. *Zuleika Dobson.* Harmondsworth/New York: Penguin: 1981.

Bellquist, John. "Ibsen's *Brand* and *Når vi døde vågner*: Tragedy, Romanticism, Apocalypse." *Scandinavian Studies* 55 (1983): 347-70.

Beyer, Edvard. "*When We Dead Awaken*: Some Notes on Structure, Imagery, and the Meaning of 'Epilogue.'" *Ibsen Årbok 1971*: 26-41.

Blixen, Karen. *Mindeudgave.* Vol. 1. *Fantastiske Fortællinger, Første Del.* Copenhagen: Gyldendal, 1964.

Dahlberg, Dag, and Urban Dahlberg. *Skillingtryck.* Stockholm: Fabel, 1986.

Dehmel, Richard. *Gesammelte Werke.* Vol. 1: *Erlösungen.* Berlin: S. Fischer, 1906.

Dickinson, Emily. *The Poems.* Ed. Thomas H. Johnson. Cambridge, Mass.: Harvard UP, 1958.

Durbach, Errol. *Ibsen the Romantic: Analogues of Paradise in the Later Plays.* Athens: U of Georgia P, 1982.

Fjelde, Rolf. *Ibsen: The Complete Major Prose Plays.* New York: Farrar, Straus, Giroux, 1978.

Flaubert, Gustave. *Correspondance: Nouvelle Édition augmentée: Quatrième Série (1854-1881).* Paris: Louis Conard, 1927.

Forslund, R. V., *Four Plays of Ibsen.* Philadelphia/New York/London: Chilton, 1968.

Gvåle, Gudrun Hovde. "Henrik Ibsen. 'Når vi døde vågner.'" *Ibsen Årbok 1968-69*: 22-37.

Haaland, Arild. *Ibsens verden. En studie i kunst som forskning.* Oslo: Gyldendal, 1978.

Heredia, José-Maria. *Poésies complètes.* Paris: Librairie Alphonse Lemerre, 1924.

Holtan, Orley. *Mythic Patterns in Ibsen's Last Plays.* Minneapolis: U of Minnesota P, 1970.

Hurt, James. *Cataline's Dream: An Essay on Ibsen's Plays.* Urbana/Chicago/London: U of Illinois P, 1972.

Ibsen, Henrik. *Samlede verker.* Ed. Francis Bull, Halvdan Koht, and Didrik Arup Seip. "Hundreårsutgave." Oslo: Gyldendal (F. Hegel), 1928. 21 vols. 1928-57.
See especially vol. 13 (1936): *Når vi døde vågner.*
See also: Vol. 1 (1928): *Kjæmpehøien.*
       Vol. 2 (1928): *Fru Inger til Østråt.*
       Vol. 4 (1930): *Kjærlighedens komedie; Hærmændene på Helgeland.*

Vol. 5 (1928): *Kongs-emnerne.*
Vol. 6 (1930): *Peer Gynt.*
Vol. 10 (1932): *Vildanden.*
Vol. 11 (1934): *Fruen fra havet.*
Vol. 12 (1935): *Lille Eyolf.*
Vol. 14 (1937): "Maageskrig"; "Med en Vandlilje."

Joyce, James. *"When We Dead Awaken."* In *Discussions of Henrik Ibsen.* Ed. James Walter McFarlane. Boston: D. C. Heath, 1962. 61-65.

Keyserling, Eduard von. *Bunte Herzen, Am Südhang, Harmonie: Drei Erzählungen.* Frankfurt a.M.: Fischer Taschenbuch, 1983.

Lawrence, D. H. *The Later D. H. Lawrence.* New York: Knopf, 1952.

Lukács, Georg. *Probleme des Realismus.* Berlin: Aufbau, 1955.

Lyons, Charles R. *Henrik Ibsen: The Divided Consciousness.* Carbondale/Edwardsville: Southern Illinois UP, 1972.

McFarlane, James Walter. *The Oxford Ibsen.* Vol. 8. Oxford/London/New York: Oxford UP, 1977. 8 vols. 1961-77.

Meyer, Michael. *The Lady from the Sea, The Master Builder, John Gabriel Borkman, When We Dead Awaken.* Garden City: Doubleday's Anchor Books, 1960.

Morgenstern, Christian. *Galgenlieder.* Berlin: Cassirer, 1920.

Northam, John. *Ibsen's Dramatic Method: A Study of the Prose Dramas.* Oslo/Bergen/Tromsø: Universitetsforlaget, 1971.

——. "Ibsen's Use of Language in *When We Dead Awaken."* *Ibsen and the Theatre: The Dramatist in Production.* Ed. Errol Durbach. New York/London: New York UP, 1980. 105-17.

*Den nyeste Visebog for Hvermand.* Kristiania [Oslo]: Alb. Cammermeyer, 1879.

Olivarius, Peter. "Henrik Ibsen. Idealismens svanesang." *Den erindrende faun. Digteren og hans fantasi.* Ed. Aage Henriksen, Helge Therkeldsen, and Knud Wetzel. Copenhagen: Fremad, 1969. 192-208.

Paul, Fritz. *Symbol und Mythos. Studien zum Spätwerk Henrik Ibsens.* Münchener Universitätsschriften 6. Munich: Wilhelm Fink, 1969.

Rilke, Rainer Maria. *Sämtliche Werke.* Vols. 1 and 2. Wiesbaden: Insel, 1955, 1957. Vol. 3: *Jugendgedichte.* Frankfurt a.M.: Insel, 1959. 6 vols. 1955-66.
See especially, the following vols.
Vol. 1 (1955): "Lieder der Mädchen." 172-81.
Vol. 2 (1956): "Sieben Gedichte." 435-38.
Vol. 3 (1959): "Weißes Glück." 454.

Rode, Helge. *Sommeræventyr. Skuespil i tre akter.* Copenhagen: Gyldendal (F. Hegel & Søn), 1897.

Rudkin, David. *When We Dead Awaken, Rosmersholm.* London: Absolute Press, 1990.

Schnitzler, Arthur. *Gesammelte Werke: Die Theaterstücke*. Berlin: S. Fischer, 1928.

Snoilsky, Carl. [SD] *Samlade dikter*. Nationalupplaga. 5 vols. Stockholm: Hugo Geber, 1903-04.

Storm, Theodor. *Sämtliche Werke*. Vol. 1. Hrsg. Albert Köster. Leipzig: Insel, 1920. 8 vols. 1899-1913.

Söderberg, Hjalmar. *Samlade verk*. Vol. 5. Stockholm: Bonniers, 1949. 10 vols. 1943-49.

Södergran, Edith. *Samlade dikter*. Stockholm: Wahlström & Widstrand, 1962.

Ustvedt, Yngvar. "Professor Rubek og Henrik Ibsen." *Edda* 67 (1967): 272-87.

Vogel-Jørgensen, T. *Bevingede ord*. 4th ed. Copenhagen: G. E. C. Gads Forlag, 1955.

Watts, Peter. *Ghosts and Other Plays*. Harmondsworth/Baltimore: Penguin Books, 1964.

Weigand, Hermann J. *The Modern Ibsen*. New York: E. P. Dutton, 1960.

Østerud, Erik. "*Når vi døde vågner* på mytologisk bakgrund." *Ibsen Årbok 1963-64*: 72-86.

Hamsun ... så ... på virkeligheten som noe fantastisk og kunsten som noe virkelig.

Harald Naess,
*Knut Hamsun og Amerika,* 1969

# Hamsun 1898-1912: Crisis and Regeneration

## Edvard Beyer

"Aa Gud, hvor dette Skriveri nu byder mig imod," Knut Hamsun wrote in a letter to Mrs. Gerda Welhaven, in July 1898, when he was just finishing *Victoria*:

> Jeg er træt af Romanen, og Dramaet har jeg altid foragtet; jeg har begyndt at skrive Vers nu, den eneste Digtning, som ikke er baade pretentiøs og intetsigende, men bare intetsigende. (Quoted in T. Hamsun 87)

As a matter of fact, the very same year Hamsun had finished his first and most ambitious enterprise as a dramatist, the trilogy *Ved Rigets Port, Livets Spil, Aftenrøde* (1895-98). It is no masterpiece, but it is typical of the *fin de siècle* and stands out as a remarkable parenthesis in Hamsun's total *oeuvre*. The main character, Ivan Kareno, is a social philosopher who in the first part stands "at the gate of the kingdom," but refuses to enter, rejecting a promising academic career because it would imply that he had to disclaim his defiant views and attitudes. In the second play, however, when he is nearly forty years of age, he is no longer capable of acting upon his own ideas, and in the final part, when he is about fifty, he is really a broken man. Again Kareno is faced with a decisive choice, and this time, pleading the experiences of a long life, he betrays the convictions of his youth in order to obtain power and a safe place in bourgeois society. For, as he once declared, "En Mand er psykisk og fysisk gammel naar han er femti Aar" (*SV* 6: *Aftenrøde* 32).

The trilogy is not at all autobiographical. But in light of its concentration on the inescapable aging process and Hamsun's preoccupation with the same theme in letters and lectures — as "Aandens Avblomstringsalder" — from the surrounding and succeeding years, there seems to be something very personal about it. The last part may even be seen as an ironic and somewhat malicious prefiguration of his own successful career after the age of fifty.

Hamsun was thirty-nine when he wrote *Victoria* and finished the Kareno trilogy. In the course of less than a decade he had produced a number of outstanding novels — as well as a few others — and in various respects led a strenuous life. That he should feel tired and drained was only natural. But the most important reason for his despondency is to be found in his books from the following years. The "poet of youth" does not himself feel young any longer. The sense of getting old and of having nothing more to say has led him into a crisis that is on the point of paralyzing him as an author.

After an interval of four years Hamsun started publishing books again, collections of old sketches, short stories, and autobiographical trifles, as well as an account of his honeymoon journey to Russia and Turkey. (The marriage, by the way, according to his son Tore, was doomed from the start, and it lasted only for a couple of years.) It is characteristic of Hamsun's uncertainty regarding his own talent, but also of his strong will to recover, that he again returned to the genre he had always detested and that his first and most ambitious work from the period is a poetic drama in eight acts, *Munken Vendt* (1902).

Hamsun always excepted *Peer Gynt* (1867) from his violent disparagement of Ibsen's works, and, to a certain extent, it has obviously been a model for *Munken Vendt*. But in quality Hamsun's work is far beneath Ibsen's great dramatic poem. In Hamsun's work the action takes place in Northern Norway in a far, indefinite past, perhaps the sixteenth century. The plot is richly coloured and varied, but circumstantial and lax. The speeches are sometimes poetic, but sometimes given to rhetoric in a negative sense of the word. In a peculiar way this drama is an offspring of *Pan* (1894) and *Victoria*, for the main character is identical with the young lover and poet of Johannes's imagination in *Victoria*, and Lady Iselin of Glahn's dreams in *Pan* has here come to life as the object of Vendt's passionate love. In other words, characters who were "doubly" fictional, are here presented as "real."

Again, as in the early novels, the hero is a stranger and an outsider, loving a proud and highborn lady. But Lady Iselin is not, like Edvarda in *Pan*, the daughter of the local sovereign, but his wife. And the sovereign turns out to be the outsider's own father. In this case the term Oedipus complex is hardly to be avoided. And Vendt the monk, who has run away from the University of Wittenberg, is not only the rival and the rebellious opponent of his own father, but a rebel against the universal order itself and against God, who does not Himself respect the moral regulations He has given mankind but pursues His own creations and forces them to submit.

Many years later, in 1910, Hamsun said that *Munken Vendt* was essentially to be the first part of a trilogy presenting three attitudes toward God: revolt, resignation, and faith. He went on, however,

> Med oprøret er jeg ferdig, det er ikke engang et standpunkt; "resignationen" er jeg ikke kraftløs nok og "troen" ikke tandløs nok til at levere endda. Det kommer nok med aarene — som hos alle. (Quoted in Winsnes 283)

Vendt the monk is the last of the young rebels in Hamsun's works. Hamsun did not continue the projected trilogy. But resignation — or the attempt to resign — is one of the main themes of the following books and remains a subsidiary one to the very last.

This period of wavering, doubt, and renewed effort is also characterized by the play *Dronning Tamara* (1903), which has a romantic theme and a medieval oriental setting, and especially by the appearance of Hamsun's only collection of verse, *Det vilde Kor* (1904). Hamsun himself later spoke slightingly of the latter book and even regretted that he had ever published it. But neither his contemporaries nor posterity have agreed with him. It is in many ways a remarkable collection, and it greatly influenced the following generation of lyric poets in Norway.

The poems were written over a long period; they reflect different artistic phases and cover a wide range of themes, moods, and forms. There is free as well as rhymed verse, and the versification is diversified and expressive. Despair, amounting to a feeling of utter loneliness and isolation in the universe, contrasts with passionate hymns to spring and nature. Some of the poems that give vent to a bold defiance of all sorts of conventions are very polemical. Extremely provocative is "Himmelbrev til Byron," in which Hamsun scornfully attacks the great social movements of the time — the labor movement, feminism, and the peace movement. This poem is, no doubt, an outspoken confession to antidemocratic, perhaps even prefascist ideas and attitudes, and much later it came to be a main issue in the discussion of Hamsun's support of Nazism. It is a bombastic poem and very different from his monumental poem of homage to Bjørnstjerne Bjørnson, the only Norwegian writer of the old generation whom he really admired.

Underlying most of the poems is a profession of life and vitality, muted or jubilant, defiant or wistful. But there is also a strain of pantheistic mysticism in some of the poems, especially in the marvellous, low-keyed little "Skjærgaardsø," which voices an intimate experience of nature, merging into a complete union, a mysterious recollection of former existence, and a surrender to Nirvana.

After this period of restless shifting between different genres, Hamsun published his first novel in six years, *Sværmere*, in 1904. The setting and the plot of the novel in a peculiar way remind us of *Pan*. The setting is again a small trading centre in Northern Norway; the ruler of the place is Edvarda's uncle; and the main character, telegraph operator Rolandsen, is in love with her cousin, but carrying on flirtations with other women. The parallels bring out the contrast between the two works in the mood and tone of narration, turning *Sværmere* into a parody of *Pan* and Rolandsen into a caricature of Glahn. Like him Rolandsen is a dreamer and a stranger who brings variation into "det stille Liv og de smaa Skjæbner" of the place (*SR* 3: 261). But he is a dreamer only in a very limited sense of the word; he is a good-natured giant, not a romantic worshipper of nature. He has a bit of Nagel's desire and capacity to make himself remarkable, but his means are queer turns of speech, not outrageous assertions. Nor are the men and women of the place enigmatic or unique in any way, but just funny types. It is a third-person novel, and the narrator looks at all the characters, the romantic dreamer as well as anybody else, with an impartial eye and a marked preference for the odd aspects of life. And if the style is as elaborate as in *Pan*, it is so in quite another way — talkative, droll, wily, excelling in stylistic extravagance and surprising turns of speech. *Sværmere* is Hamsun's first great experiment in what most readers connect with the notion "the Hamsun style." That style is, of course, indescribable in the end, and it is quite impossible to translate properly into any other language. There may be a direct stylistic influence from Mark Twain. But more important is a recognizable but more or less indefinable strain of Northern dialect mixed up with Hamsun's own felicitous phrases and inimitable whims. Hamsun never tries to reproduce the dialect faithfully, but he makes use of it by slightly exaggerating its peculiar vocabulary and ways of speaking — for instance, the frequent use and misuse of Biblical and priestly phrases, mixing them up with words and expressions from commercial correspondence and official documents, popular romances, advertisements, newspapers, etc. It is a charming mixture that remains forever fresh and keeps its power to shock and amuse again and again.

In short, with *Sværmere* Hamsun makes a new start. He bids farewell to the books of his youth, estranging himself from them by placing their dominant motives and constellations into a humorous perspective. *Sværmere* is his only completely cheerful novel. And, in it, he tries a way of writing that many years later would become his speciality. It is also a light prelude to the great social novels, which were to be the most important achievements of his later years.

That Hamsun was consciously striving to get away from the attitudes and works of his youth is obvious from the so-called "wanderer novels," *Under Høststjernen* (1906) and *En Vandrer spiller med Sordin* (1909). In the early nineties he had asked for a more complicated literature that would present the divided feelings and the unconscious life of the soul, the poetry of the nerves. In his own books he had tried to realize such a program. But as early as 1897 he talked of "at drive Livet tilbage til den Enkelhed det har udviklet sig bort fra" ("Mod Overvurdering"). And the two wanderer novels testify to his own efforts to approach that simplicity again and rid himself of the nervous hypersensitivity that he had carried to extremes and exploited in writing *Sult* (1889, 1890), *Mysterier* (1892), and *Pan*. At the same time, his efforts were the outcome of another encounter with the problem of age and his struggle to come to terms with it through accepting the role of a mere spectator at the game of life, the lot of the elderly.

Both these novels are first-person novels. What is more, the main character calls himself Knut Pedersen, Hamsun's name before he became an author, and tries to return to the sort of life he had lived in earlier, happy days.

*Under Høststjernen* is the tale of a wanderer on "den gjengrodde Sti ind gjennem Skogen" (*SR* 3: 307), away from the restless life of the town and the excitement of the nerves, or neurasthenia, as he now calls it. He tries to return to the healthy habits and the simple joys he remembers from his days as a road-builder. He also meets one of his old companions, and together they get short-time jobs on various farms. But it remains impossible for him to regain the simple life he is striving for; his neurasthenia will not let its hold on him go. Nor does he succeed in regaining the superstitions of his childhood; he should like so much to shudder for fear of ghosts again, but it is impossible for him. What is worse, he fails in his efforts as a lover as well. He still succeeds with young women who do not matter very much to him. But he himself falls deeply in love with Mrs. Lovise Falkenberg, who puts an end to all his hopes for rest and peace, but does not at all seem to share his feelings. And this is the outcome of it all, "Men ai hvor en halvgammel Mand gjør sig til Nar naar han er forelsket" (*SR* 3: 327). The typical Hamsun hero is nearly always hopelessly in love. He is so as a young man, but as he grows older, matters get still worse. Feeling that time is short, he cannot afford to be proud any longer, and he becomes more and more awkward. The years have deprived him of the excessive generosity that can lead an unhappy lover to his death — as with Nagel and Glahn. Returning to the town, at last, he drowns his disappointments and defeat in a more worldly-wise manner — in whisky. His efforts were doomed from the start; there is no way back: "Mine Herrer Neurastenikere, vi er daarlige Mennesker og til nogen Slags Dyr duger vi heller ikke" (*SR* 3: 412).

In the next volume, *En Vandrer spiller med Sordin*, Knut Pedersen tries still again, six years later, to find his way back to lost simplicity. He feels even more burdened by his age, but he can still be "besat av Stjærner og Uregjerlighet indvendig" (*SR* 5: 9). He can still fall in love as well, and he meets Mrs. Falkenberg again. But now it is irrevocably too late. Her marriage is breaking down, but he can merely look on idly, at the sad procedure, her increasing desperation, and final suicide; he is filled with sympathy and jealousy, but he is paralyzed and cannot in any way interfere.

This experience affects Knut strongly and teaches him to yield to the facts of life, to accept them with resignation. In the end he feels grateful and conciliatory:

> Det duftet av Jasminer i en Syrinskog og det bævet en Glæde gjennem en jeg vet, ikke for Jasminernes Skyld, men for alt, et Vindu med Lys i, en Erindring, hele Livet. Men da han blev kaldt bort fra Syrinskogen hadde han jo allerede faat Betalingen paa Forhaand for denne Ubehagelighet. (*SR* 5: 159)

He — Knut Pedersen or Knut Hamsun — has not only suffered a loss, but, as a poet, has gained something as well. His understanding of others has become wider and more tolerant, and Hamsun himself has gained a greater freedom in relation to his theme. In the wanderer novels we have seen how Knut is partly driven and partly draws himself away from the centre of events. Starting as the main character, he ends as the sympathetic observer. His own feelings are still engaged and colour his narration, but he has become more detached from himself and his own passions. He may even make fun of his own clumsiness, whereas he looks on the faults of others mildly. And that indulgent attitude is not here — as in *Sværmere* — the result of a farcical perspective, but the outcome of an extended interest in other human beings.

*Under Høststjernen* and *En Vandrer...* have an important place in Hamsun's total *oeuvre*, since they represent and contain the transition from the romantic, subjective, and more or less lyrical novels of his youth and early manhood to the more realistic, objective, and epic works of his later years. About the age of fifty, which he had feared so much, he finds that a creative regeneration takes place.

Between the two Knut Pedersen books, Hamsun published two other novels, *Benoni* and *Rosa* (both 1908), which may be read and regarded as a single two-volume novel. With them Hamsun has definitively entered the world he had visited in *Sværmere*, the world that from then on was to be his particular domain, the North Norwegian trade centre, or tiny coastal town, in the transition from barter economy to early modern capitalism. The action takes place about 1870. We meet some of the characters from *Pan* once more, Edvarda as well as her father. But they are hardly to be recognized, not only because they have changed in the course of the years, but also because they are seen through different eyes and placed in different surroundings. *Pan* mostly took place in the lonely woods; *Benoni* and *Rosa* at Sirilund and in the countryside nearby. The number of characters is much greater and more diversified, and they are presented with a mixture of the farcical humour of *Sværmere* and a certain sympathy. The main character, Benoni, benefits from the sympathy. He is a fisherman and a postman who turns into a deliberate status-seeker, and he often makes a fool of himself in his efforts to climb the steps of the local hierarchy and gain Rosa, the minister's daughter. The narrator views him from a double perspective, partly indulging him, partly exposing him to laughter. A similar ambiguity marks the portrait of Mr. Mack, still the mighty merchant of the place. He has become a ruthless man of business and a cynical profligate, abusing the young girls and women in his service. But he is still the aristocratic master of Sirilund, and he is seen and respected by the narrator as the rightful potentate of the place. There is hardly any criticism of capitalism in these novels, nor melancholy reflections on its destructive influence on the old order of things. But there are some hints of a serious reckoning with the ambitious aspirations of Hamsun's own early years, aspirations that drew him and many others away from earth-bound simplicity to superficial refinement and empty restlessness. Benoni may be seen as an ironic portrait of the artist as a young upstart clerk. Old age is here a secondary motive, but it is carried to macabre extremes in the portraits of two stinking old cripples. On the other hand, the author points at the child, the regeneration of the family, and life itself as immanent and paramount values. The proud and fickle Edvarda has been desperately hunting for a substitute for Glahn, whom she has never been able to forget. She is on the brink of total degradation, but in the end she is saved by realizing her joyful duty as a mother. On the whole, *Benoni* and *Rosa* show a definite shift in the author's field of interest and system of values.

Great changes occurred in Hamsun's own life about the same time. In 1909, he married again. It was to an actress, and the following year he wrote his last play, *Livet ivold*, a tragicomedy of an elderly music-hall star and a harsh satire on the profession of actors and theatrical life as a whole. The play was obviously meant as a severe warning to his wife never again to return to the demoralizing sphere of the theatre.

"Jeg er fra Jorden og Skogen med alle mine Røtter," Hamsun wrote the same year, in a pamphlet attacking modern tourism:

> I Byene bare lever jeg et kunstig Liv med Kafeer og Aandrigheter og alskens Hjærnetull. Men jeg er fra Jorden. Og man skulde ikke gaa ut fra at jeg bare "dikter" naar jeg skriver om den. ("Et Ord til os")

So far, Hamsun had not written very much about the soil. As a young man he had spoken in a condescending manner about peasants and agriculture; in *Mysterier* there is a very sarcastic passage about them; and, as late as 1908, Hamsun refuted the idea of a peasant culture in a rather insulting article. But only three years later he took the consequences of what seems, in retrospect, to have been a long development. He had left the town for good, returned to the district of his childhood, and bought a farm near Hamsund. The vagabond settled down as a farmer and the father of a family. And, at the same time, he stood forth as a polemical moralist and a chastiser of his nation, in fact as well as in fiction. To a certain extent, he took over the role that Bjørnson had left vacant at his death in 1910, as a spokesman of "riksmål," morality, and family life. But Hamsun's general view of life and society was very far from Bjørnson's democratic and optimistic humanitarianism.

Such polemical and critical attitudes are obtrusive in Hamsun's next book, *Den siste Glæde* (1912). It is a first-person novel, related by Knut Pedersen, and it is a delayed sequel to the wanderer novels. But the wanderer has become a stern moralist. He addresses himself to what on the last page he calls "den nye Aand i Norge"; the book has been written "under en Pest for en Pests Skyld," he says (*SR* 5: 346). "The new spirit" is symbolized in the setting of the novel — a farm that, with a total neglect of the soil, has been turned into a hotel for tourists. "The plague" is the general superficiality of the times, its restless excitement and lack of contact with the elementary facts and values of life. The author turns his eloquent, but venomous, sarcasms in many directions. Among his favorite targets are men of business and academics, career women, actors, journalists, sportsmen, and — as a group apart — British tourists.

Beneath the aggressive satire there is, however, "en Roman i Romanen" (*SR* 5: 345). In these parts of the book Knut Pedersen dwells on his lonely walks in the wood and his joy at the tiny wonders of nature. He is still bothered by the thought of approaching old age and dissolution, but his criticism of the times is tempered by his human inconsistencies. He mocks women with careers, but he feels very much attracted by one of them, a Miss Thorsen, "Typen Thorsen" as he slightingly calls her (*SR* 5: 247). There is, after all, a sound core in her, and she is drawn, not towards him himself, but towards a young peasant, who turns out to be her salvation — he and the soil and the children they will have. Once more, Knut Pedersen has to resign himself. "Den siste Glæde" he has to find somewhere else — in the lonely recesses of nature, in "Stemning og Vers og Ingenting," in watching children growing up (*SR* 5: 251). "Børn? Det rene Vidunder! Og naar Alderen kommer den eneste Glæde, den siste Glæde" (*SR* 5: 331).

*Den siste Glæde* is the last of Hamsun's first-person novels. In his early third-person novels there was also a strong sense of affinity between the narrator and the main figure. But in the novels succeeding *Den siste Glæde* Hamsun assumes the position of the detached, olympic, and omniscient narrator, observing and commenting on the bizarre world of his own creation, "Maurtuen" with its characters as "Typer og figurer" (*SR* 9: 9) — quite the opposite of what he intended in his early books. It should be noted, however, that the narrator's voice cannot be completely identified with Hamsun's own. The voice is, after all, part of the fiction, and it is not easy to define it. Sometimes it has a ring of what might be supposed to be general opinion or gossip, and sometimes it seems to belong to an anonymous and very critical member of society. At all events, the lyric intimacy of his former books is replaced by epic narrative, their delicate psychology by a lively depiction of life in general, of men and women, manners and events. In some of the books we still meet a philosophical wanderer, but he is no longer a central character, just a solitary observer of what is going on. He usually seems, more or less, to be the author's mouthpiece, advocating ideas closely related to those put forward by the critical voice of the narrator. The ideas and attitudes that are emphasized in these ways are clear and consistent — *for* the way of life and the values of the past, agriculture, hard work, and a patriarchal order of society and *against* all manifestations of "the new spirit," all kinds of subversive activities and ideas, industrialists, and — in particular — those representatives of parasitic occupations: officials, doctors, clergymen, lawyers, and shopkeepers.

But beneath the level of obvious ideas and attitudes there are — as in *Den siste Glæde* — undertones and contradictions. There is something paradoxical about Hamsun's own position. The art of writing itself is one of the parasitic occupations that are at odds with his own principles. More than once he speaks of laying down his pen. He should be a peasant and nothing else! But he just could not. On the contrary, at short intervals he had to leave his farm, go to a town nearby, and seek refuge in a hotel, just in order to write. His farming, on the other hand, was no success, and after a couple of years he had to give it up. In the poet's mind the vagabond is still very much alive. The vagabond's human understanding and sympathies may go far beyond the limits of the poet's reactionary ideas. And the vagabond's nervous sensibility, his fantastic whims, his artistic play with words, his irony and self-irony still modify the moralist's teaching. There are more self-contradictions and ambiguities in Hamsun's later novels than Hamsun the preacher would like to admit. And those inconsistencies constitute one of the sources of their artistic vitality and indefinable charm.

## Works Cited

Hamsun, Knut. "Et Ord til os." *Verdens Gang* 3 July, 1910: 1.

———. "Mod Overvurdering af Digterne og Digtningen." *Morgenbladet* 31 Feb., 1897: 2.

———. [SR] *Samlede romaner.* Vols. 3, 5, and 9. Oslo: Gyldendal, 1933. 14 vols. 1932-33.

———. [SV] *Samlede verker.* 2nd ed. See *Aftenrøde.* In vol. 6. Christiania [Oslo]/Copenhagen: Gyldendal, 1918. 12 vols. 1918-20.

Hamsun, Tore. *Knut Hamsun som han var. Et utvalg av hans brev.* Oslo: Gyldendal, 1956.

Winsnes, A. H. *Norges litteratur. Fra 1880-årene til første verdenskrig.* Rev. 2nd ed. Oslo: H. Aschehoug, 1961. Vol. 5 of *Norsk litteraturhistorie.* Ed. Francis Bull et al. 6 vols. 1957-63.

Sanddruhed er hverken Tosidighed eller Objektivitet,
Sanddruhed er netop den uegennyttige Subjektivitet.

Knut Hamsun, Et Forord,
*Fra det moderne Amerikas Aandsliv*, 1889

"It is perfectly monstrous," [Lord Henry] said, . . . "the way people go about nowadays saying things against one behind one's back that are absolutely and entirely true. . . . Women love us [however] for our defects. If we have enough of them they will forgive us everything. . . . "

"If [said Lady Narborough] we women did not . . . where would you all be? . . . . Nowadays all the married men live like bachelors, and all the bachelors like married men."

"*Fin de siècle*," murmured Lord Henry.

"*Fin du globe*," answered his hostess.

"I wish it were *fin du globe*," said Dorian, with a sigh. "Life is a great disappointment."

"Ah, my dear," cried Lady Narborough, putting on her gloves, "don't tell me that you have exhausted life."

Oscar Wilde,
*The Picture of Dorian Gray*, 1891

# Eros and Subjectivity: Knut Hamsun's *Pan* and Ragnhild Jølsen's *Rikka Gan*.

## Pål Bjørby

### I

> Most of the available theories of reading, writing, sexuality, or any other cultural production are built upon male narratives of gender... narratives which persistently tend to reproduce themselves in feminist theories.
>
> Teresa de Lauretis,
> *Technologies of Gender*, 1987

THE WORK OF TERESA DE LAURETIS and other feminists — Elaine Showalter, Nancy Miller, Luce Irigaray, Julia Kristeva, and especially Judith Butler, Eve Kosofsky Sedgwick, and Diana Fuss — presents a convincing case that, taken together, Western cultural discourses form a powerful voice, one that can be defined as masculinist. Such a claim is echoed in the epigraph opening this discussion of Hamsun's *Pan* (1894) and Ragnhild Jølsen's *Rikka Gan* (1904) and is also echoed in the literary scholarship devoted to these writers.

Particularly noteworthy is the latter part of the Lauretis quote, pointing to the internalization of the phallocentric or masculinist voice in writings by women. In exploring the nature of the masculinist voice in *Rikka Gan*, however, I will show how Jølsen seeks to disrupt that very voice. Feminist theoretical writings of the last two decades have argued that the only terms under which women can speak have been preordained by men: women can speak in a masculine voice, can seek to construct a new voice (the project of several women modernists), or can keep silent.

Feminist theory and criticism have shown that the figure at the center of modernity is Woman and therefore that the question to be posed is the value accorded Woman in modernity? This question has cast its shadow across my reading of these two central works of *fin-de-siècle* Norwegian literature.

One important response to the feminist view of discourse as being masculinist through and through is offered by Michel Foucault, who suggests that men's colonial grip on the relationship between language and power is not total or irreversible. The claim by Lauretis that feminist theory reproduces masculinist narratives takes an unexpected turn in Hamsun's *Pan*, in which, I believe, "masculinity" is partially contested from within, not simply by crossing boundaries into "femininity," but by rendering "masculinity" both ambivalent and fragmented, powerless to prevent what André Gide described to Paul Valéry in 1891: "L'effort pour la détruir est la mesure de cette chose. Toute chose ne se constitue que de son vide . . ." (Gide 141). The hollowing out of identity in *Pan*, the process that constitutes its claim to modernity, must be "read" again, this time by asking such questions as 1) in what way subjectivity is marked by "masculinity," 2) what the value of Woman is in *Pan*'s claim to modernity, and 3) whether *Pan* upholds its modernity in light of such questions?

The strong hints of a "feminization" process in *Pan*'s hero, Glahn, find a perverse reversal in the "masculinization" of desire in Jølsen's protagonist, Rikka. As a matter of fact, the undoing of the masculine self in *Pan* may have more to do with the presence of a crisis in the homosocial bonds than with any impasse in female/male erotic relations. This essay will propose reading *Rikka Gan* as a challenge to the masculinist nature of modernity, specifically as it manifests itself in *Pan*.

The central discourses of the latter part of the nineteenth century were controlled by men, giving them the authority to exert censorship and to set the agenda. In literary matters, men were quick to reassert what was important should a woman writer be so bold as to suggest that she be taken seriously.

To many late nineteenth- and early twentieth-century men, women seemed to be agents of an alien world that evoked anger, anguish, while to women in those years men appeared as aggrieved defenders of an indefensible order (Gilbert and Gubar 4).

Anxious to be taken seriously by the Norwegian literary establishment, Hamsun paid scant attention to feminism or the voices of contemporary women writers. In his quest for status as a writer to be reckoned with, Hamsun eagerly and strategically made himself the spokesman of the new by attacking tradition. This act and the simultaneous publication of *Sult* (1890) are viewed as indisputable breaks with the controlling Father-voice of Scandinavian realist/naturalist literature and as harbingers of modernity.

Much has been written about the *fin de siècle* as a period marked by deep crisis of the self. Discussions centered on notions of subjectivity, sexuality, femininity, and masculinity; desire figured prominently in an enormous number of publications, scientific and literary, that were staking out new territory, disputing with one another in much the same way as such publications had in the 1840s, 1850s, and in the 1880s, and as they would in the 1920s and 1930s, and again almost a century later in the 1970s and 1980s. "Love" and sexuality, each with its supposed correspondence to the appropriate gender, betokened the intensity of a crisis felt not only between the sexes but likewise within each sex. Both *Pan* and *Rikka Gan* were in large part responses to such a crisis. The pervasive authority of nineteenth-century discursive practice, be it in the natural sciences, in medicine, sexology, or psychiatry, could not be avoided by literature. Epistemological ideology became equated with truth. As George Levine has shown (3-32), it is impossible to separate the Darwinian (and Social Darwinian) debate from broader cultural, political, ideological, economic, and literary issues.

The important concept of fatigue, central to countless scientific discussions during the latter part of the nineteenth century (and analyzed by Anson Rabinbach in his book *The Human Motor: Energy, Fatigue and the Origin of Modernity*, 1990) encapsulated the paradoxes of modernity. Material progress was undermined by demands on the body and spirit; scientific and technological advances produced a dark underside, the physical and psychological exhaustion of modern life, resulting in idleness, displacement, antisocial behavior, and such antimodern sentiments as selfishness, unproductiveness, and general evasive behavior. Fatigue became identified with modernity itself, and it had such subjective manifestations as melancholy, listlessness, and ennui. It was seen as a defense against the demands made by the modern world. In a publication titled *L'Ennui* (1903), Emile Tardieu "declared that modernist sensibility and subjectivity characteristic of his generation were actually rooted in physiological, psychological infirmities of writers" (see Rabinbach 42). According to Tardieu, fatigue caused writers' excessive subjectivity — fatigue, not aesthetics, explained their profound disorder of ideas, mental torpor, irritability, and general asthenia. A subjective writer was deeply antipositivistic.

These issues are part of the framing of the narratives in *Pan* and *Rikka Gan*, two novels about the self, about love, the erotic — matters irreducibly "complicated by the historical, political, and figurative body of the woman writer" (Miller 107) and our reading of that body. We must acknowledge difference and agency in the woman writer's response not only to historic forms, but particularly to Woman in fiction. Jølsen, I shall show, challenges Hamsun's notion of the feminine in her story of thwarted erotic desire, confronting the ideological inscription and literary effects of a gender/sex system that Hamsun appears to reaffirm. There is in both these books an exchange of women, in *Pan* between men and in *Rikka Gan* between Fernanda (Rikka's sister-in-law) and Aga (the landowner of Gan), in the sacrifice of Rikka sexually to keep the family at its ancestral home.

A central aspect of the modern at the end of the nineteenth century was a concern with the individual, the subject, the self. What were its true and natural properties, and what was its destiny? The main figures in *Pan* and *Rikka Gan* are embroiled in this metaphysics of identity conflict. Both protagonists explore desire and sexuality as crucial aspects of the self's being in the world, and they are both "modern" as literary representations of a self that is being cut loose from its traditional moorings. But the result is tellingly different and has much to do with literary representation of gender and the gender of the author. Nevertheless, Norwegian literary scholarship, in its concern over Jølsen as a woman writing and a woman writing about Woman, has not sufficiently appreciated her attempt to destabilize the metaphysics of sexuality; rather, it has sought to read both writer and texts as pathological case histories.[1]

By looking at the description of men's relationship to women in *Pan*, as well as the novel's problematization of self and desire, and then contrasting it with a similar reading of *Rikka Gan*, one finds that a differing view emerges from Hamsun's literary subjectivity than from Jølsen's. The point is not to argue against Hamsun's greatness, but to recognize how his inquiry into sexuality, desire, self, and power was deeply embedded in the masculinist discursive voice critiqued by contemporaneous feminism. *Rikka Gan*, on the other hand, challenges male narratives of gender; it rebels, resists, seeks a way out of male discourse. And in doing so, it reveals how deeply internalized is the belief in the central role of a specific, but encompassing, female sexuality when the time comes to talk about the self of the novel's main female figure. Following up on the insights of Lauretis, we may find that the voice Jølsen creates through her distinctive and unusual mixing of many modes of expression not only challenges masculinist hegemony but paradoxically also remains essentialist and repressed within a patriarchal order of literature and society.

## II

> Do you wish to love? Use Love's Litany, and the words will create the yearning from which the world fancies that they spring.
>
> Oscar Wilde,
> *The Critic as Artist*, 1891

Hamsun in *Pan* speaks to men knowingly, telling a story that implies a masculine reader, in the same way as do most of his contemporaries in literature and art. I never cease to be struck by the deafening silence that descends upon scholarship every time readers of Hamsun's *Pan* arrive at the point of choosing *not* to interpret the insistence in the novel on depicting muted, ridiculed, sacrificed female figures. Granted, these figures are little more than familiar representations of stock traits of the "feminine" operating at the center of this narrative's deliberation on self, desire, sexuality, masculinity, and the relationships between Glahn, Mack, the Doctor, the Russian suitor, and — finally — the Hunter. But to reiterate, what is the value of Woman in Hamsun's modernity, in Glahn's forlorn self's resigned quest for self-realization? *Pan* is often praised for its timelessness and universality, without any reference either to the gender of its creator, other than to underline his "mandighet," or to the crucial role of gender and sexuality in the novel's drive toward that very timelessness and universality. What of the representation of marginal femininity in the female figures? What of the work's notion of femininity as it attends to a displaced and an unstable masculine subject?

How different for Jølsen. Upon the publication of *Rikka Gan*, readers and critics alike were startled by the gender of its author and protested against her transgression of gender/sex. The book was seen as too masculine, even "lodden," to have been penned by a woman. Critics were concerned with sins it committed against femininity, both in the story of Rikka Gan and in the life of the author herself. Why, then, in the case of *Pan*, was there an analytical avoidance, a refusal to look too deeply into male subjectivity, on the part of both Hamsun and his readers? By looking into the matter of female subjectivity, gender, and sexuality, although expressed within masculinist discourse, Jølsen creates a narrative of female desire/sexuality that cannot but affect the critical assessment of Hamsun's *Pan*. The latter ushers in, along with *Sult*, Scandinavian modernity, with its excessive subjectivity, its depiction of a slowly disintegrating protagonist, and its emphasis on the central role of sexuality, desire, and the erotic in writing. Could not perhaps *Pan*'s modernity be seen as a way of dealing with masculine desire and sexuality, their means of definition, their signs, the bodies of women? Nature and Woman are, after all, the territories across which Hamsun inscribes his hero's tortuous experience of increasing alienation from self and society.

Appropriate to modernity, Hamsun describes exhaustion, anxiety, and nervousness in a destabilized bourgeois male self, who is uncertain about how to live in the modern world and whose effort to salvage the self requires a return to nature (which here stands in for Origin, Truth, the Real, and the Erotic, freed of civilization's norms and conventions). The restoring of the self includes, not surprisingly, a return to uncluttered desire, sex, and Woman. There is the prerequisite "love" affair, showcasing not only Hamsun's talent but, equally, the notion of nonrealist "love" described in the then increasingly fashionable rhetoric of the unstable presence of the unconscious. To all appearances the attempt succeeds: the hero nestles into a naturalized existence posed between civilization/world and the wilderness. He is safe as long as he remains there, and because of his "dyreblikk" he need not engage the human settlement down by the boat landing; rather, women come as if drawn to his hut at the edge of the forest by the overwhelming scent of his sexual readiness. Their common self, not unexpectedly, is defined as basically a state of preconsciousness and all-sexuality.

It does not take long before the story shifts its emphasis from love, sex, and bliss to trouble in paradise. Glahn's love object, Edvarda, dutifully lives up to Eve's reputation; she leads her unassuming, bumbling lover ever closer to chaos, not only within himself but also in terms of both his place in Nature and his relationship to Civilization. The various aspects of Hamsun's hero, Glahn — who is intelligent, sensitive, but also frail, split, helpless — are deeply felt by the reader. It is also Glahn's excessive subjectivity, his passivity and apparent softness, his "feminization," that breaks with the traditional rendering of "masculinity," a process under-lined not only by his inability to take charge in love but also, and as importantly, by his failure to find his place among men. The women in the novel, however, can easily be summed up as familiar, essentialist depictions of Woman, unequal to the task of properly tending to Glahn's acutely sensitive "soul." The Henriettes, Evas, and misguided Edvardas of the world are no match for the readers' interest in the tormented inner life of modern man. They can even be read as Jungian archetypal representatives, from the preconscious Henriette; to the Madonna-Mother, self-sacrificing Eva; to the "unnatural" mix of femininity and masculinity in the too-civilized child-woman Edvarda. They can also be read as semiotic beings who betray Hamsun's desire to be modern and place him squarely in the convention of nineteenth-century misogynist representation.

In Eve Kosofsky Sedgwick's pathbreaking studies of literature, culture, and politics, she argues that the more the female figure of a narrative appears as man's other, the more one should shift one's attention to the relationships between the men (see *Between Men and Epistemology*). Most readers of *Pan* have been far more concerned with the love story between Edvarda and Glahn than with Glahn's tangled relations with the other men. The roles of "love" and Woman in Glahn's quest for authenticity are strikingly tied to, and dependent on, his ties to men. The force of the bonds, for better or for worse, between Mack, the Doctor, the Smith, Glahn, the Russian Count, and — in the end — between Glahn and the nameless male in the epilogue, is keenly felt and gives ample evidence of the marginality of the women in the narrative.

The bonds between the men profoundly affect the lives of the women, whose primary value, aside from their availability as sex objects to be hunted down, is as exchange objects between the men, a status that directly leads to the death of Eva. It is Glahn's inability to function homosocially that is ultimately as much part of his demise as is the doomed "love story." The epilogue, which was written before the rest of *Pan*, can also be read in this light. Yet another nameless woman becomes the focus of the hero's sexual desire; she appears to lead a somnambulistic existence, like some animal that responds to Glahn's "dyreblikk." All sexuality, she is indiscriminately attracted to another nameless male, who engages Glahn in a challenge; may the best man win. . . . Any notion that the author is here presenting the universal complimentarity between man and woman takes an odd turn in so far as the nameless man becomes a greater focus of Glahn's attention than the woman. The desire for Woman comes dangerously close to becoming Glahn's irresistible erotic jealousy of the other man. The very frail state of Glahn's besieged heterosexual identity, so troubled throughout the narrative, almost collapses into the unspeakable in this final encounter with naked desire, an identity only to be saved by a bullet from the other man's rifle.

Glahn's Iselin fantasy, yet another inscription of Woman as eternal and pure sexuality, prepares readers for this theme of transgression. The dream sequence is, like the locked eyes of hunter and Glahn in the epilogue, another such dangerous moment of dissolving boundaries, of possible homosocial-turned-homoerotic jealousy and voyeurism in *Pan*.

The gender-fixed nature of Hamsun's exploration of the self on the threshold of the modern world contravenes the brilliant descriptions of the hero's failure — descriptions generally taken to be so "true." Glahn cannot realize himself anew and survives neither the unbridgeable gap between Nature and World nor the split between consciousness and unconsciousness. In the end he loses out to the stronger man, just as earlier he lost out to Mack and the Doctor. Glahn, the antihero, becomes the forefather of the ineffectual, weak, straying, hypersensitive, vain, nervous, passive male that inhabits Western literature at the end of the nineteenth century.

In spite of *Pan*'s claim to fame as a herald of modernity, a claim that surely rests on its aesthetic experimentation, the novel's deliberations on the state of the self — a self that does not survive transformed — represents in the end but a minor rebellion. The narrative does not seriously transgress commonly held conceptual modes, rather it reaffirms male primacy within a mode of writing that *is* the "authenticity" to which the reader responds when acknowledging the importance of the novel. The unacknowledged, but implied, ideology of a literary experiment firmly embedded in discourses about sex, gender, sexuality, and desire figures prominently in *Pan*, as it does as the subtext of our own reading, the criticism, and the scholarly writing about *Pan*. There is the sense of the compulsory to such writing, and I believe that Foucault's suggestions for how, in the nineteenth century, sex was "put into discourse" and subsequently became "knowledge," "power," and "truth" can be of some import to our reading of *Pan*.

What does *Pan* offer its female readers? Since gender and sex, femininity and masculinity are far from interchangeable in the novel's problematization of the modern self, where and how do female readers place themselves in relation to the central theme of desire and Woman? The novel's blend of metaphysics, moral values, heightened self-consciousness, modes of ecstatic psychic and sensual experience — all operate within an economy of ahistorical, carefully retained, preordained positionings as to, and concepts of, who "he" and "she" can be in or out of fiction. Hamsun chooses not to question the cultural definition of Nature, sexuality, and desire, which he quite conventionally reproduces in the belief that he can point to a "truer" home for the self. In Rousseauean fashion Hamsun hints at a presocial or "natural" identity that has, as it were, been wounded. *Pan* is perhaps less the search for eternal truths than a familiar commentary on what life, love, and self should be, and as such it is always quick to reinforce what these things are not. But is Glahn all pose, all convention? Hardly. *Pan* does show that individualism can be a disturbing and disintegrating experience.

# III

> Lad os kvinder, Herre, faa større ret for vor
> kærlighed — at den ikke stilles mod sky som
> saa bleg og tander en vare, at jordslag saa let
> stænker den til!
> La vor kærlighed paa jord, Herre, faa jor-
> dens evige segl, mulden, stærk og rig som det
> Liv, hvoraf den udspringer — saaledes at den
> ikke behøver gemmes bort i mørke. Lad den faa
> rang og gang for hvad den i sandhed er. La den
> faa bedre kaar, Herre gud!

> Ragnhild Jølsen,
> *Hollases krønike*, 1906

Ragnhild Jølsen was an innovator in Norwegian *fin-de-siècle* literature, but her work, in ways parallel to Kate Chopin's in American literature, remained largely unknown until being briefly rediscovered half a century later. Jølsen has been increasingly seen as a major literary voice and has recently become the focal point of feminist scholarship. In the decades following her early death, however, she had little influence on those who shaped Norwegian literature.

Astrid Lorenz (135) rightly identifies *Rikka Gan* as a gothic novel that has much in common with Emily Brontë's *Wuthering Heights* (1847), but she does not elaborate further. Clearly, *Rikka Gan* is gothic: the story it tells is a dark protest, full of wildness, overwhelming erotic yearning, freakish female figures, guilt, anxiety, depression, hidden spaces, and murdered and buried newborn babies — fantasies that literally disrupt realist prose in a language chiselled like a *Jugendstil* artwork. The language is romantic, transgressive, and revolutionary. The novel's antirealism gives the author freedom from narrative restrictions, from plots that cannot tell the story of Rikka Gan's quest for self-realization and sexual fulfillment.

Jølsen inscribes a story of shocking female desire. The author insists on language's ability to materialize new ways of being and create new ways of seeing in the world. We ought not to misread the novel's discursive historical moment nor discredit the "reality" of the protagonist's violent transgression of what was defined as the true female self. Nor can we pathologize the reality of the author as woman. We do best to view the self culturally and politically, along with its nature as a cultural and historical discursive construct: the "she" of gender, class, race — the "she" of sciences, of literature, and of art. (Consider for a moment the difference *Rikka Gan* brings to the reading of *fin-de-siècle* works by Arne Dybfest, Thomas Krag, Gabriel Finne, Hans E. Kinck, and Anders Stillsoff.)

Jølsen's tale of desire turns upside down the "natural" division of masculinity and femininity, and it fractures the so-called masculinity and the singularity of the metaphorical, metaphysical, essentialist conceptualization of "feminine difference" as Woman. At the same time, the text bears witness to Lauretis's reminder that the author, as woman, is herself already a subject marked by gender, sex, and cultural differences, already caught in the mechanisms of identity — the very means by which she is enabled to write. As Susan Lanser and Evelyn Beck have argued,

> The writings of women who are struggling to define themselves but have not yet given up a patriarchal frame of reference may betray a tension so strong as to produce a virtually "double-voiced" discourse. (86)

It is Rikka's fervent belief that, to express her self, she must meet a man who can sexually free her, self and body, and only a certain man will do.

Foucault has pointed to the dissolving boundaries between the sciences and literature in their urgent concern for the individual. In *Rikka Gan* as in *Pan*, we observe the authority and hegemony of the discourse-produced, gendered individual. Both novels evidence the convergence of a variety of modes in the literary representation of self. The standardized individual urged upon the world by Richard von Krafft-Ebing, Havelock Ellis, Herbert Spencer, and their ilk further resulted in a plethora of categories, statistics, and empirical data — all involved in the re-vision of what Woman was meant by nature to be. Once more, diverging stories by such women as Jølsen about desire, sexuality, and the body were buried. If Jølsen's protagonist, Rikka Gan, is inserted here, her "deviancy" becomes all the more striking. The narrative rebels against the narrowing of literary representation for woman's self-realization. In the figure of Rikka, Jølsen creates anything but the expected feminine ideal of modesty mixed with coy seductiveness and helplessness so endearing to male readers. Rikka is no innocent heroine waiting for the hero to whisk her away to an appropriate and moral life as wife and mother. Instead, one encounters a physically and mentally strong woman with "blasse øyne," "brede hofter," and "sort hår" (*Rikka Gan* 20), whose steps are long and athletic, and whose smile reveals large white teeth. Contemporary critics were disturbed by the overwhelming, raw power of Rikka's erotic desire, which leads her to lead Aga on an erotic chase, shocking the polite "society" that bears witness: "Blesten tok i jomfru Rikkas røde kjole, og et øieblikk flagret den op, vilt som et løsrevet seil" (*Rikka Gan* 19). The encounter proves fateful for Rikka: she has somehow "betrayed" her desired self. From now on life is worthless, cursed, and without a future: "Rikka Torsen er fallen" (25). What is her crime against self? That she chose an unworthy man? That the man she expected so much from turns out to be inferior to that of her desire? In the belief that she has lost the right to realize herself as *she* should, Rikka sinks into a life of self-accusation and brooding. Her desire never abates, and in her imagination rises the fantasy figure of Vilde Vaa, her male ideal — who is slender, beautiful, sensual, desirous; part legend, part history, a dark outsider like herself. He is Rikka's Pan, the only one who can satisfy her longings, the only one who responds to her call. In conjuring him forth, she lives fully and *not* like other "normal" people.

Jølsen's *Rikka Gan* is a story about troubled domestic space and about a female power that wreaks havoc on the cherished ideal of the sanctity of home, motherhood, and natural womanliness. There is no love that is deep, tender, and life-nurturing; it is dark, criminal, wild, defiant, uncivilized, and deadly. Rikka's desire defies discursive categories and any attempt made to return it to the fold. She defies a cultural and literary logic that no longer is appropriate for the one all-powerful quest in her life. Aga's visits and the attempts to create some semblance of domestic normalcy serve only to heighten the readers' sense that something is terribly wrong with life at Gan, with its atmosphere of confinement, suffering, pent-up fury, and yearning in dark female minds, with the control of Gan by the outside modern, technological world of capitalism and men's power. The men — Rikka's brother, Jon; Aga, the owner of Gan; the groom-to-be from Herby; and the deacon — are no match for the intelligence, cunning, and forceful-ness of the two women, Rikka and Fernanda. They are two maligned furies, echoes from a distant, legendary matriarchy. And equally, they are repre-sentations of contemporary women, who, in order to "live," have had to subjugate the self to men's laws and men's desires. And the price exacted is terrible.

One must take care, however, not to reduce Rikka Gan to female pathology. Her excessive transgression, bent on erotic fulfillment, is in striking contrast to the modesty and purity of the familiar female icon, Katarina, bride-to-be from Herby, an Edenesque opposite to Rikka's Gan. Katarina's fiancé, who has a "forunderlig deilig munn" (*Rikka Gan* 32), momentarily takes the place of Vaa in Rikka's feverish imagination as "the lover," but he has not the "gnistrende øyne" (38) of Vaa that can hold Rikka. Only in Vaa does she encounter her equal in suffering, in "ondhet og heftig sinn" (38). As in Glahn's Iselin dreams, it is only in imagination that love reaches the pitch Rikka demands. Compared to *Pan's* "skogjomfruer," who cannot compete with the "brodersjæl" Glahn needs (Nærup 78-83), Rikka conjures up such a "brodersjæl" in Vilde Vaa. In life, the only person who can tame the wildness in Rikka is the equally thwarted sister-in-law, Fernanda, who "sacrifices" Rikka to Aga's desire and who murders one of Rikka's unwanted babies. Upon realizing that Aga has the upper hand, Rikka's wild nature erupts in a rage against Katarina, the female ideal, fictional as well as social, and brings about her violent death. Sinking further into despondency and darkness, Rikka is left only with the ruins of a self, whose source of development was to have been the "great" love, now denied her and for which she sees herself unworthy.

Rikka Gan is seen as mad by the people around her, and in her "madness" she attacks Aga and scratches him till he bleeds, like Vaa and like her brother, Torsen, who, when ill, develops Vaa's bleeding wound on his chest. Like the laughter of mad Bertha in Charlotte Brontë's *Jane Eyre* (1847), Rikka's is loud, accusing, taunting, and frightening. But what sort of "madness" is this? And whose? "Bedre å knuses ung og lykkelig enn tomme for tomme å visne bort fra livet —," sums up Rikka's outlook (*Rikka Gan* 79).

In remorse she acknowledges that Katarina was the one she loved, "Og henne drepte jeg" (79). When the Iron Nights, as in *Pan*, arrive in fall, darkness descends without and within. Rather than the peaceful acceptance of the "natural" as in *Pan*, Rikka, prisoner of her thwarted desire, is tortured by the truth of her life — her "madness" intensifies. She "drowns" her fantasy Vaa in the lake, and in an attempt to flee Gan, she drowns there herself, with Fernanda, sinking down into the arms of *her* "sjøorm."

## IV

> My great religion is a belief in the blood, the flesh, as being wiser than the intellect.
>
> D. H. Lawrence, letter of 1912

> Phallic consciousness . . . is the basic consciousness, and the thing we mean, in the best sense, by common sense.
>
> D. H. Lawrence, letter of 1927

Why have masculinist discourses, comprising both letters and sciences, always been concerned first and foremost with Woman? In literature, the male protagonist appears to be caught up in a feminization process. Simultaneously, *fin-de-siècle* artists produced numerous portraits of women (documented by Bram Dijkstra) as devourers of men, dangerous, threatening, even mannish. Rikka's madness and savage behavior are as much a response to the claims of truth in the fictional works preceding the novel as a response to contemporary realities outside of fiction, such as Otto Weininger's *Geschlecht und Charakter* (1903). The vision of maleness does not last, cannot be reproduced in "real" life at Gan. Rikka's desire challenges cultural and fictional representations of female desire. Her desire cannot be domesticated or simply diagnosed and treated. It was frightening for critics to accept Rikka's erotic pleasure as being for her herself alone, and that was the threat the novel posed to contemporary readers. Why do the men in this novel come up short? (Even the masculine ideal, the legend, the fantasy Vilde Vaa, fails to endure.)

Although they saw themselves as outsiders and as vanquishers of the Father, Strindberg, Munch, Garborg, and Hamsun ended up joining hands with the very bourgeoisie they vociferously claimed to detest. In their search for human nature, while armed with master narratives for what literature/society ought to be, they proved willing to step aside from their singular outsider position long enough to reinscribe male privilege and concomitant gender laws. They vigorously set about regulating and censoring what they saw as deviancy and misguided speculations by women, whether in politics or in the arts.[2]

Jølsen acknowledges what Hamsun does not, namely, that sexuality and gender are trapped within forms (social, political, historical, and literary) and that desire is rooted in notions of sexual difference having far less to do with Nature than with the civilization Hamsun flees in *Pan*. What is natural, absolute, and universal in *Pan* is under attack in *Rikka Gan*.

The attempt by critics to employ psychoanalysis in an effort to rein in the dangerous representation of an abnormal desire erases the history and the difference of such desire, as it erases the writer Jølsen in the process. They have made Ragnhild Jølsen her text, and the text her psyche. Elaine Showalter has shown that turn-of-the-century psychiatry differentiated between an English malady, associated with the economic and intellectual pressures of highly civilized men, and a female malady, associated with sexuality and the "essential nature" of women (7). Writing and a study of subjectivity cannot be seen as separate from such matters. *Rikka Gan* imagines a terra incognita and thereby threatens the borders of aesthetics and culture from within. Realism cannot contain the wildness in Rikka. The novel's scenes of "madness" are not expressed in realist prose, but in the language of legend, myth, and lore — hinting at domains beyond realism, suggesting other ways of expressing the unconscious, and revealing an authorial intensity that resulted in a mixing, a reinventing of styles and images that promised something entirely new in Norwegian literature.

Both *Pan* and *Rikka Gan* represent striking *fin-de-siècle* experiments, one aiming to stabilize the natural difference and identity of man and woman and the other enacting a possible destabilization of the metaphysics of sexuality. *Pan* can be read as, among other things, an anxiety-ridden return to Nature, away from an increasingly industrial modern world characterized by listlessness and melancholy, a world bent on destroying the cultural authority of patriarchy. Jølsen's novel can then be seen as an attack on such cultural authority. In *Pan* there is a sense of being at a loss as to what to do — instead of embryonic stirrings of a new order, there is the doomed return to Eden that ends in the death of the subject. Jølsen, along with Hamsun, believes in the centrality of sexual desire for her character in the process of attaining a self/identity. She recognizes that female sexual desire must be liberated for growth to occur. The sexual desire she unleashes in Rikka of Gan, however, has no man's as a match.

The world of *Rikka Gan* is perverse, dangerous, decadent, decaying: *fin de siècle*. Although Hamsun seeks an unequal complementarity between man and woman, between masculinity and femininity, Jølsen does not. She rightly sees Woman as the problem in literature. Men seek to reinstate their representation and authority over matters "female" and in the process fail to discuss the masculine subjectivity that needs precisely this Woman as other. Hamsun wistfully describes female sexuality as free and giving, with no reality of pregnancies or other social problems, whereas Jølsen describes secret births and infanticides as literal results of such an expression. Only in fantasies of Iselin and Vilde Vaa can both Glahn and Gan find momentary fulfillment.

## V

Je commençais à me découvrir, que je pouvais
souhaiter me quitter, sur le point de découvrir
en moi les tables de ma loi nouvelle.

André Gide, *Si Le Grain ne meurt*, 1928

The articulation of female desire in *Rikka Gan* threatens chaos and anarchy. Is the protagonist of *Rikka Gan* an "idol of perversity" (Dijkstra)? And has the novel been read by men responding to post-Darwinian sexual anxiety with re-charged misogyny? Desire figures as Rikka's all-consuming sense of identity, inner being, and purpose — and, when thwarted, ends in her sense of anguish, her violent outlashing, her demonic inner life. Hers is a powerful eroticism that clashes with the tepid bourgeois-Christian love ideal. She also sees in her sexual desire a kind of superiority to the others around her. Images of love and death are inseparable. Rikka is no "Angel in the House." There is only suppression, suffering and death, pain and murder and, finally, suicide. Freud would later see a figure such as Rikka as a violation of common sense, a bending of nature, as abnormal. If being in love epitomizes the human condition, what then of Rikka Gan's quest for self through love/desire? She finds not even a lover to be united with in death — no peace, no quiet slumber, only a violent yearning for lived passion, which is abruptly silenced. What remains is only the agony of loss: of life, of destiny, of longed-for self-fulfillment. When Glahn, through love and desire, seeks once more to connect nature and identity in his quest to free his culturally repressed true self, he seeks what cannot be; what he seeks is "always already" informed by the very culture he seeks to avoid.

The figure of Rikka Gan raises the question of the complicated processes by which sexual borders are constructed, sexual identities assigned, and sexual politics formulated, revealing how difficult it is to effect change, even in an imaginative act called fiction writing. These issues are alive in *Pan* as well. Both novels mirror discursive shifts and reactions to them, responses to paradigm tremors around them. With *Pan* the preceding realist tradition of women writers, Scandinavian as well as Continental (the Brontës, Eliot, Sand), is ignored; instead the company is sought of male writers striving to stem the tide of unnatural stirrings swamping male privilege, upon which the authority, power, and raison d'étre of the man rest.

With Rikka Gan, Jølsen not only counters the literary reign of the masculinist voice by burying the fictional heroine as icon of modesty and "normal" womanhood, she also counters discourses that seek to maintain woman as man's other. In doing so, Jølsen offers a modernity with perhaps greater consequences than Hamsun's for the conflict-ridden metaphysics of man's identity. These novels, by virtue of failing to imagine the self in any other form than desire, sexuality, and gender (that is, a compulsory heterosexual self), are limited to representing an impasse to which in these instances this ideology must come. There is an erotic logic and economy operating in these novels that must ignore the presence of an Oscar Wilde, an André Gide, and a Herman Bang — or must at least make sure that outsiders of that sort remain safely out of sight, out of mind, and out of literature.

## Notes

[1] See Bukdahl, "Den røde høst" and "Romantikk og eksistensproblematikk"; Nettum; and Nielsen. Important feminist beginnings, as in Lorenz's "Etterord" to *Rikka Gan* are often reduced to insupportable psychohistory (see Christensen).

[2] A recent study of the life and work of one such dangerous female figure substantiates this view of turn-of-the-century Scandinavian literature. Dagny Juel's threat against "family romance" and against this self-proclaimed heroism of the male outsider had serious consequences for her own self-realization as both writer and woman (see Norseng).

## Works Cited

Bukdahl, Jørgen. "Den røde høst." *Norsk national Kunst. Litterære Essays*. Copenhagen: Aschehoug, 1924. 171-221.

——. "Romantikk og eksistensproblematikk. Omkring Ragnhild Jølsen og hendes litterære baggrund." *Festskrift til Jens Kruuse, Den 6. April 1968*. Ed. Gustav Albeck et al. Århus: Universitetsforlaget, 1968. 55-86.

Christensen, Kari. *Portrett på mørk treplate*. Oslo: Aschehoug, 1989.

Dijkstra, Bram. *Idols of Perversity: Fantasies of Feminine Evil in Fin-de-Siècle Culture*. New York/Oxford: Oxford UP, 1986.

Gide, André. *André Gide — Paul Valéry — Correspondance 1890-1942*. Preface and notes by Robert Mallet. Paris: Éditions Gallimard, 1955.

——. *Si Le Grain ne meurt*. 1928. Rpt. Paris: Éditions Gallimard, 1955.

Gilbert, Sandra M., and Susan Gubar. *No Man's Land*. Vol. 1: *The War of the Words*. New Haven: Yale UP, 1988.

Hamsun, Knut. *Pan*. In vol. 1 of *Samlede verker*. Kristiania [Oslo]/Copenhagen: Gyldendal, 1918. 12 vols. 1918-20.

Jølsen, Ragnhild. *Hollases krønike*. 1906. Rpt. in vol. 2 of *Samlede Skrifter*. Kristiania [Oslo]: Aschehoug, 1923.

——. *Rikka Gan*. 1904; rev. 1933. Oslo: Aschehoug, Fontene Serien, 1981.

Lanser, Susan, and Evelyn Torton Beck. "[Why] Are There No Great Women Critics? And What Difference Does It Make?" In *The Prism of Sex: Essays in the Sociology of Knowledge*. Ed. Julia A. Sherman and E. T. Beck. Madison: U of Wisconsin P, 1979. 79-91.

Lauretis, Teresa de. *Technologies of Gender: Essays on Theory, Film, and Fiction.* Bloomington: Indiana UP, 1987.

Lawrence, D. H. Letters of 1912 and 1927. Quoted in vols. 1 and 6 of *The Letters of D. H. Lawrence.* Vol. 1: *September 1901-May 1913.* Ed. James Boulton. Cambridge: Cambridge UP, 1979. Vol. 6: *March 1927-November 1928.* Ed. James Boulton and Margaret H. Boulton, with Gerald Lacy. Cambridge: Cambridge UP, 1991.

Levine, George, ed. *One Culture: Essays in Science and Literature.* Madison: U of Wisconsin P, 1987.

Lorenz, Astrid. "Etterord." *Rikka Gan.* By Ragnhild Jølsen. Oslo: Aschehoug, 1981. 128-50.

Miller, Nancy. *Subject to Change.* New York: Columbia UP, 1988.

Nærup, Carl. *Skildringer og Stemninger.* 1897. Excerpts rpt. in *Norsk litteraturkritikk 1890-1914.* Ed. Arne Hannevik. Oslo: Gyldendal, 1973. 73-83.

Nettum, Rolf [Nyboe]. "Romantikk og realisme i Ragnhild Jølsens forfatterskap." *Edda* 72 (1972): 157-67.

Nielsen, Louise Bohr. "Drømmen, virkeligheten og døden." *Vinduet* 3 (1949): 251-62.

Norseng, Mary Kay. *Dagny: Dagny Juel Przybyszewska, the Woman and the Myth.* Seattle: U of Washington P, 1991.

Rabinbach, Anson. *The Human Motor: Energy, Fatigue and the Origins of Modernity.* New York: Basic Books, 1990.

Sedgwick, Eve Kosofsky. *Between Men: Homosocial Desire in the English Novel.* New York: Columbia UP, 1986.

———. *Epistemology of the Closet.* Berkeley: U of California P, 1990.

Showalter, Elaine. *The Female Malady: Women, Madness, and English Culture, 1830-1980.* New York: Pantheon, 1985.

Wilde, Oscar. "The Critic as Artist." In *The Works of Oscar Wilde.* Ed. and introd. G. F. Maine. New York: E. P. Dutton, 1954.

Figs. III.1-2

Edvard Munch, *Mot Skogen*, 1897 and 1915
Woodcut. © Munch-museet, 1992
Oslo Kommunes Kunstsamlinger
MM G 575 and 644

Fig. III.3

Edvard Munch, *Selvportrett med Sigarett*, 1895
Oil on canvas, 110.5 x 85.5 cm.
Nasjonalgalleriet, Oslo
(Photo, Jacques Lathion)

Fig. III.4

August Strindberg, Self-Portrait, 1886
Photograph from Gersau
Strindbergmuseet, Stockholm

# The Photograph as Esthetic Norm
## in *Fin-de-Siècle* Scandinavia

### John L. Greenway

DEVELOPING PHOTOGRAPHS on paper replaced plates after Daguerre's death in 1851 and relegated the sensation of 1839 to mere popularity. By mid-century, the photographer had become an accepted part of the popular cultural landscape, if we can judge by the technical knowledge assumed of the audience in the 1865 comedy *Le Photographe* (Lesák 133). Eventually, some photographers saw their work as art, such as Peter Henry Emerson and his *Gathering Water Lilies* of 1888 (Newhall 96). From the beginning, however, most artists, even such realists as Courbet and Flaubert, distinguished between depicting objects with the "pencil of nature," as Henry Fox Talbot described the process in 1843, and art based upon objectivity (Sobleszek 149). But in nineteenth-century science, the photograph changed from a depicting medium to a revelatory medium, and I will attempt to sketch the reaction to this change in the artistic imagination of *fin-de-siècle* Scandinavia, in particular in that of Edvard Munch.

On the Continent, the naturalist Zola enthused over photography, particularly after the snapshot allowed one to capture the moment and not just the object. "In my opinion," he said in 1900, "one cannot be said to have really seen something until one has photographed it" (Émile-Zola 6). But Zola's enthusiasm came late in the century; Baudelaire's ridicule of the passive nature of the camera in the hands of philistines was more typical. In "The Modern Public and Photography" of 1859, Baudelaire says that "an avenging God has heard the prayers of this multitude; Daguerre was his messiah" (Baudelaire 86).

An early Scandinavian reaction to the discovery came from the physicist H. C. Ørsted. Ørsted published a lecture in *Morgenbladet* on 4 March 1839, saying that "The Fine Arts, the real creator, have of course nothing to fear from an art that just reproduces by similarity, but cannot create" (quoted in Eggum, *Munch and Photography* 18). In mid-century Norway, Adolph

Tidemand probably used Marcus Selmer's daguerreotypes of national costumes as material for his romantic paintings (Erlandsen 27) but agreed with Ørsted: art should reveal "Hvad der er gjemt som anelse hos folket" (Erlandsen 27).

The debate went on, becoming increasingly sterile. Even after the introduction of chronophotography and cinematography by the Lumière brothers in the 1880s and 1890s, a writer for *Gads danske Magasin* in 1906 reploughs the, by then, tedious argument and declares that the photograph can never transcend depiction to ascend to art.

Henrik Ibsen certainly shared that view of photography. On 11 October 1857 he remarked sarcastically that an adaptation of a tale by H. C. Andersen would not have a long run, for it was poetic and did not have a photographic resemblance to reality (Meyer 168). More memorable is Ibsen's characterization of the feckless Hjalmar Ekdal in *Vildanden* (1884). We see Ekdal at the beginning of Act Three retouching photographs (to make them resemble reality less), and we hear him constantly prattle about his never-described "invention" that will raise photography at once to an art and to a science.

But ignored in this debate about photography and art was a fact in the history of photography that radically extended the imaginations of *fin-de-siècle* scientists and artists alike: the photographic plate is sensitive to light that the retina is not. The popular imagination had increasingly to deal with the reality of the unseen world of energy, particularly as it left the arcane world of Maxwell's field equations and became dramatically practical. The telegraph and the radio contributed to an unprecedented sense of simultaneity (Kern 68-70), and we need only recall Henry Adams's "The Dynamo and the Virgin" (*The Education of Henry Adams*, 1907/1918), in which he records his stupefaction at the world of energy at the Paris Exhibition of 1900, when he sampled the flavor of that new world.[1]

The ability of the photographic plate to fix ephemeral images of the invisible world provided dramatic evidence not only of its reality, but of the limitations of our senses. Spectral photography, introduced by Vogel in 1873 and applied to astronomy by Huggins in 1875, had, as far as I know, little effect upon the artistic imagination (although, the topic would certainly be worth exploring). August Strindberg uses spectroscopy to establish the Captain's moral authority in *Fadren* (1887). As part of Laura's plot to convince others of her husband's insanity, she says the Captain is using a microscope to see what is on another planet.

The Captain is actually using a spectroscope and is quite up to date in that regard. When spectral analysis revealed water in the atmosphere of Mars, it enhanced a widespread debate about life on other planets, particularly Mars. The approaches of Mars in 1888 and 1892 produced sketches of "canals," and speculation about the canal-builders culminated in Wells's *War of the Worlds* in 1898. In Scandinavia, Otto Asmussen, the science writer for *Gads danske Magasin*, uses evidence from spectroscopy in "Er Mars beboet?" (1907-08) and cannot resist the power of the Argument from

Design (If God created Mars, He must have created Martians) to suggest that we are not alone.

The narrator in Sigbjørn Obstfelder's *En prests Dagbok* (1900) shares some of Henry Adams's bewilderment that reality at the *fin de siècle* seems accessible only through apprehensions of the invisible:

> Hjernens tanke, øiets syn, mikroskop, teleskop, spektroskop, de drog teppet bort for en tegning, et net, et væv bag stoffets tåge. (Obstfelder 2: 184)

The poet Johannes Jørgensen uses the spectrograph as a metaphor for defending science (as he understood it) against materialist reductionism. Even as our eye sees but a small fraction of the spectrum, he argues, the research into psychic phenomena shows that we know but a small fraction of the self, which extends into other dimensions than the visible (Jørgensen 250-65).

So scientific photography showed that the images of reality are confined, but not by the eye, a fact that the announcement by Röntgen of his discovery of X-rays in January of 1896 made stunningly clear. X-ray photography was simple to do, and most laboratories had the equipment necessary: a cathode tube, an induction coil, and a photographic plate. And, as X-rays are of too high a frequency to be felt, the dangers of dosage did not become evident until later.[2]

The drama of "photographing the invisible" was not lost on the artistic imagination, either. In "Jord og Sjæl" (1918), the Danish poet Sophus Claussen recalled the heady days of Bohemian artistic life in the Paris of the 1890s in terms of X-rays and the dematerialized cosmos:

> mens aandelige og tekniske Eksperimentatorer gennemtrænger Tingenes Involde med deres Søgelys og vinder Magt i hidtil hemmelige Verdener, X-Straaler, Lydbølger m. m. (14),

the "new poetry" already knew the creative law of everything from within, so that in a sense, he concludes, "Poesien har ventet paa Videnskaben" (Claussen 15). Frans Lasson, in his edition of Claussen's letters, agrees, seeing the effect of Röntgen's announcement as a metaphor for modernism:

> Man kan med en vis ret sige, at det tyvende århundredes herskende evne har været — ligesom Røntgen-strålerne — at gennemlyse overflader for at finde ned til skjulte strukturer, til sindet og det organiske livs hemmelige mønstre. (Lasson 1: 71)[3]

If the spectrograph implied the effacing of the distinction, obvious to everyday experience, between the organic and the inorganic, X-rays showed that opacity is relative as well. Engineering journals reported on numerous sideshows involving X-ray exhibitions, with human subjects vying for popularity with illusions making bedroom walls transparent (Greenway 31).

The ability to photograph through wood fueled a concern over the voyeuristic in the popular imagination but had an impact upon the artistic imagination as well. Edvard Munch's 1915 woodcut *Mot Skogen* (fig. III.2) has an interesting predecessor from 1897, when imaginative speculations concerning X-rays were at their highest (fig. III.1). Note that in the early version he lets the grain of the wood show through, giving the illusion of loss of the wood's opacity, and the figures are nude, suggesting the stripping of physical surfaces.

Munch will be an integral part of the subsequent discussion of experimental photography. He had no interest in physics, but he shared with his friend August Strindberg a fascination with photographing the invisible. In 1888, Munch had objected to the limitations of photographic naturalism, criticizing the renderings of "lifeless nature" (quoted in Eggum, *Munch and Photography* 45). By the 1890s, however, photography had risen to his challenge and he to its, owing in part to the role of photography in the *fin-de-siècle* interest in the occult.

Occultists seized upon X-rays to legitimize a host of other speculative forms of photographing the invisible (Krauss). Indeed, as Didi-Huberman puts it in the *History of Photography* (1987), "a magic or mediumistic use of X-rays was even written into the scientific birth certificate of the phenomenon" (75). The announcement of the discovery in *Stockholms-Posten* (28 January 1896) was a translation of "Photographing the Invisible" by the French astronomer Camille Flammarion and explicitly linked X-rays to occultism. Flammarion and Strindberg, by the way, were the two honorary members of Jolivet-Castelot's Alchemical Society in Paris, which found radiation a confirmation of its "Hyperphysics."

In 1896, for example, concurrently with the exhibitions of photos taken with the "Röntgen rays," Dr. Hyppolyte Baraduc exhibited four-hundred "soul photographs."[4] According to Stanislaw Przybyszewski, chronicling the bohemian days of Berlin in the 1890s, Munch devoured Alexander Aksakow's *Spiritismus und Animismus* (1894) in one evening (Przybyszewski 222-23). The book had several photos of the invisible spirit world, one of which is in the Strindberg archives in Stockholm.

As we read, say, *The Coming of the Fairies* (1922), chronicling Arthur Conan Doyle's belief in fairy photography, and his two-volume *History of Spiritualism* (1926) we need to bear in mind the faith that the camera plate objectively rendered a spectrum of invisible reality, a faith anchored in X-rays, spectroscopy, and infrared photos. That Doyle, who could create such a powerful debunker as Sherlock Holmes, could uncritically accept obvious photographic fakes (the "fairies'" clothes are from a contemporary fashion magazine) should let us put aside our quibbles about questionable lenses and experimental developing techniques, not to mention outright fraud.

Stanislas Meunier, the science writer for *La Nouvelle Revue*, remarked, in February 1896, that the "universal emotion" stemming from recent brilliant achievements of physics had to make us take seriously the "sensitives" who could see through opaque objects (Meunier 366). If we define clairvoyance with the Theosophist C. W. Leadbeater, who declared clairvoyance to be "the power to see what is hidden from physical sight" (Leadbeater 5, 11), we can understand why the prestigious *Journal of the American Medical Association* (*JAMA* May 1896) could print a note on "The Roentgen Ray and 'Second Sight,'" reporting that

> the supposed power of seeing through opaque media, etc., which is claimed by certain hysteric somnambulistic or trance subjects, may have some objective basis in the light of the recent discoveries by Roentgen. (1065)

In this context, one can see that occultists and spiritualists could use science to suggest that certain sensitive individuals might be able to see into a spectrum normally accessible only to the photograph. The psychologist Eduard von Hartmann took the suggestion seriously in *Der Spiritismus* (1885, see 46), although he was skeptical of the spirit photograph (97-98).

The sensitive, wasted young man became a cliché in the literature of the *fin de siècle*. We need only recall the famous "Exit Niels Lyhne" line of Jens Peter Jacobsen's 1880 novel or the bleak figure of Jarmann in Hans Jæger's at that time lurid *Fra Kristiania-Bohêmen* (1885), whose funeral is conducted by a figure apparently modeled on Norway's leading spiritualist (Eggum, *Munch and Photography* 35).

Munch, however, saw himself as one of those sensitives and took the implications of the "new photography" for art quite seriously. And at that point he sees himself as changing from a feckless lad of retarded development to a man with a new view of painting, informed by experimental photography. A poem in the Munch archives, published by Arne Eggum, Curator of the Munch Museum in Oslo, reads thus:

> Gives der Ånder?
> Vi ser det vi ser — fordi vi har
> således beskafne Øine —
> Hva er vi?
> En Samling Kraft i Bevægelse —
> et Lys der brænder — med Væge —
> så den Indre Varme — så den ydre Flamme
> — og endnu en usynlig Flammering —
> Havde vi anderledes beskafne Øine —
> vilde vi som med Røntgenstraaler
> blot se vore Væger — Bensystemet —
> Havde vi atter anderledes
> beskafne Øine —
> kunde vi se vore ydre Flammeringe —
> og se Mennesker i andre Former —
> Hvorfor skulde altså ikke andre
> Væsener
> med lettere oppløste Molekyler
> færdes om os og i os —
> Afdødes Sjæle —
> Vore kjæres Sjæle — og onde Ånder
>           (quoted in Eggum, *Munch og fotografi* 36)

Why not use the proven sensitivity of the photograph to reveal such entities?

In 1895, Meridith B. Little, a converted skeptic, had described how this process works, in an article on "Spirit Photography" in *The Photographic Times*:

> The success of a spirit in its attempt to manifest its presence on the sensitized plate of the photographer depends greatly upon its ability to impress on the unseen spirit artist a correct conception or idea of its own mental picture of itself. When this mental representation becomes sufficiently tangible to the unseen spirit artist, he prepares a very thin mask in which he reproduces this idea; the mask is of semi-material atoms and is covered with a semi-luminous substance emitting sufficient light to affect the plate in a long exposure, but not sufficiently material to be perceptible to human sight. (Little 147)

We see how Conan Doyle could believe that fairies could be photographed.

Munch's experience with speculative photography and the occult was mediated through his friend August Strindberg, the leader of the bohemian group in 1890s Berlin. Strindberg painted, and he exhibited with Gauguin, but he influenced Munch not through his painting but through his photography.

Strindberg, an ardent photographer, did not venture into spirit photography, though he seems to have respected it. In a photograph of the poet Paul Verlaine on his deathbed, Strindberg saw a demon, noting in the border, "Märk vid fötterne denna!" (Söderström 175).

Strindberg did share the contemporary scientific view of photography as a revelatory medium, however: through the photograph, Strindberg believed, one could capture the essence of the person, but not in the naturalistic sense of Zola. Strindberg was particularly interested in Rochas's *L'Extériorisation de la sensibilité* (1881). Rochas claimed that human beings exuded invisible, but colored, psychic auras, which he believed Crookes had discovered with the cathode tube and which were accessible to the spectrograph and the photograph (Rochas 53, 117).

Though Munch used photographs as sources, in the 1890s he did not actively participate in Strindberg's interest in the occult. But he shared the interest in rendering the invisible. Munch's friend Gustav Schiefler said of Munch that "to him the figure often seems surrounded by an 'aura,' which envelopes it as a colourless flame" (quoted in Eggum, *Munch and Photography* 198).

Eggum has noticed an influence of Strindberg upon Munch that illustrates both their similarities of interest and difference in artistic goals (Eggum, *Munch and Photography* 60). In Strindberg's self-portrait (fig. III.4), taken in Gersau in 1886, we notice the penetrating quality of the eyes, a technique that Strindberg called "själefotografi." In Munch's *Selvportrett med Sigarett* (fig. III.3), from 1895, we see how Munch uses the smoke to efface the distinction between foreground and background, the corporeal and the incorporeal, projecting the substance of the body into a demateri-alized aura. He had done the same, of course, in *Skrik* (1893), in which he transformed a pedestrian postcard photo of Oslo, rendering it into a huge spectrum of emotional reality by fusing the figure on the bridge with the anguished world outside.[5]

So Munch went beyond Claussen's maxim of "Alt indefra" (Claussen, *Indledning, Heroica*) to infuse the flat world of early photography with a representation of an external world of psychic reality invisible to the insensitive eye, but not to the experimental camera. Paul Thompson describes "post-naturalism" as a rejection of materialism, but not of science (71). The change in the photograph from a depicting medium to a revelatory one provided what at the time was thought to be a scientific tether from the scientific to the artistic imagination.

As Thompson points out, the next generation's conceptual conundrums of quantum mechanics and the logical paradoxes of relativity were not as accessible to artistic imaginations untrained in mathematics (71). While postmodern narrative style has attempted to absorb reality as understood by modern science, the drama of the experimental photograph in the *fin de siècle* made it possible for Claussen's jaunty declaration that "Poesien har ventet paa Videnskaben" and the beginning of our era, in which the image is more real than the object.

## Notes

[1] Zola particularly enjoyed photographing the Palace of Electricity, and journalists outdid each other to describe the fairgrounds lit at night by "the fairy electricity."

[2] A clinic in France used a ninety-minute exposure to diagnose pregnancy, and a German physician recommended X-rays for removal of unwanted facial hair. See Greenway, "Penetrating Surfaces."

[3] For a sample of Baraduc's work, see Greenway 37. Strauss reproduces many of these photographs.

[4] The idea seems to have caught on, particularly in Scandinavia, or at least others saw Scandinavia as a frontier of the imagination. When Ernst Weiss needed a quintessentially modern hero for his 1913 novel *Die Galeere*, he created Erik Gyldendal as a Scandinavian radiologist whose love life is considerably enhanced when he is bathed by "Röntgenrays."

[5] For the postcard view from Ekebergveien, see Eggum, *Munch og fotografi* 50. The mental hospital into which Munch's sister had shortly before been committed lay below, surrounded by slaughterhouses.

## Works Cited

Adams, Henry. *The Education of Henry Adams*. Boston: Houghton Mifflin, 1974.

Asmussen, Otto. "Er Mars beboet?" *Gads danske Magasin* 2 (1907-08): 627-37.

Baudelaire, Charles. "The Modern Public and Photography." *Classic Essays on Photography*. Ed. Alan Trachtenberg. New Haven: Leete's Island Books, 1980. 83-89.

Claussen, Sophus. Indledning. *Heroica*. See below.

——. "Ny Aand. Forbindelsen mellem Fantasi og Videnskab." *Heroica. Nye Digte.* Copenhagen: Gyldendal, 1925. 11-19.

Didi-Huberman, Georges. "Photography — Scientific and Pseudo-scientific." *A History of Photography: Social and Cultural Perspectives*. Ed. Jean-Claude Lemagny and Andre Rouillé. Trans. Janet Lloyd. Cambridge: Cambridge UP, 1987. 71-75.

Doyle, Arthur Conan. *The Coming of the Fairies*. Toronto: Hodder and Stoughton, 1922.

——. *The History of Spiritualism*. 2 vols. New York: George H. Doran, 1926.

Eggum, Arne. *Munch og fotografi*. Oslo: Gyldendal, 1987. See also translation below.

——. *Munch and Photography*. Trans. Birgit Holm. New Haven: Yale UP, 1989. See also original above.

Émile-Zola, François. *Zola Photographer*. Trans. Liliane Emery Tuck. New York: Seaver, 1988.

Erlandsen, Roger. "Maleri og fotografi i norsk kunst rundt 1860." *Skandinavisk kunst og fotografi*. Ed. Arne Eggum and Bodil Stenseth. Munch-Museets skrifter 4. Oslo: Oslo Kommunes Kunstsamlinger, 1988. 9-32.

Greenway, John L. "Penetrating Surfaces: Strindberg, X-rays and *The Ghost Sonata*." *Nineteenth-Century Studies* 5 (1991): 29-46.

Hartmann, Eduard von. *Der Spiritismus*. Leipzig: W. Friederich, 1885.

Jacobsen, Jens Peter. *Niels Lyhne*. Copenhagen: Gyldendal, 1880.

*JAMA*. See "The Roentgen Ray."

Jæger, Hans. *Fra Kristiania-Bohêmen*. Oslo: Gyldendal, 1974.

Jørgensen, Johannes. "Overgreb af Videnskaben." *Gads danske Magasin* 3 (1908-09): 260-65.

Kern, Stephen. *The Culture of Time and Space 1880-1918*. Cambridge, Mass.: Harvard UP, 1983.

Krauss, Rolf H. *Jenseits von Licht und Schatten: Die Rolle der Photographie bei bestimmten paranormalen Phänomenen — ein historischer Abriß*. Marburg: Jonas Verlag, 1992.

Lasson, Frans. *Sophus Claussen og hans kreds. En digters liv i breve*. 2 vols. Copenhagen: Gyldendal, 1984.

Leadbeater, C. W. *Clairvoyance*. London: Theosophical Publishing Company, 1899. 5, 11.

Lesák, Barbara. "Photography, Cinematography and the Theatre: A History of a Relationship." *Fin de siécle and Its Legacy*. Ed. Mikulás Teich and Roy Porter. Cambridge: Cambridge UP, 1990. 132-46.

Little, Meridith B. "Spirit Photography." *The Photographic Times* 26 (1895): 142-47.

Meunier, Stanislas. "Sciences." *La Nouvelle Revue* 98 (1896): 365-67.

Meyer, Michael. *Henrik Ibsen: The Making of a Dramatist 1828-1864*. Vol. 1. London: Rupert Hart-Davis, 1967. 3 vols. 1967-71.

Newhall, Beaumont. *A History of Photography*. New York: Museum of Modern Art, 1964.

Obstfelder, Sigbjørn. *Samlede skrifter*. 3 vols. Oslo: Gyldendal, 1950. See *En prests dagbog* in vol. 2: 121-234.

Przybyszewski, Stanislaw. *Erinnerungen an das literarischen Berlin*. Munich: Winckler, 1965.

Rochas, Albert de. *L'Extériorisation de la sensibilité*. Paris: Éditions Pygmalion, 1977.

"The Roentgen Ray and 'Second Sight.'" in [*JAMA*] *Journal of the American Medical Association* 26 (1896): 1065.

Sobieszek, Robert A. "Photography and the Theory of Realism in the Second Empire: A Reexamination of a Relationship." *One Hundred Years of Photographic History: Essays in Honor of Beaumont Newhall*. Ed. Van Deren Coke. Albuquerque: U of New Mexico P, 1975. 146-55.

Söderström, Göran. *Strindberg och bildkonsten*. Uddeballa: Bohusläningens, 1972.

Thompson, Paul. "In Search of Faith and Fixing-Points: Strindberg, Obstfelder and the Age of Post-Naturalism." *Scandinavica* 28 (1989): 55-73.

Weiss, Ernst. *Die Galeere*. Berlin: Ullstein, 1913.

# Fartein Valen: Atonality in the North

## John Weinstock

THE END OF the nineteenth century saw the culmination of a long development in the history of music, the breakdown of tonality. From the middle of the seventeenth century to the end of the nineteenth century music was tonal, that is, it was written in one or another of the twenty-four major and minor keys. This is not to suggest that the underlying structure of music was static; rather, it had evolved through the diatonic tonality of the eighteenth century to the chromaticism of the nineteenth century and was gradually breaking down. At the turn of the century the last vestiges of tonality were being abandoned by the most avant-garde composers. In other words, 1900 represented a major break with the classical music traditions of the preceding two and a half centuries. The Norwegian composer Fartein Valen was one of the few who stepped across the boundary to write atonal music, eventually arriving at what has been called his dissonant polyphonic style. In this article we will look at Valen's path to a mature style, touch on his life along the way, and examine in some detail his third symphony as a testimony to his unique achievement.

## Biographical Background

Valen was born in Stavanger on August 25, 1887, while his missionary parents were home on vacation from Madagascar (now Malagasy).[1] Valen (meaning "shallow water") is the name of the original farm in Valestrand parish in the Haugeland area. The composer came from a family that had been there for generations. His father, Arne, survived a shipwreck at age twenty and subsequently devoted his life to God by becoming a missionary. As a student Arne displayed enough musical talent in violin and theory that a teacher suggested he concentrate on music. Fartein Valen's mother, also musically inclined, was reputed to be a fine singer.

When he was two, the family returned to Madagascar for six years. The early experience of living in a different culture was crucial to the shaping of his character in many respects. He developed a great love of nature, of plants and of animals, which later on became so evident in his music. His love of language manifested itself when, at a young age, he learned Malagasy, a language of Indonesian origin, from a nursemaid; later in life he would eagerly become proficient in a number of European languages. It was noticed early on that he had an excellent ear, and when his father purchased a slave boy named August, who became Fartein's foster brother and who was himself very musical, Valen used to listen to him play the organ in church. Valen's strong piety and his wider than customary horizons, from his having lived abroad when young, are two of his strongest character traits.

Back in Stavanger, as he attended private school, musical experiences began to play an increasingly important role for him. Beethoven, especially, captivated him. He began violin lessons but was not strong enough to keep up with both them and his school work. He had had numerous illnesses in Madagascar, including malaria, which left him frail his entire life, and classmates were later protective of the sickly boy. Pleurisy at age fifteen meant an entire year out of school. In spite of his early frailty, it had not been long before he had learned to play the piano on his own. He had a number of piano teachers during his school years, including Jeannette Mohr, whose sons were to become his best friends and benefactors. (One is reminded of another Norwegian composer whose early bout with pleurisy had such an impact on his life, that is, Edvard Grieg.)

Valen liked to write, not only music, but poetry and prose. He was very good in other school subjects as well and even skipped one grade. He always did more than was asked of him and liked everything but math; this bias is curious since musical talent often goes hand in hand with linguistic and mathematical ability. He wrote his first musical composition at age eleven, and by the time he entered the *gymnasium*, he knew he wanted to be a composer. His father was opposed to the idea for the "right reasons" (you could not, for example, earn a living by writing music), but his mother supported him in his aspirations. A compromise was reached for his first year at the University of Oslo: he would study philology as well as music.

Up to that point his knowledge of composition had largely been auto-didactic. Then, from 1906–09, he studied theory with Catharinus Elling and subsequently passed the organist exam. His fast friend Otto Laus Mohr, who provided invaluable information about Valen during his University of Oslo days (Gurvin, *Fartein Valen* 35–36), considered Valen, who was of a deeply religious nature, to be without a doubt the most innocent person he had ever met. Valen's shyness — which even made him afraid to eat, believing everyone would take him for a fool — nearly turned into a persecution complex, and the merest trifles could take on violent dimensions in his fantasy. The whole time he continued working intensively, playing piano and composing, while at the same time suffering from a severe lack of sleep. He finally became sick and the doctor ordered a complete bed rest. He was in terrible torment when he at last went to a publisher with his first manuscript. Mohr noted that although Valen was very critical of the artistic efforts of others, he never expressed those feelings except to such a close friend as Mohr himself, but also that Valen himself was afraid of doing anything trivial; he demanded the extraordinary of himself. His lack of self-confidence ultimately proved to be disastrous to his commercial success.

On Elling's advice Valen went to Berlin to study music. The outcome of his studies there was mixed. He himself wrote that he had learned a lot technically, but little about the aesthetic, ethical, and intuitive nature of music. "Jeg trodde jeg var kommet til et kunstens tempel, men så var det et seminarium for musikanter" (Gurvin, *Fartein Valen* 44). He did not get to know many other students, for he was alone most of the time. Significantly, though, he did get to hear a lot of music that he could not have heard in Norway, but he left disappointed, just as Grieg had left Leipzig. Valen had not yet found his style.

Summers and other vacations were mostly spent at Valevåg, the old family farm, where his mother and sister lived after his father's death and where he was later to spend a large part of his life. In 1911, he was asked to do some arrangements of chorales for a missionary songbook. He worked hard, using Bach as his model, but not surprisingly Valen refused to allow his name to appear in connection with the work. When word nevertheless got out, there was somewhat of an uproar. Soon afterward he received an offer to go to America but turned it down, saying he was afraid of spending his life among people who were so conventional and who had such a poorly developed and uncomplicated spiritual life (Gurvin, *Fartein Valen* 47). He returned to Berlin to study on his own, finding it easier to escape attention in the large city. He gave private lessons to make ends meet and spent his free time studying the works of composers from as far back as the Renaissance. It was during that time (1913, to be exact), that he first heard a piece by Arnold Schoenberg, the still-tonal A-Minor Quartet. He found that he particularly liked its linear structure.

Dreams and mysticism always played an important role in Valen's life and in his composition; in 1913, he had a dream that he believed to be of great significance: he dreamt that Bach was at his side saying, "Glem ikke forholdet mellom akkordene" (Gurvin, *Fartein Valen* 53). He woke up immediately with a revelation. He had been struggling to compose a violin sonata for some time, and he now changed a number of the chords as a result of his dream. From that point, the process of composing was somewhat easier for him.[2] He had completed his opus 1 in 1907, yet his opus 5 was not finished until 1924. His meager production during seventeen years was primarily due to the fact that he was striving hard to find his own personal style.

In 1914, Valen had to return to Valevåg because of his sister Sigrid's nervous breakdown. He began to work on a setting for the *Ave Maria*, which was to become his opus 4 seven years later (Gurvin, *Fartein Valen* 57). There were brief sojourns in Oslo in 1917, 1919, and 1921. Although a few women were attracted to him during that period, he rejected both them and the idea of marriage and family, partly because he was so frail and also partly because his erotic feelings — according to Gurvin — had possibly been sublimated in his art and in religion. He gradually withdrew from the external world and its events and devoted himself to his own inner life. He did have occasions to go abroad, in 1922 to Italy and in 1932 to Mallorca. The trips lifted his spirit. In Italy he was still searching for a definitive style and found inspiration in Italian art and architecture. The Mallorca trip resulted in one of his most productive years. Nevertheless, by 1924, his failure to promote his own work had left him in serious financial straits. No more job offers from America were forthcoming, and he went to Oslo, and lived with his sister Magnhild and her family, and finally managed to get a job at the music library. The small salary there, plus income from private students, enabled him to get by, but the commotion created at his sister's home by all her children made composition difficult. In 1928, pleurisy forced him to return to Valevåg.

Some of Valen's works at last began to be performed, but they invariably received poor reviews. His artist friends frequently came to his defense. Henrik Sørensen promoted a "Valen evening" in 1931, for which the three performing artists were promised lithographs of Werenskiold, Sørensen, Revold, and Heiberg. In 1934, Valen's application for a state salary for composition had been turned down in favor of another composer. But, the following year, with the help of friends and testimonials from abroad, he was successful. The salary eventually enabled him to move permanently to Valevåg where he spent the rest of his life. There, his sister Sigrid, making many a personal sacrifice — such as giving up her own piano playing because it disturbed his composing — spent much of her time caring for him. All his years of private teaching did have a positive effect on future generations of composers: he would have no part of the trendy Norwegian nationalist movement in music, and he had trained so many young musical talents so well that they were able to see through a great deal of dilettantish music. For his efforts, he was accused of corrupting youth.

Until 1933, Valen had an ally in the music publishing business, Sigurd Kielland of Norsk Musikkforlag, where many of his early works were published, even if the royalties for them did not amount to much. After Kielland left the company, there was no longer any interest shown in printing Valen's compositions. Valen, who was simply tossed out the door in 1938, had hastened his move to Valevåg for good. Valen was once asked about his many unpublished and unperformed works, and he replied, characteristically: "Det er vel viktigst at de blir skrevet" (Gurvin, *Fartein Valen* 111). Not until 1947 did Valen find a suitable publisher, Harald Lyche, after which his works, new and old, again began to appear.

In 1936, Valen had another mystical experience, the night before his beloved nephew Arne died of tuberculosis at age twenty. As a child of five or six, Arne would sing atonal melodies; that was precisely when Valen was struggling with his own style, looking for a sign that would allow him to reject classical tonality completely. Valen prayed for Arne that night and felt strongly that his prayer had been answered and that Arne would recover. When he learned that the boy had died, Valen decided that God had a more glorious fate in store for the boy. Valen reported the experience to his sister and to Dagny Knutsen, the pianist who had performed a number of his works; she suggested he write music about it. Though at first considering the experience too intimate, he soon afterward wrote a chorale, which was eventually incorporated into the coda of his Violin Concerto (1947). The work is reminiscent of Alban Berg's Violin Concerto (*To the Memory of an Angel*, 1935) which was written in memory of Manon Gropius, Alma Mahler's eighteen-year-old daughter. Valen knew the work but denied any mutual influence between Berg and himself.

A modicum of fame came to Valen after the war and toward the end of his life. His *Sonetto di Michelangelo* (1932) was performed to great acclaim at the 1947 meeting of the International Society of Contemporary Music. The Violin Concerto (1947) was equally successful at the following year's festival. Valen died in 1952 from double pneumonia. He had been a most remarkable person, deeply religious and extremely sensitive, and his unusual life had a profound effect on his music.

Valen reminds one of the protagonist of Hamsun's *Sult* (1890), the starving artist whose commitment to his metier is sorely tested in his isolation. Valen, because of his very nature, chose a lonely path from which he never strayed, despite his many setbacks. If another musician suggested possible alterations in his scores, Valen tended to evade the issue, knowing full well that he would not change a single note. He was also close-mouthed about his personal life and his art, speaking about such matters only occasionally and then but to a few intimate friends. His sources of inspiration are not difficult to discover — in order of importance: nature, religion, and poetry. Much of his music seems to derive from his profound love of nature and his way of experiencing it. In the summer of 1948, the composer Øystein Sommerfeldt spent some time in Valevåg taking lessons from Valen; he was able to witness Valen's connection with nature at first hand. He could understand that the boundless and all-embracing in nature had been transformed into resounding overtones in Valen's many symphonic poems, that it was nature that had colored his music and given it its special atmosphere, and that for this purpose Valen needed to use the chromatic scale as his point of departure (Sommerfeldt, 54). As an example, he mentions Valen's first symphonic poem, *Pastorale for orchestra* (op. 11, 1930, pub. 1933), for which the composer's fantasy was nourished by nature, poetry, and painting (Sommerfeldt, 45). He wrote no fewer than nine motets on various texts, some other works inspired by religious ideas and thought — for example the *Ave Maria* — and thirteen songs on poetic texts.

## Compositional Analysis

Valen began as did most of the great composers: he composed in the style of his predecessors before finding his own.[3] Wagner had pushed tonality to the limit: there were long stretches without cadences; there was frequent enharmonic reinterpretation of dissonant chords; and what had been passing chords became independent harmonies. Yet, in Wagner's music there was always an underlying fundamental tonic, or harmonic, "home base." Max Reger also composed tonal music, but he often used melodies with as many as ten, eleven, or all twelve notes of the chromatic scale. Scriabin went a step further than Wagner or Reger. Instead of the tonic triad, he used the dominant ninth as the point of departure or chord center. Consonances were almost nonexistent, as were cadences. But his chords were triadically built, so that his music was marginally tonal. Debussy's introduction of the whole-tone scale, in what came to be called "musical impressionism," was very important. The octave was divided into two tone-rows (F, G, A, B, C$\sharp$, E$\flat$ and F$\sharp$, G$\sharp$, A$\sharp$, C, D, E); within each row there was no tension from the traditional dissonant-consonant functions at all. He made frequent use of parallel chords and augmented triads, ninths, and elevenths. An entire piece could be based on the whole-tone scale with a brief tonal section as contrast. Bartók and Stravinsky abandoned tonal harmony as well but kept diatonic scales for melody and used rhythm to provide form, as in the latter's *Le Sacre du printemps* (1913). Schoenberg, in his early works, weakened the force of dominant tension and the dominant-tonic cadence, and in his "atonal expressionism" he gradually shifted the weight and tension to all twelve of the notes in the chromatic scale, so that harmonically and melodically they were without tonal value. He referred to the "emancipation of the dissonance": dissonances and consonances were no longer distinct subsets of intervals; dissonances would now become "comprehensible," just as consonances had always been (Dahlhaus 120-21). He began to use the twelve tone-row as a basis of harmony; his chords were largely tetrachords derived from the row. Before he finally arrived at his serial technique in the 1920s, the main compositional principle for Schoenberg and most of his contemporaries remained the avoidance of any hint of tonality. Schoenberg's first serial work, his *Fünf Klavierstücke*, was published in November of 1923, three months after Fartein Valen published his first work in a pure atonal style.

Being Norwegian meant an additional dilemma for Valen: Norway was young as a nation, and national self-assertion had been very important to several generations of Norwegian composers. Edvard Grieg, for example, began composing music in the continental idiom, but his fame is based on his compositions with roots in Norwegian folk music. Valen, though, never felt compelled to move along that national romantic path. His first work was typically late-romantic, in the fashion of Brahms and Reger, but with a good bit of dissonance and chromaticism. His opus 2 (1912, pub. 1914), one of his two piano sonatas, is also in the late romantic vein, with heavy chords and lots of modulation, but with even more dissonance and weaker cadences, though still largely tonal. His melodic lines gradually became more chromatic, a development that is not surprising when you consider the fact that, from the time of his childhood on, he had been very sensitive to overtones. Even then he had been able to hear the dissonant overtones accompanying a low-register triad. He studied acoustics in 1921 to gain a better understanding of the principles of sound.[4] Then things began to make more sense; he could see that even the sharpest dissonances were derived from the fundamental tone and that the difference between consonance and dissonance was a matter of degree rather than kind.

Valen's Violin Sonata (op. 3, 1916, pub. 1920) showed considerable progress; it was freer rhythmically; final dissonances were not resolved; and in the last movement a theme that employed all twelve notes of the chromatic scale was used. His *Ave Maria* and *Trio* (opp. 4 and 5, respectively) each took seven years, during which he experienced his most difficult crisis of style. In the midst of that crisis he remembered the story of Liszt's playing Bach's C-Minor Prelude and Fugue for Beethoven in the 1820s and Beethoven's asking Liszt if he could play it in another key, which Liszt did without difficulty (Beethoven was certainly deaf by that time but could tell what Liszt was doing by watching him). Valen decided to work on Bach's *The Well-Tempered Clavier*. He practiced the forty-eight preludes and fugues until he could play them all equally well. Then he wrote six fugues in each key, an effort that cost him two years, until he realized that he had to create his own style. Finally, a higher power seemed to intervene: he dreamt that Bach visited him and pointed to a book on the bookshelf and then left. Valen knew immediately that the book had to contain Bach fugues. He thought about that idea for a long time and at last became convinced that he could write counterpoint with dissonance as a basis.

Valen's opus 5, begun in 1917, is his real stylistic breakthrough; it was rewritten nine times and not completed until 1924. In this piece, tonality is abandoned for good, and the mode of expression is for the first time completely atonal. From then on all his music would be atonal. For Valen the move toward an atonal style had been protracted and fraught with difficulty. But in his atonal "dissonant polyphony" he at last found a style that was completely his own. Opus 5 represents the beginning of Valen's second period. His dissonant polyphony operated in a kind of reverse fashion from baroque counterpoint, in that the independent melodic lines met in dissonances rather than consonances. He would create a twelve-tone melodic line, which contained no hints of tonality, and write counterpoint, in the form of another twelve-tone melodic line, in such a way that the vertical harmonies were dissonant. Dahlhaus, in discussing Schoenberg and dissonant polyphony, says:

> Dissonance should be understood as the way the notes move apart, and therefore as an effective element, not as the chance result of an uncompromising use of counterpoint in which the sonorities are incidental. (123)

In decreasing order of dissonance, the intervals m2, M7, 5+, 4+, M2 and m7 were most important to Valen. A third melodic line could be added (and a fourth as well); the latter lines did not necessarily have to stand in a dissonant relationship with the first two. The dissonant sonorities had to change frequently so that no vertical sonority might be construed as primary. Parallel seconds, sevenths, fourths, fifths, or octaves were not allowed. Thus, Valen abandoned tonality with respect to both melody and harmony. He abandoned all traditional cadencing as well. He did, however, use the classical forms (for example, sonata, ternary) and genres (for example, concerto, symphony).

In Valen's third, or serial period, he uses dodecaphonic themes as a point of departure and then develops his music using dissonant polyphony with an occasional foothold in a main tone or tone complex, for example, two themes might be introduced a fifth apart. In fact, the fifth relationship is used often. This last period does not differ essentially from the second one, although Valen had begun to write in larger genres as, for example, in his Violin Concerto and the last three of his four symphonies. His music had become a union of twentieth-century tone language, a rich baroque polyphony with its free rhythms, Viennese classical form, and a hint of romantic color in the instrumentation and dynamic nuancing (Gurvin, *Fartein Valen* 189; Huldt-Nyström 34). The music flows along smoothly with a sparkling clarity that often seems dreamlike. Whatever attention had been paid to harmony and harmonic development has been given over to rhythm and the interplay of the lines. He builds from small to larger units with clear intervalic-rhythmic motivic development. He does not use varied compounding of portions of the twelve-tone row, as did Schoenberg and Berg, nor could he rigidly preserve the order of the row, as did the serialists; he needed themes and motives that would not upset the rhythmic center of gravity. It is interesting to note that Valen had arrived at his twelve-tone method before he became acquainted with Schoenberg's. Valen worked on his twelve-tone melodies daily for seventeen years before he felt comfortable with them; he did not "leap" to a twelve-tone style as so many of the composers of this century did. Finally, in 1928 in Paris, he heard a performance of one of Schoenberg's twelve-tone compositions, which impressed him. He realized, though, that serial techniques would not work with his dissonant polyphony.

Valen began composing his third symphony on January 12, 1944, more than a month before he completed his second symphony. He was apparently eager to start putting new ideas on paper. It was the only one of his four symphonies that he was to hear in concert, and that was in Oslo on April 13, 1951 (Gurvin, *Fartein Valen* 209). The symphony was begun while the Germans were still occupying Norway. A year before the Germans had marched into Poland, Valen dreamt that a friend of his parents who was no longer alive came to him and said, "Fienden vil komme, og Haugesund vil bli tatt. Folk vil flykte, men du kan ta alt helt rolig. Du kan være trygg" (Gurvin, *Fartein Valen* 125). The war meant that Valen was deprived of much that he needed, most significantly kerosene for lamps, since there was no electricity in Valevåg until 1950. He used to take short daily tours in the environs but had to curtail even them after an odd incident. When a neighbor expressed a strong hate for the Nazis, Valen replied that he could not hate anyone. Such tolerance was not surprising in so deeply devout a person; however, rumors soon began to spread that he was a Nazi sympathizer. In 1945, after a Norwegian military officer and friend had been to visit him, Valen came to be considered a hero because he knew such an important person.

Valen's third symphony is largely a positive work, celebrating the beauties and vicissitudes of nature. This celebration is most evident in the first and fourth movements. The second movement, the Larghetto, Valen planned as a memorial to those lost during the war. While working on the latter half of the movement, he received word that a good friend had drowned when the ship he had been on was struck by a mine. Valen, strongly moved, visualized the sea when, after the mine blast, it had calmed down. He could feel the silence in the air and over the ocean surface, the silence of sorrow (Gurvin, *Fartein Valen* 139). While working on the movement in December of 1944, some targets near Valevåg were bombed, and Valen could hear the cries of the shipwrecked sailors (Maegaard and Vollsnes 8). In a letter Valen described the symphony "as a kind of 'Pastorale,' in which he had tried to use some of the things the painters had taught him" (Maegaard and Vollsnes 13). He may have been alluding to the fact that contemporary painters and composers had to rely on the tried-and-true tools (the oils of the painters being equivalent to the scales of traditional composers) to express their abstract and atonal ideas. Gurvin preferred not to call the symphony a "pastorale" because of the third movement, the Intermezzo. This movement represents the stormy weather that occasionally strikes the west coast of Norway:

> Stormen kunne ta tungt i huset så det ristet, den hylte kraftig i hjørnene og trærne, og sjøen slo så det braket og dundret fra strand og knauser. (Gurvin, *Fartein Valen* 138)

But the two outer movements were inspired by the summer in Valevåg. According to Gurvin, Valen got the themes from the moods he was in when he was making the rounds of his garden or on his walks. The symphony ends on a jubilant note, which may reflect to some extent the defeat of the Germans and their departure from Norway in May of 1945.

The first movement, marked *Allegro moderato*, can best be described as a modified sonata form. This is polyphony in the best sense, only here it is dissonant polyphony, with atonal melodies woven together contrapuntally in masterly fashion. The exposition (mm. 1-51) contains six themes or motives, all of which play important roles in the movement. These six themes are largely chromatic or atonal in character: one of them has nine notes of the chromatic scale, three have eleven, and two have all twelve. Four of them are presented within the first five bars of the primary theme group (mm. 1-17). The movement opens with a motive in the horns (Ex. Ia).

Ex. Ia

Note the initial interval of a fifth from D to A; in the absence of tonal relationships in most of his music Valen often resorts to the fifth: successive statements of a theme might begin a fifth apart or, as is the case here, a melodic fifth may be the first interval heard. This is also the case for the second and third movements. This motive leads into the main melody in the first violins (Ex. Ib).

Ex. Ib

Together with this melody the cellos have a theme (Ex. Ic) that will reappear in the secondary theme group (mm. 18-32).

Ex. Ic

The last of these four ideas soon follows in the clarinets (Ex. Id).

Ex. Id

In the rest of the primary section the themes recur in various combinations and modifications; for example, the initial motive, Ia, immediately followed by the main theme, Ib, is in stretto with itself (mm. 7-9), after which the initial motive occurs together with its inversion (m. 11). The secondary theme group begins with a plaintive *pianissimo* theme in the flutes (Ex. Ie).

Ex. Ie

This secondary theme group is accompanied by the bassoon, which plays the Ic idea from the primary theme group. This new theme is taken up by the first violins reaching a dynamic level of *forte*, again together with the Ic theme in the cellos and violas. The closing theme group (mm. 33-51) begins with a soft, fanfarelike theme in the oboes, which is continued by the second violins (Ex. If).

Ex. If

The clarinets repeat the theme at a higher dynamic level, after which the theme is inverted in the first violins and is in stretto with the normal version in the cellos. The theme is then played *fortissimo* in the flutes and first violins. The closing theme group ends with the Ie theme of the secondary theme group, accompanied by variants of the rhythmic motive of the If theme, again at a *fortissimo* dynamic level.

The brief development section (mm. 52-72) opens with variants of the If theme at a *pianissimo* level, followed by the Ic theme against the inversion of If. Then the Ic theme is inverted itself and followed by variants of the latter half of the Ib theme. Next come three variants of the Id theme in stretto, one of which is inverted. The end of the development contains a number of examples of the Ia motive, all inverted (mm. 70-72). The recapitulation begins in measure 73 with the Ia theme in normal position and on D, as at the beginning, followed by a variant of the main theme, Ib on C♯, as at the beginning, and then fragments of the main theme. The Id theme reappears in measure 78. The Ic theme is inverted in measure 80, but in its normal position when it accompanies a variant of the main theme, Ib; Ic begins as it did at the start, on E; however, the Ib variant is one half step lower. Then comes the Ia motive inverted, followed by the Ie theme up a fourth from where it began in the secondary theme group. The beginning of the Ia theme occurs together with the end of the same theme in measure 94. The If theme reappears in measure 98 partly inverted and then in measure 101 in its normal position. Beginning in measure 105, the If theme occurs with its inversion. Most of the rest of the movement is in a finely wrought invertible or double counterpoint. The Ie theme returns again, but now, for the first time, together with the Ia motive. The Id theme returns and the movement ends with the Ie theme on *ppp*. The recapitulation is not a mere repetition of the materials presented in the exposition, although all the themes are there and in roughly the same order. The principle of inversion, which was so important in the development section, is often used in the recapitulation. It should also be noted that the half step or semitone plays a role: the primary theme group ends with the first violins on an F♯. After an eighth rest the flute begins the secondary theme section on F. Likewise, the secondary theme section ends with the oboes on a C, whereafter they immediately move to a B to begin the closing theme section. Also, in the development section there are several examples of a general theme (Ex. Ig) in which every other interval is a half step.

1 X 1 X 1 X . . .

(in which 1 = a half step and X can be any interval from 2 to 11 half steps)

Ex. Ig

One might compare measures 66-71 in the cellos and violas. These half steps are not of any significance in the first movement, but they can be considered to be a stylistic seed that will grow in importance in the other movements, especially the second and fourth. It is interesting to see on what note successive statements of a particular theme begin. Sometimes they begin on the same note, sometimes up a fifth. But these successive statements are widely enough separated that no tonal implications can be drawn. Themes Ie and Ic appear together three times: first, Ie begins on F, while Ic comes in a measure later on E; then, they begin together on C and E, respectively; finally, Ic begins on E♭, followed less than a measure later by Ie on F.

The second movement, Larghetto, a ternary form, is another contrapuntal tour de force. The first A section (mm. 1-28) presents the main theme (Ex. IIa).

Ex. IIa

The theme occurs in the flutes and first violins, together with two rhythmically simple contrapuntal accompaniments (Ex. IIb and IIc).

Ex. IIb

Ex. IIc

The IIa melody uses all twelve notes of the chromatic scale; the two countermelodies have eleven and twelve. The counterpoint is soon inverted, with IIa in the cellos and basses and IIb and IIc in the upper voices. There quickly follows a canonlike progression with the main theme, IIa, its inversion, and the latter half of the main theme. The A section ends with the first violins playing the beginning of the main theme inverted, followed by the IIb countermelody. The contrasting B section — in itself ternary — (mm. 29-54) begins with a long theme, the first part of which is a rhythmic motive that is in sharp contrast with the long, flowing, lyrical theme of A (Ex. IId).

Ex. IId

This theme sounds almost tonal with its A-minor triad. However, it is accompanied by a countermelody similar to IIb and IIc in the A section (Ex. IIe).

Ex. IIe

Played by the cellos and basses, the F#, B, F, and G♭ undermine any firm tonal basis of theme IIc. In the middle part of B, a rapid melodic idea occurs four times in canon (Ex. IIf).

Ex. IIf

This idea and the theme IId each contain all twelve notes of the chromatic scale. IIc now returns, this time on A, up a fifth from its first appearance on E. There are other instances of the rhythmic motive with which IIc begins and which closes out B. The final A section begins with the main theme, IIa, in the violas, while the countermelody is in the violins, inverted from the opening of the Larghetto. The remainder of the movement is highlighted by numerous appearances of the theme IIa in its normal position, inverted, in double counterpoint, in stretto with itself, and in partial diminution. The movement ends with the rhythmic motive of theme IIc. There are numerous examples of the 1 X 1 X 1 X general theme mentioned above; they are mostly part of the contrapuntal structure of the movement.

The third movement, entitled Intermezzo, is at an *allegro* tempo. In a letter, dated December 1945, Valen reported that he had been humming Brahms's Intermezzos to himself during the autumn while working on the middle two movements (Maegaard and Vollsnes 7). The movement is not in any of the standard musical forms, unless it is considered as a type of theme and variation. There are actually three themes presented in the first few measures, all of which reappear in many guises, coming together at the end of the movement in a beautiful *fortissimo* conclusion. The first two themes each contain all twelve notes of the chromatic scale (Ex. IIIa, IIIb).

Ex. IIIa

Ex. IIIb

The third is a rhythmic motive (Ex. IIIc).

Ex. IIIc

IIIc opens the movement in the cellos, and after IIIa and IIIb are presented by the horns and first violins, respectively, a slightly altered IIIc appears in the bassoons and cellos and, later, in the basses. The last third of IIIb comes in the violins, and then the complete IIIb moves to the cellos and basses in double counterpoint with an altered IIIa. In the course of 94 measures IIIa is altered, split up, inverted; the initial ascending fifth sequence recurs in various forms. The IIIb theme is sliced up roughly into initial, middle, and final motives. Some of these are inverted and in canon. The IIIc theme is inverted, altered, and in canon with itself. All three themes frequently move back and forth between the voices. They come together for the first time at the very end, on their original pitches. Every instrument participates in this powerful and intricate contrapuntal display. Again there are instances of the 1 X 1 X 1 X general theme, for example, the first violins in measure 59 or the cellos in measures 67-69, none of which plays a key role in the overall structure.

The Finale, an *allegro*, is in a modified sonata form similar to the first movement. It begins with a sprightly theme in the first violins (Ex. IVa) with counterpoint by the clarinets and bassoons (Ex. IVb).

Ex. IVa

Ex. IVb

The main melody has all twelve notes of the chromatic scale. This melody is followed by a motive (Ex. IVc) that is rhythmically based on IVb.

Ex. IVc

The rhythmic motive (Ex. IVd) will reappear in various forms.

Ex. IVd

Then the counterpoint is inverted with the main theme in the cellos and basses and the accompaniment in the second violins and violas. The IVc motive now appears in canon in the first violins, violas, and second violins. The main theme is heard again, but with different accompaniment both rhythmically and contrapuntally. The first section (mm. 1-28) ends with IVc in canon again in the violas, cellos and violas. In this first section there are several examples of the 1 X 1 X 1 X generalized accompaniment seen in the previous movements. This accompaniment now becomes the theme (Ex. IVe) of the second and closing theme section (mm. 29-76).

Ex. IVe

The theme first appears in the oboes at a *pianissimo* dynamic level, and again all twelve notes of the scale are included. A few measures later a signallike motive is heard in the oboes (Ex. IVf), completing the material of the closing section.

Ex. IVf

The IVe theme and IVf motive move among the voices, both are inverted, and IVf is in canon several times as the section closes *fortissimo*. The development (mm. 77-100) begins *pianissimo*, with the IVa theme in the cellos, and consists of variants of the two main themes IVa and IVe. The recapitulation opens with the IVa theme in the oboes and something similar to the original accompaniment in the second violins and violas. The flutes repeat the IVc motive, and the main theme returns in the cellos with the accompaniment in double counterpoint. A whole-tone passage in the horns leads to a repetition of the IVe theme in the first violins. A new motive, similar to IVf rhythmically, appears in canon three times in the recapitulation (Ex. IVg).

Ex. IVg

IVf also appears in canon and inverted. The dynamic level increases, and the symphony ends in a stirring climax, with the main themes IVa and IVe and the motive IVf coming together for the first time.

Gurvin has stated that the third symphony is, without a doubt, one of Valen's most significant works. The movements are each distinctive, but tied together stylistically into a whole (Gurvin, *Fartein Valen* 139). Hampus Huldt-Nyström wrote that the polyphony was on a par with the best baroque polyphony, the formal scheme and motivic work reminded him of the classical period, while the beautiful sound could be called romantic (34). This is magnificent music; it has an ethereal, dreamlike nature.

Valen's life and music are both enigmatic and unique. He was indeed an ascetic; his upbringing, his convictions, and his philosophy had an inordinate influence on the development of his musical style. He did not receive much recognition during his lifetime, nor for that matter has his music made much headway since his death. Both facts are unfortunate, because he was an innovator and deserves to be ranked with the lions of early twentieth-century music, including Debussy, Schoenberg, Bartók, Stravinsky, Berg, and Hindemith. However, Valen came from a small country on the periphery of Europe. Although his geographic isolation hindered his music from being more widely heard, it provided the environment that facilitated his growth as a composer. Olav Gurvin calls him a pioneer in modern Norwegian music, and so he was. Valen challenged the very foundations of music and was not satisfied until he had come up with a system that could express that which was in his very soul.

One of Valen's friends, Sven-Eric Johanson, wrote a poem about how to listen to Valen's music (Thommessen), and I quote it here, in the original and in my own translation, in the hope that it will inspire others to listen to music that deserves to be heard:

> Molnkurvor
> En himmelsk metamorfos av linje
> efter linje, som händer mot solen.
> Stränger av rosgirlander spännas mot
> jorden, väntade eolsfingrars beröring.
> För ett ögonblick stannar tiden och lyssnar,
> djuren höra upp att beta
> och jordträlen rätar sin rygg i stum häpnad.
> Allt som växer håller andan, ja till och med
> de döda stenarna söker fånga ekot.
> Ty det var Gud själv
> som gick förbi.

> Clouds
> A divine metamorphosis of melody
> after melody like hands toward the sun.
> Strings of rose garlands stretch toward
> the earth, awaiting the touch of aeolian fingers.
> Time stops for a moment and listens,
> the animals stop grazing
> and the globe arches its back in silent amazement.
> Everything that grows holds its breath, even
> dead stones try to capture the echo.
> For God himself
> passed by.

## Notes

[1] See Gurvin, *Fartein Valen*, for biographical information. Olav Gurvin was a pupil of Fartein Valen before Gurvin's being appointed to the university chair of musicology in Oslo. Valen's third symphony (1946, pub. 1949) is dedicated to him.

[2] Sonata for Violin and Piano, op. 3, was finished in 1916.

[3] Gurvin, "Frå tonalitet." This, his dissertation, contains a good discussion of the development of Valen's musical style.

[4] A former school friend, Carsten Lea, introduced Valen to Hermann Helmholtz's *Die Lehre von den Toneempfindungen* (1863). Lea had calculated the various overtone possibilities and provided Valen with tables that aided his own harmonic studies.

## Works Cited

Dahlhaus, Carl. *Schoenberg and the New Music: Essays by Carl Dahlhaus*. Trans. Derrick Puffett and Alfred Clayton. Cambridge: Cambridge UP, 1987.

Gurvin, Olav. "Frå tonalitet til atonalitet." Diss. U of Oslo, 1938.

————. *Fartein Valen. En banebryter i nyere norsk musikk.* Drammen: Lyche, 1962.

Huldt-Nyström, Hampus. "Fartein Valen og hans tredje symfoni." *Nordisk Musikkultur* 1 (1952): 30-34.

Maegaard, Jan, and Arvid O. Vollsnes. CD. Liner notes, Fartein Valen. Symphony nos. 2 and 3. CDN 31001, Oslo, 1987. 4-8.

Sommerfeldt, Øystein. "På sporet av komponisten Fartein Valen. Atonale tonetrinn i Valevåg, sommeren 1948." *Ballade* 2.91 (1991): 45-55.

Thommessen, Olav Anton. Jacket's liner notes, Fartein Valen. Concerto for Violin and Orchestra, op. 37; *Epithalamion*, op. 19; Trio for Violin, Violoncello, and Piano, op. 5. Philips 6507 039, 1974.

Valen, Fartein. *Symphony No. 3.* Op. 41. Drammen [Norway]: Harald Lyche & Co's Musikkforlag, 1949.

Jeg blaaser med Tuten min egen Besked,
til Noter en lønskriftkode.
Og vær det til Himmels min Sjæl følger med
og finder sig ilende frem
    mellem Klode paa Klode.

Knut Hamsun, "Basun"
*Det vilde Kor*, 1904

IV. *Fin de Siècle*: The 1800s — In Scandinavian America

In Tribute to *Maridal* —

Like the musician, the painter, the poet, and the rest, the true lover of flowers is born, not made.

One blossom . . . breathes a glory of color into sense and spirit which is enough to kindle the dullest imagination.

Celia Thaxter, An Island Garden, 1894

Fig. IV.1

Childe Hassam, *In the Garden* (Celia Thaxter in Her Garden), 1892
Oil on canvas, 22 1/8 x 18 1/8 inches. National Museum of
American Art, Smithsonian Institution, Washington
Gift of John Gellatly
1929.6.52

# Celia Thaxter and the Norwegians of
# the Isles of Shoals

## Einar Haugen

THE ISLES OF SHOALS are a group of eight treeless islands off the New England coast, nine miles from Portsmouth, New Hampshire. According to Celia Thaxter (1835-93), their first poet, they are "stern, bleak, and unpromising" to "eyes that behold them for the first time" (*Among the Isles* 7).[1] But, she adds, there is also "a strange charm about them, an indescribable influence in their atmosphere."

There was much in the nature of the landscape that was reminiscent of the Norwegian west coast. Shortly after the end of the Civil War, Scandinavian settlers, especially Norwegians, discovered the Shoals. Celia Thaxter ends her account of the Isles in her book of 1873 with the following favorable observation:

> The slight sprinkling of inhabitants yet remaining on Smutty-nose and elsewhere, who seem inclined to make the place a permanent home, are principally Swedes and Norwegians; and a fine self-respecting race they are, so thrifty, cleanly, well-mannered, and generally excellent that one can hardly say enough in their praise. It is to be hoped that a little rill from the tide of emigration which yearly sets from those countries toward America may finally people the unoccupied portions of the Shoals with a colony that will be a credit to New England. (*Among the Isles* 184)

Before turning to Thaxter's much admired Scandinavians, one should first put in place some general historical background. Since the 1600s the Isles had been visited by assorted pirates, sailors, and fishermen, and by 1800 there were several small English settlements on their shallow soil. Local people referred to the Isles as the "Shoals" and the residents as "Shoalers." The lighthouse was needed because the Shoals lay directly in the course of ships' traffic down the New England coast, and the seas, which teemed with fish, could be rough, especially in winter. The Shoals were rocky, and winter storms were often ferocious. The charm of the Shoals kept Celia Thaxter there for much of her life. In 1839, when Celia was only four years old, her parents, Thomas and Eliza Laighton, had decided to accept a post as lighthouse keepers on White Island, at first as a temporary, but then as a longtime, residence. But Celia grew up to become a lover of the island nature, which was lush and adventure-filled for a young girl. Her book about the Shoals is largely devoted to descriptions of the beauty of its flora and fauna.

In 1847 the Laightons moved from the lighthouse to the curiously named Smutty-nose Island. Celia was then twelve, and her brothers, Cedric and Oscar, six and eight (Laighton 21).[2] The family built new buildings, chiefly with the idea of promoting fishing, but also of providing rooms to rent. Visitors began coming to the island. One of the most important was Levi Lincoln Thaxter, who arrived from Watertown in 1846. Levi was a Harvard Law-School graduate, with no taste for the law, but with a fascination for the Shoals. Thomas and Levi got along famously, and between them they conceived the idea of a summer hotel to be built on nearby Appledore Island, which had previously been known as Hog Island. As Oscar Laighton put it,

> Appledore is an island of nearly three hundred acres, clothed with bay and huckleberry bushes, wild roses, and endless vegetation. After White Island, of hardly two acres of bare rock, our new home seemed illimitable. . . . (Laighton 22)

The hotel became the Appledore House, which was opened for business in June of 1848, as the first summer resort in New England. Being within easy reach of Boston, it quickly became very popular among the prominent people of the region. Among the early guests were presidential candidate Franklin Pierce, poet James Russell Lowell, poet and reformer John G. Whittier, historian T. W. Higginson, as well as authors James T. Fields and Thomas Bailey Aldrich.[3]

In 1849 young Celia Laighton became engaged to the fifteen-year-older Levi Thaxter, over the strenuous objections of her father. Although at fifteen she enrolled in the Mt. Washington Female Seminary in South Boston, the two were married at Appledore in September 1851. After some years of flitting about, they returned to Appledore for the birth of their first child, Karl, who would be the first child born in the Shoals in more than a century. It was there that the author Nathaniel Hawthorne, who was a guest at the hotel, visited the Thaxters and partook of apple toddy in a group of young men and women who "all were very mirthful and jolly" (Hawthorne quoted in Rutledge 82).

But of all the visitors to the Shoals, Whittier, who lived not far away in Amesbury, Massachusetts, was the closest to the Thaxters. He encouraged Celia to write about the Shoals. Her first poem appeared in 1871, and her book about the Shoals was serialized in the *Atlantic Monthly*, appearing in book form two years later. She wrote to Whittier's biographer:

> His sympathy and interest in all I did were invaluable to me.... Our correspondence continued from the first year of his coming here through the whole thirty years. (Quoted in Rutledge 131)

Celia won recognition as a writer, and she conducted a kind of literary salon, with her flower garden as a center. Her husband did not share her interests, and they lived apart for long periods of time.

When, in 1866, Norwegians had begun to settle on the Shoals, the first to arrive had been Ingebret Ingebretsen and his son Julius, who came to Boston in 1866 (Gjerset 138). Here they were met by Christian Johnson, who worked on Smutty-nose and persuaded them to join in the fisheries. A year later Johnson's wife and younger children followed, and in 1869 they settled on Appledore Island. On Smutty-nose lived both Captain John C. Hontvedt, who owned and sailed a fishing schooner, and his brother Matthew. With them lived Even [or Ivan] Christensen from Larvik, his newly-wed wife, Annette [or Anethe], and his sisters, Karen and Maren, the latter of whom Captain Hontvedt married. Another family, Bernt Ingebretsen, his wife, Karen, and their children, who called themselves Berntsen after their father, also lived on the island for a time (Gjerset 138-39). A Ben Berntsen, possibly of the same family, settled with his wife and six children on Smutty-nose Island (Laighton 73-74).

Norwegian artists also made their way to the islands and stayed at Appledore House. Olaf M. Brauner from Christiania painted at Appledore for a time; he married Nikoline Berntsen; and in 1900 he became a professor of art at Cornell University. The most prominent Norwegian artist to visit the Shoals, however, was violin virtuoso Ole Bull (1810-80). His reason for coming was no doubt to rest up after a busy season of concerts. Bull often went to resorts for relaxation. Oscar Laighton was present on the occasion of Bull's visit and wrote,

> I remember how splendid Ole Bull appeared as he stood with his violin before the great gathering in our Music Room. He played divinely and the audience was delighted. (Laighton 74)

Bull was playing at a benefit to raise money to aid the Norwegian families on the islands. According to Laighton, "Three hundred and sixty-five dollars were realized for our Norwegian friends." Such a benefit was a frequent practice of Bull's.

We also have Whittier's testimony to Bull's presence at the Shoals in a letter to a friend, Annie Fields, written August 15, 1882, after Bull's death. He thanks her for letters from her and Sarah Orne Jewett describing a visit to Lysøen with Sara Thorp Bull:

> I enjoyed both letters — the pictures they gave of the Enchanted Island — a spot made forever memorable by the great genius of Ole Bull.... (Whittier 3: 460)[4]

Neither of these sources dates Bull's visit, but it seems probable that it was in 1869, just after Bull had appeared at the Boston Peace Jubilee, designed to celebrate the end of the Civil War. It was an enormous festival, at which Bull functioned as the concert master of an orchestra of 1,094 players.

The hope expressed by Celia Thaxter for a permanent colony of Norwegians was not to be realized, and one might say that such a hope was dealt a cruel blow with a tragic event in the same year as her book was published. In 1873, a German immigrant named Louis Wagner, who had joined in the fisheries and had been befriended by the Norwegian colonists, met three of the men from Smutty-nose in Portsmouth on March 5, 1873. He learned that the men would not be able to return to the Shoals that day. In the night he made an excursion to Smutty-nose with the intent of robbing the Christensen family. He was unexpectedly startled by the barking of the family's dog and in his frenzy proceeded to murder Annette and Karen Christensen, left unattended on the island. Karen's sister, Maren, escaped in her nightgown into the snowy winter and hid in a niche on the island. In the morning she managed to attract the attention of the Ingebretsen children, and she was quickly rescued and brought to Appledore. The murderer managed to escape and catch a train to Boston but was caught before taking a ship to England. In spite of a threatening mob that wanted to execute him on the spot, he was not hanged until April 17.

Two years later Celia Thaxter published the story of the murder in the *Atlantic Monthly* under the title "A Memorable Murder," a dramatic account that attracted wide attention. According to Lyman V. Rutledge,

> both author and publisher were criticized at the time for desecrating the pristine pages of the *Atlantic* with the vivid narration of this horrible crime, "using the names of real people." (Rutledge 103)

But the critic Laurence Hutton, in *Talks in a Library* (1905), called it "one of the strongest pieces of prose in the English language" (quoted in Rutledge 104).

Even Christensen worked for Celia Thaxter for a year after the murder and gradually recovered from its terror. Then he married Valborg, a daughter of Jacob Abrahamsen Moss, from Drammen, Norway, a widower who from 1873 or 1874 had made his home with the Ingebretsens. They moved to St. John's, New Brunswick, where he worked as a carpenter and a cabinetmaker, later settling in Boston. One of their daughters married Professor Ingebret Dørrum of Luther College in Decorah, Iowa. Their other children stayed in the Boston area. Captain John C. Hontvedt continued to sail. His last vessel, the *Mary S. Hontvedt*, foundered in 1895, after which the captain retired and made his home in Portsmouth, New Hampshire (Gjerset 141).

Nothing seems to have remained of the Norwegian colony in the Shoals. The Thaxters died in 1884 and 1894, and the Appledore House burned to the ground in 1914. Although a hotel on Star Island had been built by John

Poor in 1873, it had soon been taken over by the Laightons. In 1897 Thomas H. Elliott of Lowell, Massachusetts founded a nondenominational (Unitarian and Congregational) conference that was held there each year, at least until 1960.

About the people caught up in the tragedy, Celia wrote that

> they were all Norwegians. The more I see of the natives of this far-off land, the more I admire the fine qualities which seem to characterize them as a race. Gentle, faithful, intelligent, God-fearing human beings, they daily use such courtesy toward each other and all who come in contact with them, as puts our ruder Yankee manners to shame. The men and women living on this lonely island were like the sweet, honest, simple folk we read of in Bjørnson's stories, full of kindly thoughts and ways. The murdered Anethe might have been the Eli of Bjørnson's *Arne*.... The Norwegians are an exceptionally affectionate people; family ties are very strong and precious among them. (*Atlantic Monthly* 35: 602)

Celia Thaxter continued to publish. *An Island Garden* appeared just before her death in 1894. It has recently been reprinted with an informative introduction by Allen Lacy. Lacy observes that, after the notable Appledore House burned down in 1914,

> The island fell on bad times. The U.S. Navy used it for many years as a target range for cannon-fire.... Thaxter's garden lived on only in the pages of her book — and in [Childe] Hassam's paintings. But the story of this fabled garden has a happy ending. There is now an outpost of Cornell University on Appledore, and its director in 1978, Professor John Kingsbury, undertook to restore the garden Celia Thaxter had made, using the plans in her book. Today the garden is lovingly tended from early spring until late fall by Virginia Chisholm of Rye Beach, New Hampshire. There is regular boat service from Portsmouth to Star Island.... On request, the marine station will fetch visitors from Star Island in a whaleboat and make the choppy crossing to Appledore. Here, in a cleared area in front of the old foundations of Celia Thaxter's summer cottage, stands the replica of her garden, bright and beautiful with the same flowers she planted and celebrated in *An Island Garden*. (xiv)

Celia said about her flowers that the successful gardener had to have

> an ineffable something that will be missing if you do not love them, a delicate glory too spiritual to be caught and put into words. The Norwegians have a pretty and significant word, "Opelske," which they use in speaking of the care of flowers. It means literally "loving up," of cherishing them into health and vigor. (*An Island Garden* 5)

The word is indeed a well-known Norwegian word (now "oppelske"), which can be translated as "cherish, foster, nurture." One wonders if Celia Thaxter might even have heard it from Ole Bull when he stayed at Appledore and played his benefit on behalf of its Norwegian immigrants? Perhaps years after his death serendipity did its mysterious work.

## Notes

[1] On Celia Thaxter see James, under her name. I owe thanks to Gloria Nielsen Esharte, who first called my attention to the Isles of Shoals, and to Carla Wengren Ricci, who sent me a copy of the Lawson review of Thaxter's 1894 book.

[2] More accurate figures are found in Rutledge.

[3] A roster of the more important visitors is in Rutledge (175-84).

[4] A footnote (3: 462) states that Whittier met Ole Bull at Appledore House.

## Works Cited

Gjerset, Knut. *Norwegian Sailors in American Waters*. Northfield, MN: Norwegian-American Historical Association, St. Olaf College, 1933.

James, Edward T., et al. *Notable American Women 1607-1950: A Biographical Dictionary*. Cambridge: Harvard UP, 1971.

Laighton, Oscar. *Ninety Years at the Isles of Shoals*. Boston: Beacon Press, 1930.

Lawson, Elizabeth. Rev. of *An Island Garden*, by Celia Thaxter. In *Fine Gardening* [Newtown, CT] 1 (1990): 12-14.

Rutledge, Lymon V. *The Isles of Shoals in Lore and Legend*. Barre, MA: Barre Publishers, 1965.

Thaxter, Celia. *Among the Isles of Shoals*. 1873. Rpt. Boston/New York: Houghton Mifflin, 1901.

——. *An Island Garden*. 1894. Rpt. Boston: Houghton Mifflin, 1988.

——. "A Memorable Murder." *Atlantic Monthly*. 35 (1875): 602-16.

Whittier, John Greenleaf. *Letters of John Greenleaf Whittier*. Ed. John B. Pickard. Vol. 3. Cambridge: Harvard UP, 1975. 3 vols.

Fig. IV.2

Childe Hassam, *Isles of Shoals*, c. 1890
Oil on canvas, 15 1/2 x 17 3/4 inches. Signed, lower right
Collection of Mr. and Mrs. Merton Shapiro
Courtesy of Graham Gallery, New York

# Norwegian-American Mutuality in the Iron Decade: "Nordlyset" of Chicago

## Odd S. Lovoll

"THIS SOCIETY'S PURPOSE shall be mutual aid in case of sickness and death," the constitution of the Norwegian Sick Benefit Society "Nordlyset" of Chicago stated simply in paragraph two ("Den norske Sygeforening 'Nordlysets' Love" — hereafter NSNL). Furthermore, at the first general meeting in May 1893, it was resolved as a second aim "to promote enlightenment and sociability through meetings, lectures, books, and newspapers" ("Record af Den norske Sygeforening 'Nordlyset'" — hereafter RNSN). The society was an immigrant expression of what the social theorist Anthony Oberschall has called the associational mode of solidarity, which replaced the traditional communal benevolence of rural life and the bonds and succor of large extended families as these disintegrated. Such societies as Nordlyset flourished toward the end of the nineteenth century. They were in fact the most common form of immigrant organization; they responded to the needs, uncertainties, and demands people encountered in an unfamiliar and perilous urban and industrialized environment. Their emphasis was on mutuality, benefit functions, and — frequently — male camaraderie. Organizational structures and ritualistic practices in secret societies and voluntary associations, as well as their social and cultural objectives, owed much to American fraternalism and system of lodges.[1]

What will be considered here is the intimate fellowship and internal proceedings of one particular society, Nordlyset. Its place in the Norwegian community in Chicago provides entrance into the urban immigrant experience in general during the years around the turn of the century. Preliminary steps to organize the Norwegian Sick Benefit Society "Nordlyset," originally as a branch of the fraternal order of the S.W.A. or Scandinavian Workers Association of America (Den skandinaviske Arbeiderforening af Amerika), were taken at a meeting at Scandia Hall, January 22, 1893, on the initiative of the officers of the latter organization. It became Nordlyset, Branch No. 10, one of S.W.A.'s several units in Chicago; it was located in the Norwegian neighborhoods centering on Milwaukee and Grand Avenues (the latter then Indiana Street) on the West Side. As its first regular meeting site, Nordlyset rented Staubs Hall on the corner of Milwaukee and Racine Avenues (the latter then Center), in the heart of the Norwegian "Milwaukee Avenue" colony.[2]

Scandia Hall, the building of the Scandinavian Workers Association, lay just a few blocks further south, on the corner of Milwaukee Avenue and Ohio Street. The opening of the fraternity's own structure on March 12, 1891, was, according to Chicago's Norwegian-language newspaper *Skandinaven*, celebrated not only by the Norwegian, but by the entire Scandinavian colony in that city. Open to all Scandinavians, S.W.A.'s foremost, though not exclusive, appeal was nevertheless to a Norwegian membership. Its hall, situated in a district with a heavily concentrated Norwegian-American population, was for some time even beyond the dissolution of S.W.A. in the mid-1890s an important social and cultural center, used for theater performances and lodge meetings, and it had its own restaurant. The ornate architecture and lofty dimensions of Scandia Hall gave evidence of the renewed vitality and growth of S.W.A. after 1886, when it expanded into offering life insurance and began organizing branches in Illinois and Wisconsin. Fraternal benefit societies, which provided life insurance for their members in large predetermined amounts, became an important part of the American fraternal movement during the final quarter of the century. The Scandinavian Workers Association consequently simply emulated a pronounced trend in American fraternalism. It had emerged in the Scandinavian community in Chicago in June 1870, as a paternalistic venture by people outside the working class who desired to exercise social control by educating and influencing the common laborers of their own nationality. It was not unlike the many "arbeidersamfunn" (workers' societies) organized by middle-class benefactors in Norwegian urban areas in the 1860s and 1870s, and like them exhibited, albeit in an immigrant setting, a rising social consciousness; S.W.A. had sick and funeral funds from its inception. Not a single Scandinavian-American workingman, however, sat in its leadership. Internal controversy reduced membership until the 1880s, when S.W.A. gained popularity with the many newcomers arriving in Chicago from Scandinavia and attracted a young leadership. By the time of its transformation into a fraternal life insurance society in 1886, it had lost much of its initial middle-class paternalism and attracted about six-hundred members, mainly men in solid working-class occupations, but also white-collar workers and professionals.[3]

The closing years of the nineteenth century, because of their perceived wickedness, selfishness, and degeneracy, earned the epithet "the Iron Decade," echoing the final iron age of classical mythology. The decade began on a promising note, except of course for the civic-minded people concerned with moral uplift, who represented the strong reform spirit of the era. In Chicago vice and corruption flourished, prompting urban moralists like William T. Stead to take direct action; he orchestrated the event that led to the formation of the Chicago Civic Federation in November 1893. Stead's moral tract *If Christ Came to Chicago* (1894) directed its attacks against the ubiquitous saloons and brothels in the city, but it also concerned itself with the prevalent political wrongdoing of profiteers and corrupt city officials. Most people were, however, more concerned with the prosperity of the early 1890s and the prospects and excitement surrounding the World's Columbian Exposition in 1893. But economic reality quickly changed public attitude from one of optimism to one of despair. When the "White City," as the fair was called, closed at the end of October, a bleak winter replaced the euphoria it had engendered. Already then the early shock waves were being felt of the "Panic of 1893," a financial crisis and beginning industrial depression. The journal *Public Opinion* in 1894 noted the despair of the nation, its industrial structure paralyzed. Wages were lowered and three million demoralized workers were reduced to idleness. It was a decade of national discontent. Economic recovery did not take hold until just before the end of the century.[4]

Nevertheless, regardless of hard times and deepening economic woes, the Norwegian colony in Chicago from all appearances achieved maturity during those troubled years. That judgment can be made even though the depression manifestly adversely affected ethnic organizational and cultural life. There were obvious victims; and there were counterforces. Advances and growth were most clearly evident in charitable and benevolent endeavors. An example is the much heightened activity of the Norwegian Relief Association or "Relief'en" (Den norske Hjælpeforening), which had been organized in 1886 "to give deserving countrymen, who are placed in temporary need, a helping hand" (*Skandinaven* Dec. 6, 1893). Developments on this front gave credence to the supposition that during periods of hardship ethnic groups pull together and mount relief efforts; such efforts in turn promoted social interaction, public events, and a sense of community. The Relief Association raised funds by arranging "evening entertainments" to aid needy Norwegians in Chicago. Several benevolent institutions gained permanence. By 1900 they served a Norwegian-American population of 41,551, counting the first and second generations. Those with one or both parents born in Norway numbered 19,546. The Norwegian-born group had not expanded much since 1890; the depression had caused an extreme drop in immigration. On the other hand there were about 9,000 more in the American-born category. Obviously, many were migrants from Chicago's hinterland, but the increase is also evidence of greater family life and a sign of a maturing community. The move to the Wicker Park and Humboldt Park neighborhoods, which had begun shortly after the Great Fire of 1871, intensified. By the beginning of the new century the latter district became, at the expense of the diminishing importance of the Milwaukee Avenue neighborhood, "the great Norwegian center."[5]

The decade saw the firm establishment of such benevolent institutions as the Norwegian Lutheran Tabitha Hospital,[6] the Lutheran Deaconess Home and Hospital, an orphanage for poor and neglected children, and a home for the aged — where deserving indigent compatriots as well as those willing and able to pay would receive care. These many efforts "to show Christian charity among the Norwegian people" (Lovoll 218), were expressions of the social role of the church. Bazaars, lawn parties, fund-raising efforts, donations, and a network of support groups secured the operation of these institutions. Originating in the mission of the church, they appealed to the entire immigrant community on the basis of a common nationality. Leading men and women, taking their cue from Americans in similar social positions during this heyday of the charity organization movement, assured the fiscal solvency and growth of benevolent institutions. It was frequently wives of men from this level of the Norwegian-American community who played a leading role in charitable activities. Showing solidarity with their compatriots in more ordinary or even impecunious circumstances, prosperous Norwegian Americans nevertheless identified with an emerging American middle class, as defined by Robert H. Wiebe in his *The Search for Order* (1967), and were people like the banker Paul O. Stensland; like medical doctors Niles T. Quales and Ingeborg Rasmussen, the latter illustrating the new professional opportunities for women; and like industrialist Andrew P. Johnson of the Johnson Chair Company. There was as well an imported elite of Norwegian-trained architects and engineers, men like Joachim G. Giaver, who won prominence as assistant chief engineer at the World's Fair. The arrival of men with technical skills, an aristocracy among the immigrants, further exposed cleavages, which were accentuated during the depression of the 1890s, within the Norwegian-American social world in Chicago.[7]

Nearly all immigrant organizations in the city, secular as well as religious, and whether or not it was their primary function, provided assistance to their members when need arose. The practice reflected the severe reality of urban life. Societies organized specifically for mutual assistance were in a certain sense merely an institutionalization of traditional concepts evident in social situations experienced in the homeland. The Order of the Knights of the White Cross (Ordenen af Riddere af det Hvide Kors) began as the Nora Society in 1862, but already by the following year was transformed into an order along Masonic lines, with a supreme lodge and sublodges, Nora becoming lodge number one. Nationalistic and strongly secular, it assembled men from the budding commercial and professional elite. They became *knights*, and though displaying ethnic unity, placed a distance between themselves and working-class Norwegian Americans. From 1886 on, in the manner of the S.W.A. imitating American fraternalism, the Order changed to a mutual insurance society and moved its headquarters to Milwaukee. Its original lodge, Nora Lodge No. 1, "old Nora," as Chicago Norwegians called it, with its own lodge hall in the Milwaukee Avenue neighborhood on Ohio and Green Streets, continued to play a central role in Norwegian immigrant life. It persisted as a purely Norwegian lodge even after the Knights of the White Cross abandoned Norwegian membership qualifications; after 1881 the Order permitted national or mixed Scandinavian sublodges. Nora gave attention to the Norwegian cultural and historical heritage and gained great popularity, losing much of the extreme exclusivity of its early history, though maintaining preeminence among the four Chicago lodges of the Order. The other three were also nationalistic, designated as Leif Erikson, Tordenskjold, and Dovre, and organized to assemble men who had settled in the new Norwegian neighborhoods to the west and north. In the 1890s various societies vied for an elitist membership and a position of prominence within the immigrant community; a number of the groups were professional associations. But there were also elitist social organizations, such as the Norwegian Quartet Club formed in the mid-1890s; these same professionals and specialists, who according to Wiebe exemplified the new middle class, met there and in similar settings to cultivate an elegant social life reminiscent of customs and practices in comparable social circles in Norway. Still, Nora had established, and continued to maintain, a model for culture and learning and for immigrant fraternal organization.[8]

During the early 1890s the Scandinavian Workers Association competed with considerable success with the Knights of the White Cross as the prime secular ethnic institution. The association's name identified its broad social appeal to all working people. It soon became a casualty of several adverse circumstances, some of them predictable: not anticipating the depression, it had overextended resources; and there were accusations of mismanagement; but also a "problematic" Norwegian patriotism, fueled by the escalating conflict over the union between Norway and Sweden, became a factor in S.W.A.'s demise. Indicative of the inner dissent and fiscal grief was the withdrawal in late 1893 of the S.W.A. branch in Eau Claire, Wisconsin, Norden No. 8, founded in 1889.[9] Nordlyset, organized as Branch 10 earlier in 1893, resolved unanimously (see RNSN) on August 16, 1894, "to withdraw from the central administration" and to have its delegate "recalled . . . and released from all commitments he might have made to the central administration." Low morale, acrimonious exchanges, and a decline in interest accompanied these moves. Several of S.W.A.'s branches discontinued all activity. Nordlyset's attendance suffered to the extent that a merger with other lodges seemed to be a logical step. Serious consideration was given to merging with Branch 1 of S.W.A., the original society from 1870, which carried on after the discontinuance of S.W.A. Instead, following the severance from the Scandinavian Workers Association, it joined as Nordlyset Branch 1 a new mutual insurance society; "Grand Logen," as Nordlyset referred to it in its minutes, took the name the United Scandinavians of America (U.S.A.). This attempt to organize a successor to S.W.A., in spite of its striking initials, was a disappointing and short-lived experiment. U.S.A. soon fell into disfavor and passed by the board. On June 4, 1895, Nordlyset severed all ties and, on July 25, met in the home of Olai Höitomt, a fireman, and organized as an independent lodge, the following year receiving its charter from the State of Illinois. Its decision necessitated a discontinuation of offering life insurance; its membership was less than fifty, and, at its height in 1929, only 179. As a small society with the limited goal of providing sick and funeral benefits, Nordlyset was nearly an anachronism when it was brought to an end in 1944, and long before then it had in reality been superseded by large fraternal life insurance companies.[10]

In 1895, appearing as an independent Norwegian lodge, Nordlyset limited its membership to "any man of Norwegian birth or ancestry, healthy in body and soul, and not engaged in unseemly business" (RNSN Jan. 4, 1898). It pointedly excluded other Scandinavians, most specifically Swedes, as the conflict between the two homelands waxed and waned until the final dissolution of the union in 1905. Patriotic passions were inflamed and produced similar discrimination in other Norwegian immigrant societies and clubs. The Norwegian-American Gymnastic Union (Det norsk-ameri-kanske Turnforbund), formed in Chicago in 1893 and the beginning of a major institutional growth in Norwegian athletic activity, decided that, "as the turners are patriotic Norwegians who do not wish any mixing," Danish and, under the circumstances, surely Swedish turners would have no place there (Lovoll 135). The membership of Nordlyset had likewise been nearly all Norwegian from its start that same year, in spite of its larger Scandina-vian affiliation, and after 1895 would be exclusively so (Lovoll 255).

Forty men qualified as charter members of the original society. Their average age is surprisingly high, in the mid-thirties, and again reflects the seriousness both of the situation and of their purpose. Fourteen were in the age range of 21 to 29, thirteen between 30 and 39, and thirteen between 40 and 49. The greater risk of insuring older members dictated age limits of 18 to 45, later expanded to 50. The S.W.A. recommended a category of "social members" for men who were uninsurable. Exceptions were made, as — for instance — with Magnus Jensen, "a few months past fifty," when the examining physician approved and a sponsor attested that he "was well and strong and had never been sick" (RNSN Mar. 1, 1893). There was a broad spread in occupations. Twenty-seven may be considered to have been blue-collar workers, including a day laborer and a sailor, two tailors, a baker, a butcher, and a fireman, with the remainder working as carpen-ters, furniture-makers, painters, and machinists and thus reflecting com-mon pursuits for Norwegian-American men. The white-collar category numbered ten members, and these men were clerks, druggists, a detective, and a bar inspector. Considering the moralistic tone of Nordlyset's consti-tution, reminiscent of the language of urban reformers of that day, one finds it unexpected to discover two saloonkeepers and one bartender as mem-bers. Paragraph four specifically disallowed sick payments to men who "directly or indirectly had acquired venereal disease through debauchery and use of alcohol, or for accidents incurred while intoxicated" (NSNL). The first president of the society, Ole A. Hedvig, was listed in the respectable and common occupation of "machinist."[11]

A civil engineer and two young physicians, Anthony Christensen, twenty-nine, and Thor Warloe, twenty-six, joined Nordlyset as charter members. Nordlyset, like other beneficiary societies, required a physical examination prior to admission, and sick benefit payments were subject to a physician's approval. In addition to income from these services, the lodge was an important way for doctors to recruit patients. Such opportunities were especially of consequence to young doctors starting out in practice. As Mary Ann Clawson states it, "the usual quid pro quo was that the doctor had to lend his prestige and standing to the lodge by becoming a member" (214-15). Apparently in the case of Nordlyset the two men's expectations were not met, as both men eventually resigned, and only Dr. Warloe functioned for a period of time as the examining physician.[12]

In true fraternal fashion members addressed each other as "brothers," and after 1895, when it became an independent lodge, Nordlyset expanded its membership. Some, like its initial president, Ole Hedvig, who had left during the time of dispute, rejoined. The new president, Olai Höitomt, and secretary, John H. Haugen — listed as an upholsterer — were both charter members of the original society. They were joined by Jens Höitomt, age twenty-three and a piano-maker, who was admitted to membership in August 1895 and shortly afterward elected to serve as marshal and later as president. These men, all in respectable, but common, occupational pursuits, became a leading force in the enterprise. The marshal had important functions at the ceremonial rituals associated with the acceptance of new members; as a secret society with a password, Nordlyset required an inner guard and an outer guard to protect the inviolability of its deliberations. A member who had forgotten the password, which of course shifted, was admitted to the proceedings of the society only after having presented himself to the vice-president. The strict adherence to the formality of secret orders, even in a small society like Nordlyset, where everyone presumably knew one another, bears witness to the appeal of fraternal practices and the significance members placed on ritual and ceremony and the use of official emblems and regalia. "Lodge night" satisfied social needs and a desire to rise above the mundane demands of everyday life.[13]

The greater reality of the brotherhood to its membership nevertheless lay in its material benefits. Care was consequently exercised before admitting new members; candidates recommended by the examining physician were voted on by members casting white balls in favor of, and black in opposition to, admission. An installation fee of $2.00 and dues of 50 cents monthly were continued after 1895, with special assessments for, and contributions to, the funeral fund; sick payments were prorated at $6.00 weekly for a maximum of thirteen weeks. Extension of payment was not uncommon, though apparently contingent upon a member's standing. At the meeting on March 15, 1894, Nordlyset granted "Brother [Louis] Olson reprieve with payment of two assessments and two months' dues" (RNSN). Olson was a carpenter by trade and during the hard times suffered unemployment as well as illness in the family. He had once earlier received a postponement and "had paid punctually." The brothers therefore approved his request unanimously. On the other hand, the brothers had earlier suspended C. Field, who also, because of a lack of work, was in arrears to the society.[14]

When the brothers were informed, however, of the straitened circumstances in which their fellow member Nils Olsen found himself, they not only gave him reprieve, "because it was an impossibility for him to pay," but also recommended that a collection should be taken "to help him out of his difficulty" (RNSN Nov. 3, 1896). In April 1897, "Brother Swanson," who was "in a very hard situation," received $7.50 through a collection taken among the brothers (RNSN Apr. 20, 1897). The concise lodge minutes provide no further particulars beyond the obvious mutuality evidenced by the acts themselves.

In word and deed the members were expected to treat fellow members with fraternal respect and, as stated in the constitution (RNSN May 22, 1893), "not in any manner speak badly of or slander one another," but demonstrate "a worthy conduct outside as well as inside the society." Furthermore, "any member who has fulfilled his obligations to the society and who presents a certificate of illness from a capable physician and the sick benefit committee [to the effect] that the illness was not contracted through debauchery will enjoy sick support." That benefit, phrased in moralistic terms, was understandably the most common direct aid. The ability of the treasury of Nordlyset to sustain it was, however, always in some doubt. Its sick benefit fund mostly hovered around $50.00; the precise amount when it organized independently was $40.21. It would require only a minor disaster or epidemic to deplete the fund entirely; but payments were seemingly made automatically to members who qualified. At its meeting on February 15, 1894 (RNSN), for instance, it was resolved to give Brother Ole Nielsen benefits for two weeks, and on March 1, an additional one-and-a-half weeks were granted him, for a total of $21.00, or about 40 percent of the entire fund. Nielsen, who was a carpenter, was himself present at the last meeting, "nearly well again from an axe cut in one foot" (RNSN Jan. 5, 1898). Not withstanding this drain on scarce resources, on July 6, the same year, Brother Sigurd Friedrichs, a painter, received two weeks of sick leave benefits. The treasury — sick and funeral funds — improved, mainly through the regular payment of dues and assessments, so that by July 1898, it stood at a total of $204.80, of which $45.00 belonged to the funeral fund, yet to be drawn on.[15]

A "stag party," as the minutes of May 4, 1898 (RNSN) referred to the event, which was arranged for that same month to promote sociability and to attract new members, disclosed the surfacing of tensions even within a society dedicated to brotherly harmony. The expense of "the little party," which appears to have been a success, was $11.78, including $1.00 for printing two- hundred tickets, $1.28 for lunch, and $9.50 in liqueurs and cigars (RNSN June 1, 1898). As recorded by the secretary himself, Brother H. Olsen, a member's complaint at a subsequent meeting of Nordlyset, of not knowing about the party, gave Olai Höitomt, "with his big mouth," an opportunity to criticize Olsen "in as coarse a manner as possible." He, according to Olsen, "immediately jumped up like a deranged person," claiming that "it was sad when people accepted offices for which they did not qualify" (RNSN June 15, 1898). Olsen left Nordlyset, and at the next meeting his minutes were not approved, with the comment by several, including John H. Haugen, who functioned as temporary secretary, that "personal feuds should not be entered into the protocol" (RNSN July 6, 1898).

Olai Höitomt had by this time moved to California Avenue by Humboldt Park, the emerging "Little Norway," and changed his occupation from fireman to that of manager of a chocolate and cigar store there. Within Nordlyset he was of course one of the founding fathers, though in 1898 still in his mid-thirties, and perhaps, as some of the newer members claimed about many of the originators, he had assumed a nearly proprietary attitude. Nordlyset had itself moved most of its meetings to the Odd Fellows Hall farther west on Chicago Avenue, as a consequence of the pattern of movement in the Norwegian community. People in the new Norwegian-American clusterings in the Wicker Park and Humboldt Park areas in time adopted a superior attitude toward those who remained in the decaying and crowded Milwaukee Avenue district, an attitude that indicated the increasing stability and status of the new neighborhoods. As reported in the minutes, however, the social events arranged by Nordlyset through the years produced minimal discord. Most were designed to include the men's families, picnics at which children were welcome and dances, always designated as balls, to which wives and women friends were invited; or Nordlyset participated in public celebrations of May 17th, Syttende Mai, Norway's Constitution Day. In 1899, for instance, the society joined the charitable efforts of the Tabitha Hospital (later called the Norwegian-American Hospital) to commemorate

Norway's great day in a manner that will do honor to all Norwegians and at the same time with the noble goal of assisting the less fortunate of our countrymen. (RNSN Mar. 21, 1899)

It was a popular May 17th festival at the impressive Chicago Auditorium for the benefit of the hospital, with "the participation of all Norwegian societies in Chicago." It led directly two months later to the formation of the Norwegian National League, a union of member organizations, which, from 1900 on, arranged May 17th festivals and coordinated other concerted actions. These advancements were again the indices of a maturing and self-confident Norwegian-American subculture (Lovoll 241).

Ad hoc committees served when an "Entertainment," as the secretary recorded it, was deemed desirable. Only later did someone settle on the rather unusual Norwegian equivalent "Fornöielseskommité," or "Amusement Committee," if translated directly. The minutes are in fact sprinkled liberally throughout with Americanisms — and English terminology. Fraternalism was plainly a part of the American experience of the members of Nordlyset and not a transplant from Norway. They did not belong to the classes that would have taken part in Masonic practices before emigrating, and consequently their concepts and idioms expressed an American fraternal tradition. The mixed English-Norwegian usage and the unusual orthography of both Norwegian and English words in their recorded transactions bring to light the limited formal education of the society's members and the cultural and social environment created by in the Norwegian community in Chicago.[16]

Christmas balls and entertainments, regular features of secular societies, were among the most applauded events. In 1899, Nordlyset rented Nora Hall, which continued to be in use by Nora Lodge No. 1 of the Knights of the White Cross, for such an event, at a cost of $20.00 for the facilities and music. An invitation to join the Order as a sublodge and the consequent advantages had been considered in late 1897, but rejected on a motion that the question be dropped. Favoring an independent status did not, however, prevent extensive interaction with compatible organizations. The brothers favored participating in the Knights' "PicNic" in June 1901, to which they had been invited, and they reciprocated with similar cordial offers. For paid events, a few complimentary tickets with an invitation to purchase more were regularly exchanged with other groups. Nordlyset cultivated a wide array of relations with other lodges and relief societies, singing societies — like Bjorgvin and Normennenes — and received "Kamp-Tickets" (competition tickets) from the Norwegian turners, as well as to a concert and ball arranged by the Minnehaha Temperance Club. The brothers also gave support to the Leif Erikson Monument Society and participated in the unveiling of the statue of the Norse discoverer in Humboldt Park on October 12, 1901, a major symbolic and historical moment for Chicago Norwegians. The strength of fraternalism and the vitality of the secular urban associational movement in general, though not necessarily opposed to organized religion, gave a base for urban Norwegian Americans outside the framework of the church.[17]

An essential social network was built that gave emotional and material security. Nordlyset persisted in providing sick benefits to members who legitimately qualified. A sick benefit committee consisting of three elected brothers visited the ailing member to determine eligibility; the visitors were a source of comfort to him, and they reported to the assembled group on his illness and recovery. A sense of belonging to an extended family was thereby clearly established. Not until 1902, at the death of Brother Henry Johnson, did Nordlyset have to draw on its funeral fund. By that time the society felt sufficiently mighty to require that its examining physician should be a member. Dr. William Hanshus, age thirty, joined in return for the boon his association with Nordlyset would be to his medical practice.[18]

In 1898, serious thought was given to possible funeral arrangements, and Nordlyset decided to purchase "some kind of badges for pallbearers in case of a member's death" (Oct. 19). The concern and solicitude of the brothers during Brother Johnson's prolonged illness and death are clearly recorded in the society's minutes. He was admitted to the hospital for the insane at Kankakee in December 1900 and lingered there throughout 1901 and until his death in August 1902. His sick benefits were obviously exhausted, but extra assistance was forthcoming, and the brothers paid regular visits. In March 1901, the members of the sick benefit committee received reimbursement for fourteen trips to the hospital by streetcar at 10 cents per round trip. In September of the same year President Jens Höitomt reported that "Brother Johnson ate and slept but no longer spoke to anyone" (RNSN Sept. 15, 1901). His deteriorating condition was described as "hopeless" on July 16, 1902 (RNSN). At his funeral, on September 1 at Mount Olive Cemetery, a Norwegian burial place on the Northwest Side of Chicago, there was full participation by the brothers. His widow, Anne Marie Johnson, received $47.00 in death benefits and the society's deep condolences. Nordlyset's charter was draped in black for a period of three months, and a eulogy to the departed brother was inserted in Norwegian-American newspapers and a resolution entered into the minutes with a copy to the widow. The latter stated,

> Be it resolved that it is only simple justice toward the memory of the deceased to say that we grieve for a brother who in all respects was worthy of our brotherhood and our esteem. (Sept. 19, 1902)

The fraternal idea was eloquently and poignantly expressed in those words. They reveal the means by which some immigrants adjusted, sought security, and prevailed at a particular time and under difficult circumstances in their American experience.[19]

## Notes

[1] The NSNL and RNSN are in the archives of the Norwegian-American Historical Association (NAHA); see also Clawson (211), who discusses Anthony Oberschall's views on social conflicts and movements. See Oberschall as well.
All translations of the above-mentioned laws and records are by the author.

[2] RNSN Jan. 22, Feb. 15, 1893; *Skandinaven*, an undated clipping from 1938 in the "Nordlyset" Collection; see also Lovoll, 139-44.

[3] Clawson 221; Lovoll 166-67, 208, 260, 262. *Skandinaven* (June 17, 1896) contained a report on the 26th anniversary festivities of Branch No. 1 of S.W.A., which continued after the dissolution of the grand lodge. *Norden* (June 16, 1894) reported on S.W.A.'s 24th anniversary. The first society of Norwegian workers was organized in Christiania in 1864 by the pioneer sociologist Eilert Sundt in order to protect the common laborer against "pernicious influence" and to enlighten him. See both Sundt and H. O. Christophersen.

[4] See Boyer 184-87; Lindsey 1, citing the *Public Opinion*; and Lovoll 184-85, 188.

[5] See Lovoll 145-49, 210, 229; *Skandinaven* Dec. 6, 1893; *Norden* Nov. 10, 24, Dec. 8, 1894.

[6] In 1910 the hospital became a nonsectarian institution; its current name is the Norwegian-American Hospital.

[7] A second home for the aged and a children's home-finding society gained permanence after the turn of the century. For a discussion of these developments, see Lovoll 212-21. See also the Wiebe chapter titled "A New Middle Class," 111-32.

[8] Lovoll 87-89, 130, 205-06, 258. The Order of the Knights of the White Cross eventually had thirty-five men's lodges, and, starting in 1911, six women's lodges were introduced throughout the Upper Midwest.

[9] The S.W.A. branch Norden, after its withdrawal, organized the Independent Scandinavian Workers Association and operated as a mutual insurance company with branches throughout the states of the Upper Midwest. The idea to organize the Sons of Norway in Minneapolis in 1895 most likely came from Eau Claire.

[10] RNSN June 21, July 5, Aug. 2, 16, 30, Sept. 20, Oct. 24, 1894; and May 7, 21, and June 4, 1895; Charter, dated Apr. 13, 1896; and Articles of Dissolution, dated Feb. 29, 1944, in "Nordlyset" Collection; in same collection clipping from *Skandinaven*, 1937.

[11] Also see RNSN Mar. 1, 13, 1893; Mar. 18, 1894; Aug. 18, Oct. 6, 1896.

[12] RNSN Mar. 1, Dec. 20, 1893.

[13] NSNL; RNSN Oct. 24, 1894; Aug. 6, Sept. 3, Dec. 17, 1895; Aug. 18, 1896; Lovoll 209.

[14] See RNSN Aug. 28, Nov. 2, 1893.

[15] The original constitution was retained throughout the society's history with amendments and minor revisions. See also RNSN Aug. 30, Dec. 12, 1894; Jan. 15, Apr. 2, July 30, 1895.

[16] RNSN Feb. 13, Nov. 2, 1893. Examples of English-influenced, frequently misspelled usage would be: "i god standing," "aprovel," "blodpoisen," "application," "blanks," "kjarter," "fri car fare."

[17] RNSN Sept. 15, Oct. 6, Nov. 3, 1897; May 21, July 16, Aug. 6, 20, Sept. 3, Oct. 1, 15, 1901.

[18] RNSN May 6, 21, Sept. 3, 1902.

[19] See also RNSN Jan. 15, Mar. 19, 1901; Jan. 21, Mar. 18, Apr. 16, May 6, Sept. 3, 1902; Lovoll 198, 209. Mount Olive Cemetery was founded in 1886 as a Scandinavian cemetery by Norwegian businessmen in Chicago. It was used mainly by Norwegians and to some degree by Danes.

# Works Cited

Boyer, Paul. *Urban Masses and Moral Order in America, 1820-1920.* Cambridge: Harvard UP, 1978.

Christophersen, H. O. *Eilert Sundt. Humanist og samfunnsforsker.* Oslo: Det Norske Studentersamfunds Kulturutvalg, 1959.

Clawson, Mary Ann. *Constructing Brotherhood: Class, Gender, and Fraternalism.* New Jersey: Princeton UP, 1989.

Lindsey, Almont. *The Pullman Strike: The Story of a Unique Experiment and of a Great Labor Upheaval*. Chicago: U of Chicago P, 1942.

Lovoll, Odd S. *A Century of Urban Life: The Norwegians in Chicago before 1930*. Northfield, MN: Norwegian-American Historical Association [NAHA], St. Olaf College, 1988.

*Norden* [Chicago] June 16, Nov. 10, 24, and Dec. 8, 1894.

"Nordlyset" Collection. Norwegian-American Historical Association [NAHA]. Northfield, MN. St. Olaf College.

[NSNL] "Den norske Sygeforening 'Nordlysets' Love." In the Norwegian-American Historical Association [NAHA]. Northfield, MN. St. Olaf College. See "Nordlyset" Collection.

Oberschall, Anthony. *Social Conflict and Social Movements*. Englewood Cliffs, NJ: Prentice Hall, 1973.

[RNSN] "Record af Den norske Sygeforening 'Nordlyset.'" In the Norwegian-American Historical Association [NAHA]. Northfield, MN. St. Olaf College. See "Nordlyset" Collection.

*Skandinaven* [Chicago] Dec. 6, 1893; June 17, 1896; and an undated clipping from 1937 (see "Nordlyset" Collection).

Stead, William T. *If Christ Came to Chicago*. Chicago, 1894.

Sundt, Eilert. *Om Piperviken og Ruseløkbakken. Undersøgelser om Arbeiderklassens Kaar og Sæder i Christiania*. Christiania [Oslo]: Selskabet for Folkeoplysningens Fremme, 1858.

Wiebe, Robert H. *The Search for Order, 1877-1920*. New York: Hill and Wang, 1967.

Fig. IV.3

Blue Mounds Pioneers
Ragnhild Gulbrandsdatter Elseberg (1846-1931) emigrated from Valdres,
Norway, to Dane County, Wisconsin, in 1848; in 1864 she married Civil War
soldier and later stagecoach-driver Tideman Knutson Grøndalen (1842-
1933), who had emigrated from Valdres in 1862. Their daughter Minnie
Knutson (1883-1973) was a schoolteacher.
Photograph, courtesy of local historian Lawrence Berge
Private collection, Mrs. Charles Jones
Blue Mounds, Wisconsin

A SPRING DANCE IN THE OLD LOG HOUSE ON THE FARM

Fig. IV.4

Spring Dance
A drawing by artist Knut Kleven (1862-1942), carpenter, contractor, and
president of the Wisconsin Silo and Tank Co. The Kleven family emigrated
from Valdres, Norway, in 1867, and Knut lived both in Klevenville and Mt.
Horeb, Wisconsin, until ca. 1915.
Photograph, courtesy of local historian Lawrence Berge
Private collection, Mrs. Charles Jones
Blue Mounds, Wisconsin

# "I Was Scared to Death When I Came to Chicago": White Slavery and the Woman Immigrant

## Janet E. Rasmussen

RECENT RESEARCH ON WOMEN immigrants has helped us to appreciate the many similarities in experience and motivation between the men and the women who left Scandinavia for new lives in North America. The "myth of the reticent immigrant woman," to use K. Marianne Wargelin Brown's apt phrase (18), has, for example, been debunked by the testimonies of Scandinavian women who describe their eagerness for personal adventure and economic betterment in terms that previously were attached to men. In other respects, too, we are learning that women's encounters with American culture and their contributions to the community often paralleled those of their male counterparts. This is true both for the specific contours of immigrant life and for the broader themes of separation, adaptation, and ethnic loyalty.

While continuing to stress the similarities, it behooves us also to illuminate the areas where the immigrant experience held a somewhat different shading for women than for men. White slavery constitutes one such area, since the threat of white slavery was a dilemma specific to the woman immigrant. She traveled with warnings ringing in her ears and with offers of assistance from concerned organizations. She experienced a gender-related vulnerability, which intensified the vulnerability she shared with all immigrants as they moved from the familiar to the unfamiliar. The present discussion considers organized as well as individual responses to white slavery, drawing for the latter upon oral history interviews with women who emigrated from Scandinavia between 1905 and 1930.

The term white slavery appeared with great frequency at the turn of the century. Some employed it as a synonym for prostitution; others meant by it an extreme form of prostitution in which the woman was often exploited through some form of physical coercion or even kidnapping. The focus upon women as innocent victims of male sexual exploitation fit in well with both the feminist agenda of freeing women from male domination and the Victorian image of women as passionless beings. Yet white slavery was much more than a convenient ideological way to account for some, if not all, prostitution. It functioned as a terrifying specter of the sin and corruption awaiting innocent young girls who ventured into strange environments; as such, it stimulated a flood of pragmatic, but typically moralistic, advice concerning appropriate female behavior. Although the point has been debated, white slavery also appears to have been a terrifying reality that ensnared countless unsuspecting women, among them immigrants from East Asia and Europe. Furthermore, if Kathleen Barry is correct in her documentation of *Female Sexual Slavery* (1979), we must acknowledge that white slavery remains an appalling feature of our present-day world.

In *The Lost Sisterhood* (1982), Ruth Rosen argues that historians, in part, have been reluctant to take the matter of white slavery seriously because books, films, and posters from the early twentieth century tended to exaggerate and sensationalize the subject. Rosen believes, however, that

a careful review of the evidence documents a real traffic in women: a historical fact and experience that must be integrated into the record. (116)

Then-current investigations by governmental commissions and civic organizations uncovered strong evidence of the white slave trade. Because the traffic in women had international dimensions, reformers in many countries worked cooperatively to enact legal sanctions and to curb the number of incidents through aggressive intervention. Perhaps the best known of these reformers was Jane Addams, founder of Chicago's Hull House. Addams collected her articles on the subject in *A New Conscience and an Ancient Evil* (1912), in which she argued,

It is obvious that a foreign girl who speaks no English, who has not the remotest idea in what part of the city her fellow-countrymen live, who does not know the police station or any agency to which she may apply, is almost as valuable to a white slave trafficker as a girl imported directly for the trade. (26)

Organized activity on behalf of young emigrant women began in Scandinavia in the 1880s, during the period of peak emigration. In 1886, four Norwegian women formed "Unge Pigers Veninder" as a branch of "L'Union internationale des amies de la jeune fille," based in Neufchatel, France. The Norwegian organization lasted at least until 1914 and probably longer (Ræder 2: 50-52); a Danish branch also formed (Liljefalk 125-26). The primary functions undertaken by the Norwegian group were to register its members as "friends" for young women planning to work or travel in Norway and to provide Norwegian women with information and addresses as they prepared to go abroad. Close ties were maintained with the Norwegian YWCA and with the Travelers' Aid Society throughout England and in New York, the most popular destinations for Norwegian women.

Writing in 1914 about the work of Unge Pigers Veninder, president Thora Ræder lamented the fact that more had not been accomplished and suggested that while some of the blame rested with the organization's members, some also rested with the population they served:

> Mange av vore unge piker er ogsaa meget selvstændige og forsmaar den beskyttelse, som de utenlandske selskaper og herberger byr dem. Flere vil nødig underordne sig disse selskapers reglement. Der klages ofte fra utlandet over, at det er vanskelig at hjælpe de norske. (50-51)

She did go on to report, however, that a heightened awareness of white slavery had in recent years made young women more receptive to the societies' advice.

The principal trace of the efforts of Unge Pigers Veninder is a booklet first published in 1887, which appeared in at least seven new and expanded editions. *Veiviser for unge Piger* had a heavy moralistic tone and included references to Bible passages along with practical advice and addresses. The booklets were distributed to emigrant women at emigration offices, on trains, and on the steamships of the Norwegian-America Line; they were also advertised in the journal of the Norwegian Feminist Society (Ræder 51; Rasmussen 100-11). The guides recommended that, among other things, women travelers refuse to converse with strangers, seek out the emigrant pastor immediately upon their arrival in New York, and stay in touch each with her designated "veninde" at the new place of residence.

Another sign of early Scandinavian concern about the safety of young emigrant women may be found in the reports of the Finnish feminist Alexandra Gripenberg, who visited America in 1888 and whose published accounts of the trip were widely disseminated in feminist circles. In one article she noted that a young woman's "good friend" on the emigrant ship might become her worst enemy upon arrival in North America. As evidence, Gripenberg (173-74) cited a visit in Chicago to a home for unwed mothers, where she met Danish, Norwegian, and Swedish women who had been in America less than a year and who could speak little or no English.

The channels for combating white slavery and the number of persons involved with them increased after 1900. National anti-white-slavery committees formed in Copenhagen and Christiania [Oslo]; in Stockholm an organization known as "Vaksamhet" championed the cause. Axel Liljefalk, President of the Danish National Committee for the Suppression of the White Slave Traffic, noted that the Norwegians had been successful in obtaining a ministerial directive to all pastors; henceforth, training of female confirmation candidates was to include a discussion of both the dangers associated with foreign travel and the sources of assistance available to women (Liljefalk 127). The Norwegian affiliate of the International Council of Women also took up the matter. After the ICW established a special international committee to work against the traffic in women, the Norwegian chapter petitioned the Norwegian-America Line to engage a woman inspector for each of its ships in order to provide greater protection for young women passengers. Their letter to the cruise line, printed in *Nylænde*, the journal of the Norwegian Feminist Society, argued,

> Det er blit oplyst at det ikke sjelden hænder at de paa selve overreisen indleder forbindelse med samvittighetsløse og snedige agenter — hvad der senere blir til ulykke for dem. (15 Oct. 1912: 384)

Along similar lines, Christian Stephansen, compiler and publisher of *Den hvite Slavehandel i Europa og Amerika i det 20. Aarhundrede* (1912), noted that Norwegian Americans were among those functioning as agents for the white slave trade from Norway (15-16). Stephansen expressed his opinion, undoubtedly shared by others, that "der findes ikke et farligere sted i verden for unge piker end Amerika . . ." (16). Using supposedly official statistics, leading Bergen feminist Nico Hambro reported that, during the year 1909, 15,000 young women had been "imported" to the United States for immoral purposes, four-fifths of them against their own will (*Nylænde*, 15 Apr. 1912: 154).

The very experience of stepping ashore in a strange land intimidated the typical immigrant. Bewilderment at the crowds and procedures, confusion at the language and monetary system, and naiveté concerning assistance proffered rendered the final stages of the journey especially traumatic. White slavery was one among several types of exploitation to which a woman immigrant might be subjected. Bergljot, who left Norway in 1922 at the age of twenty, suggests this scenario when she describes her train trip from New York to Tacoma, Washington:

> There was a girl that went on the same train, and she sat by me. Well, the first thing, there was the porter; he came and threw candy bars in your lap. And there was a man who could speak English and Norwegian sitting in front of us, and he kind of helped me; he said, "If you don't want it, don't touch it." So I didn't touch it. Then they would charge you fifty cents for a nickel bar. And then I ordered a cup of coffee for me and my girlfriend, and I gave him [the porter] a whole dollar; the coffee was ten cents, and he said, "That'll be eighty cents." I said to the man sitting in front of me, "I gave him that big money and look the little I got back." "Oh," he said, "you wait, I'll catch him." And the porter came back, and he said, "You give the lady her money." And he said, "Oh, I thought she paid for those six fellas over there." I said, "That'll be the day. . . ." Mother said to me, you don't talk to anybody on the way or do anything. . . . In those days, they had white slavery and they used to throw pillow cases over the girls' heads and kidnap them. . . . When we came to Oregon, we went off the train, and there was another one that wanted me to send a telegram. Ja, sure, I sent one, will arrive so-and-so time. Four dollars for those few words. Well, I didn't know any better. You just paid, that's all. (SPEC T 102-03)[1]

In supplying concrete examples of how she was cheated monetarily, the narrator suggests that other young women were cheated of far more than their money.

Bergljot's mother had warned her to be cautious and not become involved with strangers. Ellen, an eighteen-year-old Danish emigrant, received her warnings from fellow travelers. The year was 1925:

> We left Copenhagen on a ship, and it was a nice trip. There was a couple ladies on board that kept talking to me — I was a young girl alone — kept warning me against the white slave trade, all those things. One lady said, "Oh, you've got such pretty rosy cheeks, you'll lose them when you get to America." (SPEC T 160)

Some women felt more isolated and helpless than others. Henny was silenced by both her fears and her linguistic limitations:

> It was a beautiful trip until I came to Ellis Island. And I would just as soon have gone home. Oh, I was scared. I was *so* scared! Here was this new country; I was scared witless. . . . We got on the train in New York and I didn't talk to anybody on the train 'cause I couldn't talk English, not a single word! (SPEC T 146)

Pearl went without food during much of her trip across Canada:

> I was only eighteen years old, you know, and all you heard on your trip was, don't talk to strangers. All you heard was, don't talk to strangers, because there was so much white slavery going on. And boy, I was so scared and even so hungry. I didn't have breakfast, I didn't have lunch. (SPEC T 7)

Pearl had the money for food, but she did not dare get off the train to buy anything, nor did she trust anyone to buy food for her and give her the correct change.

The first encounter with someone of another race could intensify the woman immigrant's feeling of vulnerability. Esther arrived from Finland in 1920. She misinterpreted the protective gestures of the black railroad employees and viewed them instead as oppressors:

> They put a slip on my chest, and they always escorted to the train. So I got to the train all right. But then the "nigger" boy. I never seen before. Finland those days, you never see any black people. Every time when they stopped the train, they put me in some room and locked the door so I can't go anywhere. Then when the time came, they came and took me out to the train. I don't know if they changed the train or what. I never understood. Soon as I go to the train, there was that black man again; 'course it was a different guy, but the blackest you can imagine. I wanted to get orange. I wanted so badly the orange . . . well, I went to the step, the "nigger" boy pulled me back. He wouldn't let me go. I had to go back to my seat. He escorted me to the seat and ordered me to sit there. (SPEC T 81)

In San Francisco, Esther slipped away from the train. Luckily, two women (Esther calls them policewomen, but they were probably from a protective agency) discovered her, installed her in a safe hotel for the night, and gave her a letter for the conductor. The next day she boarded a train again, for the final leg of the journey to Eureka, California. The letter admonished the conductor not to let her go anywhere. Esther explains:

> Because, those days, there was a lot of girls, they just disappear, to those road houses, and . . . My sisters, they wanted to make sure I got safely to Eureka. That's why they had protection everywhere. (SPEC T 81)

Assistance was available from a number of sources. Like Esther, other Scandinavian women mention the police, travelers' aid societies, and the YWCA as avenues through which they received an escort, information, and sometimes more extensive help. Alva, who was sixteen when she left Sweden, remembers:

> I was scared to death when I came to Chicago. And I just sat there. And finally a policeman found me and wanted to see my ticket. You know, it's pretty hard when you don't understand anything. So he put me on the train. (SPEC T 40)

When Astrid traveled across country in 1930, she relied heavily on a network of YWCA representatives:

> I arrived in New York, and a lady from the YWCA met us, and she talked Swedish. And we were just herding around; there were lots of immigrants. Well, she took care of us and put us on the train then. And we rode the train to Chicago, and in Chicago we changed trains to go to St. Paul. And when I got to St. Paul, there was a man that came and called my name at the train depot, and he said, "Fröken Rehn! Fröken Rehn!" And he took hold of me like that on my back, and I ran to beat the band to talk to the YWCA lady. I said, "There's a man that's coming and he wants me." "Well, don't be afraid," she said. "He knows your name, he must know you." So then he came up. And he couldn't talk very good Swedish so I couldn't understand him. . . . He was my great uncle, my mother's uncle, and he was a free missionary minister from Sweden. . . . There was a lady from the YWCA in New York, one in Chicago, and one in St. Paul. And one of them met me in Yakima. They all spoke Swedish. They were notified ahead of time that we were coming. It was through that lady that I got my first job here in Yakima. (SPEC T 254)

Johanne, a 1927 Danish immigrant, tells in great detail how the YWCA assisted her, first when she missed the scheduled train out of Quebec and later when she boarded the wrong train and took a three-hundred-mile detour through eastern New Brunswick. To quote part of her narrative:

> I sat with my map, and each time that train stopped, my heart stood still. Instead of going down to Grand Falls, we went around clear out to the coast . . . and when we got down to Moncton, the conductor came in, a big, stout man in a heavy overcoat, and he spoke a little with me. Then he took my suitcase and said, "Come on." I thought, where my suitcase go, I go. I

followed him, and I see another YWCA lady, and so I felt pretty good. And he called out, "I've got a Danish lady for you." And so I come to her, and they asked me questions, and I told her I was supposed to go to Grand Falls and meet my husband. Well, they took me to the YWCA. This was Monday afternoon, and I stayed there until Wednesday. I couldn't understand, because in Denmark, a little country, trains go all the time, so I couldn't get this in my head. Well, there was nothing to do about it, so I just prayed to God and give it in His hands. So, I stayed there, and they put me on the last train, and she put it very clearly to the conductor, "No off till she get to Grand Falls." (SPEC T 201)

A joyous reunion with her husband took place in Grand Falls. Johanne concludes, "The conductor seemed very relieved. And that's how I got to Grand Falls, New Brunswick" (SPEC T 201).

The role of travelers' aids in assisting Polish immigrant women has been researched by Lucille O'Connell. According to O'Connell, the YWCA was instrumental in launching the travelers' aid program. In 1907, YWCA President Grace Dodge established a separate organization called the Travelers' Aid Society of New York City, "for the purpose of aiding both rural American girls and immigrant girls who came to the city alone" (O'Connell 16). All agents possessed foreign language skills, volunteered their services, and helped immigrant women with many practical details. The anti-white-slavery thrust of the work was clear, and Grace Dodge's name figures in the literature of the international movement (see, f. ex., Coote). O'Connell lists Swedish, Danish, and Norwegian as languages spoken by Society agents.

The oral history narratives treat white slavery as a threatening danger, but none offers clear evidence of an attempt at seduction or abduction.[2] In some sense the extent, or even the reality, of the white slave trade may be regarded as irrelevant. We have clear evidence that women immigrants traveling alone felt threatened by the prospect of abduction and that their fears in that regard intensified the feeling of vulnerability they shared with all immigrants. Negotiating the journey to their new home in America was only the first hurdle that the women needed to clear. As Maxine Schwartz Seller points out (117) in her book *Immigrant Women* (1981), many potentially exploitative challenges awaited them when they entered the labor market and began to develop social networks. We should also remember that the campaign against white slavery took place within the framework of a large-scale assault on prostitution during the Progressive Era. That reform movement fostered and fed some nativist sentiments, owing to the identification of aliens as a source and symptom of rampant prostitution. Nevertheless, the overriding image of the immigrant woman, portrayed both by the yellow press and by sober reformers, was that of victim or potential victim, rather than perpetrator (see Feldman).

The specter of white slavery reshaped the active, more widely ranging behavior of the woman immigrant. Her right to conscious choice and self-determination were to some extent compromised. Instead of active agent, she was labeled passive victim. While she could take certain steps to protect herself, they consisted primarily of placing herself under the authority of an official or agency. The extensive and direct involvement of women's organizations in the campaign against white slavery did something to mitigate the labeling of women as passive victims, however, for much of the work consisted of women actively assisting other women. Given the widespread emphasis upon the possibility of prostitution being forced upon women of the first generation, it is interesting to note in closing that women of the second generation were in fact more likely to be engaged in prostitution than were their mothers (Feldman 199; Butler 13-14).

## Notes

[1] All interview numbers in the text refer to the oral history tape catalogue in the Scandinavian Immigrant Experience Collection, Robert A. L. Mortvedt Library, Pacific Lutheran University. A grant from the L. J. Skaggs and Mary C. Skaggs Foundation of Oakland, California, made possible the "New Land — New Lives: Scandinavian Experiences in the Pacific Northwest" oral history project. The bulk of the interviews were recorded between 1981 and 1983.

[2] For a more explicit account, see Guttersen and Christensen, 202-05.

## Works Cited

Addams, Jane. *A New Conscience and an Ancient Evil*. New York: The MacMillan Company, 1912.

Audiotapes. "New Land — New Lives: Scandinavian Experiences in the Pacific Northwest." Scandinavian Immigrant Experience Collection, Robert A. L. Mortvedt Library, Pacific Lutheran University. Catalogued by SPEC T number. Interviews cited: SPEC T 7, SPEC T 40, SPEC T 81, SPEC T 102-03, SPEC T 146, SPEC T 160, SPEC T 201, SPEC T 254.

Barry, Kathleen. *Female Sexual Slavery*. Englewood Cliffs, NJ: Prentice-Hall, 1979.

Brown, K. Marianne Wargelin. "The Legacy of Mummu's Granddaughters: Finnish-American Women's History." *Women Who Dared: The History of Finnish-American Women*. Ed. Carl Ross and K. Marianne Wargelin Brown. St. Paul, MN: Immigration History Research Center, 1986. 14-40.

Butler, Anne M. *Daughters of Joy, Sisters of Misery: Prostitutes in the American West, 1865-90*. Urbana: U of Illinois P, 1985.

Coote, William Alexander. *A Vision and Its Fulfillment, Being the History of the Origin of the Work of the National Vigilance Association for the Suppression of the White Slave Traffic*. London: National Vigilance Association, 1910.

Feldman, Egal. "Prostitution, the Alien Woman and the Progressive Imagination, 1910-1915," *American Quarterly* 19.2 (1967): 192-206.

Guttersen, Alma A., and Regina Hilleboe Christensen. *Souvenir Norse American Women 1825-1925*. St. Paul, MN: Guttersen, 1926.

Liljefalk, Axel. *Den hvide Slavehandel*. Copenhagen: E. Jespersens Forlag, 1911.

*Nylænde*. 1 June 1889: 173-74. Summary of Alexandra Gripenberg's impressions of conditions in the U.S. for immigrants.

*Nylænde*. 1 Mar. 1912: 86-88; 15 Mar. 1912: 116-17; 1 Apr. 1912: 126-28; 15 Apr. 1912: 153-55. Text of a speech by Nico Hambro.

*Nylænde*. 15 Oct. 1912: 384. Letter from Norske Kvinners Nationalraad to The Norwegian-America Line.

O'Connell, Lucille. "Travelers' Aid for Polish Immigrant Women." *Polish American Studies* 31.1 (1974): 15-19.

Ræder, Thora. "Unge Pikers Veninder." *Norske Kvinder. En Oversigt over deres Stilling og Livsvilkaar i Hundredeaaret 1814-1914*. Vol. II. Christiania [Oslo]: Berg & Høghs Forlag, 1914. 3 vols. 1914-25.

Rasmussen, Janet E. "*Nylænde* Presents America." *Scandinavians in America: Literary Life*. Ed. J. R. Christianson. Decorah, Iowa: Symra Literary Society, 1985. 104-13.

Rosen, Ruth. *The Lost Sisterhood: Prostitution in America, 1900-1918*. Baltimore: Johns Hopkins, 1982.

Seller, Maxine Schwartz, ed. *Immigrant Women*. Philadelphia: Temple UP, 1981.

Stephansen, Christian. *Den hvite Slavehandel i Europa og Amerika i det 20. Aarhundrede*. Bergen: Stephansens Bokhandels Forlag, 1912.

# Emigration: The Dream of Freedom and Land — And an Existential Quest

## Ingeborg R. Kongslien

THE MOST WIDELY READ and critically acclaimed Scandinavian novels on the emigration theme seem at first sight to be starkly realistic. Works by the Norwegian writers Johan Bojer and Alfred Hauge, the Swedish Vilhelm Moberg, and — last but not least — the Norwegian-American Ole Edvart Rølvaag have become, for Scandinavian readers, important interpreters of the emigration process.[1] At the peak of their careers, with their thorough knowledge of the historical background and their artistic skills fully developed, these authors, in their emigrant novels, have presented broad pictures of the emigration process, combining realistic accuracy with a deep understanding of the experiences of the individuals in changing homelands and cultures.[2]

Bojer, belonging to the period of "new realism" of the 1910s and '20s in Norwegian literary history, takes the decade of mass emigration from Norway, the 1880s, as his point of departure in his book *Vor egen stamme* (1924) and then moves his characters to the North Dakota prairie in the 1880s and '90s. In Bojer's Norwegian-American contemporary Rølvaag's tetralogy — *I de dage* (1924), *Riket grundlægges* (1925), *Peder Seier* (1928) and *Den signede dag* (1931) — the focus is on the settling of the South Dakota prairie in the 1870s and on the immigrant society as it grows and develops through the same 1880s and '90s. Moberg's epic, written about three decades later, in the 1950s, spans almost the entire period of Swedish emigration and settlement in the nineteenth century, from the pioneer days in the late 1840s up until 1890. The titles indicate the emigration and acculturation process: *Utvandrarna* (1949), *Invandrarna* (1952), *Nybyggarna* (1956), and *Sista brevet till Sverige* (1959). Moberg's Swedes homestead in the woods and among the lakes of Minnesota. In the 1960s, Hauge wrote his stories on Cleng Peerson and the Quaker emigration, the pioneer Norwegian emigration of 1825; he

featured that group — as well as other groups emigrating in the decades of
the nineteenth century leading up to the Civil War — in the three-volume
work *Cleng Peerson. Hundevakt* (1961), *Cleng Peerson. Landkjenning* (1964),
and *Cleng Peerson. Ankerfeste* (1965).

These works of fiction have in common not only their thematic basis in
the historical process of Scandinavian emigration to America in the previous century, but also some distinctive structural features. The term "emigrant
novel" thus indicates the historical basis and the thematic structure em-
bodying the emigration process.

The emigrant novels mentioned describe individuals and groups leav-
ing their homelands because of material need and social or spiritual
oppression. They have a dream of freedom. These people have heard
about the new world beyond the ocean where material gain is possible
and, thus, freedom can be obtained. They journey from that which is
known into the unknown. The settling, first over-wintering, and then the
whole process of acculturation for the emigrants are described. The double
perspective, that is, the relating of the literary characters to two countries
and two cultures simultaneously, is inherent in the text as both a structural
and a thematic element.

The Scandinavian writers Bojer, Moberg, and Hauge devote considerable space and attention to descriptions of the home countries and the
characters' reasons for emigration. Bojer underlines both the social aspect,
in his portrayal of a young man named Morten who seeks emigration in
order to win his sweetheart by improving his community standing, and the
material aspect, in the description of the poor cottager Kal Skaret who,
through emigration, seeks the means to feed his family. Moberg's epic does
likewise, but on a broader scale and with more depth, not only in its social
but also in its psychological description. His small farmer, Karl Oskar,
wishes to "förkovra sig," to make a living for himself and his family, but also
to bring his children to a country where societal classes, that is, "de fyra
stånden," do not exist. The younger brother Robert's main concern is that
emigration can give freedom. Freedom is also Danjel's quest, and for him
it means religious freedom. In Hauge's Cleng Peerson novels, the search for
religious freedom is the main motif, based on the documented history of the
Quaker emigration and that of other sects and expanded to a general
embodiment of freedom and a search for identity.

The main parts of these works of fiction, including the novel series by
the Norwegian-American writer Rølvaag, depict the emigrants' lives in the
new country and their creation of a new existence. These people have to start
from scratch in building up their new lives — materially, socially, and
culturally. Each of these four writers' thematic renderings of this process of
acculturation has a number of striking similarities with the others, but also
quite different aspects that come to the fore according to the different
historical bases of the works and the world view of each individual author,
as well as the structure of each of the works of fiction.

The only immigrant in this group of writers, the Norwegian-American Rølvaag, starts his story in the new country when his little group of immigrants is heading west towards the open and unsettled prairie of South Dakota. The husband-and-wife motif, embodied in the depiction of Beret and Per Hansa, unfolds to show in how totally different a manner two souls, united with strong ties, can experience their common life as immigrants and pioneers. Per sees life on the prairie as a continuous challenge, while Beret finds it frightening and dehumanizing and suffers a mental breakdown as a consequence of its physical and mental hardships. The irony of the story is that Per, the heroic builder of a new life, dies, and Beret has to stay in the new land in order to fulfill his visions of the future. In spite of the heroic dimensions in the character of Per Hansa and in his confrontations with the prairie, the overall impression made by the story is that the emigrant experience is tragic. Here fiction carries the same message as do Rølvaag's articles and speeches, in which he speaks of the tragedy of the immigrant. Part of this tragedy is owing to the cultural conflicts experienced by both first and second generations in the ongoing process of acculturation. Of the four writers mentioned, the immigrant Rølvaag is the only one to go beyond the first generation of emigrants or immigrants in his depictions.

Moberg matches Rølvaag in many ways, for example, in his use of the husband-and-wife thematic structure to depict the homesteading experience in the new land, this time in Minnesota. But his emigrant couple, Karl Oskar and Kristina, are less contradictory, even if they add different dimensions to the emigration theme. Kristina must place her life as an emigrant within a religious dimension in order to bear it and understand its meaning. Karl Oskar gets his farm and gains the freedom to provide for his family, but it takes his entire life and a lot of hard work. Towards the end of his years, he looks back to his youth. Even in this book, so dominated by the linear structure involved in reaching one's goal, the cyclical element is present.

The structural element of the double perspective in Moberg's emigrant epic is brought very much to the fore by Kristina's concept of home as still being in Sweden, and that perspective also underlies the social theme. Karl Oskar continuously refers to his progress in America in comparison to the stagnation of his life in Sweden. His namesake in Bojer's novel, the poor cottager turned rich farmer, never forgets his points of reference in his background. With Rølvaag, the double perspective mainly concerns cultural and psychological aspects. The fictitious works by Bojer and Moberg, as well as those by Rølvaag, have mainly linear structures. A character's wishes to realize a new life are mainly expressed along chronological lines: years go by in the process of reaching such goals. Some fail, and some succeed, but for them all the attempt costs a lifetime of physical toil and psychological strain, including — for many individuals — an everlasting homesickness. Another interesting thematic element in Moberg's world is the broad time dimension for his emigrant characters. It is not only an exodus that has several forerunners reaching back to Biblical times, but it is also the inevitable pivot of history, with the hungry and unpropertied of Europe coming to a rich and open land. Their presence is justified by their gaining their freedom and cultivating the land, but the native people, the Indians, are sacrificed in the process.

Hauge's three-volume novel about the adventurous Cleng Peerson and the pioneer Norwegian emigration differs quite a lot from the works of the three other writers mentioned. His is a documentary novel in the sense of using authentic characters and happenings as material for the story. It is also a novel about searching for identity and meaning, expressed in Cleng's often repeated question "Hvem er jeg?" and in the many tales of other groups of people, Quakers as well as Mormons, Rappites, Janssonites, and so on. The story alternates between two time levels, with Cleng, the narrator, in his old age at the time of the Civil War, looking back to the years before and after the first Norwegian emigration in 1825. Together with the story of Cleng's own life, the lives and destinies of the emigrant Quakers constitute the story line. Freedom, in this case freedom in religious beliefs and practices, is the goal.

In between the movements back and forth in time, the story line is quite linear as long as it deals with the settlement story of the Quakers. But soon, the narrative turns its attention to new groups of immigrants or people going west, and the structure of the novel becomes the repetition of a pattern — through several stories — of people searching for a new life, even a new Jerusalem or utopia. The emphasis is on being in the process of continuously searching for a meaningful existence, rather than on the specific goal to be reached after space and time are overcome. A cyclical structure is established, through which is expressed a quest for meaning and identity. Thematically, this is quite typical for Norwegian literature in the early 1960s. In this fascinating tale, the emigration theme, although deeply rooted in authentic material, is largely existential in nature. The linear structure is replaced by a cyclical structure of repeated attempts at establishing a new life.

Two other Nordic novels touching on emigration are highly interesting to consider in this context. They are not by any means "emigrant novels" in the sense that has been described when dealing with the works of Bojer, Rølvaag, Moberg, and Hauge — written with emigration as their historical basis and thematic structure and apparently with the intention of giving an extensive interpretation of the individuals' emigrant experiences. The two novels in question are *Paradísarheimt* (1960) by Halldór Kiljan Laxness and *Din stund på jorden* (1963), a later work by Vilhelm Moberg. Each of the books has an emigration story as a framework for the fiction, but emigration seems to be more of a vehicle to examine the question of existence and to express the theme of an existential quest than it is to depict the emigrant experience. Both novels came out in the 1960s, in the mature years of their writers' careers. These literary works are contemporary with Hauge's Cleng Peerson novels, with which they share some important characteristics regarding thematic aspects typical of the early 1960s.

Moberg's novel, like Hauge's book, alternates between two time periods, the summer and fall of 1962 and the first two decades after the turn of the century. It is a first-person novel, with the main character, Albert Carlsson — a Swedish American in his sixties — as the narrator. He spends his days after retirement in the town of Laguna Beach on the coast of California, after having come as an emigrant from Sweden in his youth and having spent his adult life in the new country. He is now trying to straighten out the records of his life, the ones that have to do with his rather unsuccessful pursuits as not only a business man but a family man; however, his reckoning gradually goes farther. He tries to analyze the meaning of his own life, what it was that shaped his destiny and formed his existence. A leitmotif is Albert's position "emellan staden och havet," that is, he lives out his remaining years between the man-made city and the powerful ocean, an eternal element of nature.

This Swedish emigrant and immigrant has tried to return to his native country but realized that his destiny was that of most emigrants, to be "en vilsen främling," a ghost in one's original homeland: "Till det landet gives det ingen återvändo för någon människa," and "Efter sex veckor som gengångare i mitt gamla fosterland återvände jag till det land, där jag skall dö" (Moberg, *Din stund på jorden* 12 and 21, respectively). Albert Carlsson's days of reckoning coincide with a fateful time for the world, namely, the days of the Cuban Missile Crisis in 1962. Moberg uses this element — the threat of annihilation when Kennedy refused to give in to the Soviets concerning atomic weapons on Cuban soil — in order to broaden his depiction of the terms of existence. His theme is here played through both on the macrocosmic and the microcosmic level: what is happening in Cuba and what had happened in Albert Carlsson's childhood days when his beloved brother, Sigfrid, had died.

Alternating between descriptions of past and present, childhood/youth and old age, the "I" of the novel tries to come to terms with the meaning of life. This existential quest is placed within the framework of an emigrant story, thus endowing the theme with the double reference typical of such stories. Upon realizing that his brother, who was by nature a pacifist, had become enrolled in the military to fulfill the wishes of his elders and had lost his life because he refused to obey military orders, Albert is so thoroughly shaken that he finally rebels against his father and becomes an emigrant. The theme of the search for an understanding of the conditions of life is in this way strengthened by being linked to the motif of emigration and the emigrant's existence.

To some extent, this character and this novel can be seen in the context of Moberg's other emigrant novels.[3] Albert shares with Kristina and with Karl Oskar's brother, Robert, the realization of the futile character of human life, and has "förlikt [s]ig med [s]in lott," as well as with the false assumption that a man can have two homelands:

> Människan bör ha ett fäste i världen. Hon skall höra till någonstädes.
> Hon kan inte överge det land, där hon är född och uppleva ett annat som

sitt fosterland. Talet om det gamla och nya fosterlandet är falskt,
genomfalskt. Antingen har jag ett fosterland eller har jag det icke.
Fosterlandet är singularis. Det kan aldrig bli pluralis för dig. (Moberg,
*Din stund på jorden* 259)

The ending of the book shows the old man — an emigrant — walking along
the beach. His traces upon the surface of the earth are washed away, but that
does not frighten him anymore because he has realized that he is both at the
beginning and at the end and therefore safe:

> Jag fortsätter min vandring längs stranden om kvällen och går med lugna,
> långsamma steg över dynerna. Tätt efter mig kommer vattnet och fyller
> hålen efter min fot i sanden. (Moberg, *Din stund på jorden* 299-300)

Laxness's chronicle of the Icelandic farmer turned Mormon in
*Paradísarheimt* is by no means a typical emigrant story, if — as we have
assumed — such a thing does exist. It has, though, several elements of
structure in common with what has been labeled an "emigrant novel," and
the very plot line is an emigration story: The farmer Steinar Steinsson leaves
Iceland for Utah in order to find a new life. He has heard about the new land
and thinks it promises nothing less than a fulfillment of his wish of finding
a new paradise for his children now that they will soon have to leave that
of their childhood. Steinar reaches Utah, the new Zion; there he learns both
the ideology and the practice of Mormonism, the new religion. His children
eventually join him in the new land, but by then time has gone by and, with
it, their innocence, which was exactly what Steinar had struggled to preserve for them. He does indeed deliver paradise to his children, but
afterward he himself finds nothing meaningful to do in the new land. He
therefore returns to Iceland, and he ends — or the book ends — where he
began, tending to the beautiful stone wall behind his farm, in order to repair
and keep it up.

The book is both a documentary novel and a fairy tale, written in the
style of a saga pastiche, but with a prevailing ironic attitude on the part of
the narrator. Some will see the story in the context of Laxness's own
development concerning ideologies, be they religious or political.[4] As so
often was the case with this writer, he has used documentary material from
Icelandic history as a foundation for his novel. Steinar Steinsson's story, in
concrete detail, is modeled on the Icelandic farmer Eiríkur Ólafsson á
Brúnum, who, at the thousandth-year anniversary for *landnám* in 874, sold
a horse to the visiting Danish royalty. He likewise became a Mormon,
traveled to Utah in the 1880s, and stayed there for some years but returned
home towards the end of the decade and resettled in Iceland. Even the
fictitious bishop seems to have his counterpart in real life, an Icelander who
became a Mormon missionary. Laxness's own impressions from his travels
in Utah and of the accomplishments of Mormonism, together with a
fascination with "utopian" models of different kinds, are intertwined with
the documentary material, and, together, these elements have been the basis

for the creation of *Paradísarheimt*. In the depiction of a search for the promised land, the Mormon settlement story offered a framework, and in the authentic experiences of Eiríkur, Laxness found the story line.[5]

In spite of the saga tone and of the ironic attitude of the narrator, the descriptions of the poverty and the social differences in the Icelandic society of the time are quite harsh. Such elements are well known in Laxness's earlier writings, as well as in the emigrant novels examined. A particular scene in which such social criticism is voiced is in a discussion of polygamy. The Mormon missionary defends it as a formalized system, contrasting it with the reality in Iceland, where powerful men have illegitimate children without any care for, or protection of, them or their outcast mothers. The general social aspect of the novel deals with the poverty and decline in culture and the exploitation of the poor and unprotected by the strong and wealthy. This thematic line climaxes with the fate of Steinar's beautiful young daughter, Steina, who, after having been abused and humiliated by several men, becomes the Mormon's fourth wife.

The fairy-tale aspect of the book, in which the text is interwoven with myth and legend, shows that a childhood paradise has a limited existence. The father's search for a new paradise, for which Mormonism seemed to offer a possibility, was a failure. It failed partly because Mormonism could not be a substitute and partly because, in the process of finding the promised land, so much had changed that his children's youthful innocence was gone. Seen in the context of the characteristic features of the emigrant novel, this book's circular structure contrasts with the dominant linear structures found in most and thus underlines the protagonist's feeling of resignation. Steinar's goal was to give the promised land to his children, so they could continue to live happy lives, just as they did in their childhood. He had had to reject the saga illusion as inadequate and thought that settling for a religious ideology might help him reach his goal. But when even this attempt fails — in spite of the fact that his children are actually brought to the new world — Steinar returns to his homeland and must settle for the contentment of everyday life and work.

This ending echoes Voltaire's *Candide* (1759) — as has been pointed out by several literary critics writing about Laxness — and the famous expression "mais il faut cultiver votre jardin." In Steinar's case, in the Icelandic landscape, it takes the form of restoring a stone wall:

> Hver ert þú, spyr þessi ferðamaður.
> Hinn svarar: Ég er sá maður sem heimti aftur Paradís eftir að hún hafði leingi verið týnd, og gaf hana börnum sínum. Hvað er slíkur maður að vilja hér, spurði vegfarandinn.
> Ég hef fundið sannleikann og það land þar sem hann býr, áréttaði vegghleðslumaðurinn. Það er að vísu allmikils vert. En nú skiftir mestu máli að reisa við aftur þennan vallargarð.
> Síðan heldur Steinar bóndi áfram einsog ekkert hefði í skorist að leggja stein við stein í hina fornu veggi uns sólsett var í Hliðum undir Hliðunum.
> (300-01)

Resignation prevails in the ending, although there is an element of value in the good work Steinar is able to preform. This ending is set against the story as a whole, the irony and the humor of the narrative, and the social criticism and the two-sided presentation of Mormonism. But first and foremost it is set against the bitterness of the tragedy of Steina and the rest of the family for whom Steinar had tried to provide. The conclusion seems to be either that the new and better life across the ocean did not materialize or that one cannot obtain the promised land for others.

The novels discussed here show highly varied descriptions of emigrant lives and use their historical frameworks in very different ways. The first group that I have dealt with offers interpretations of the emigrant experience on a broad basis, taking into account historical and social, as well as cultural and psychological, aspects. These works of art give readers unique opportunities to learn about the historical process and to experience the emotional impact of emigration. To get hold of a piece of land is often the material goal of the emigrant, and, thus, to gain freedom is most often the ultimate goal.

As we get further away in time from Scandinavian emigration as a historical entity, it seems to provoke an interest in its inherent existential content. This is how emigration is mainly used in the last two books considered here. The Cleng Peerson-trilogy, though, is an interesting example of a work belonging in both groups. It gives a most authentic picture of the Norwegian pioneer emigration to America, in broad outline and with innumerable details. At the same time, Hauge's novels are permeated with a search for identity and meaning. When Laxness and the later Moberg make these aspects the main issues in their "emigrant novels" from the 1960s, it shows an interesting shift in the use of emigrant material as points of reference for fiction.

A later work, from the early 1980s, in which emigration is one motif within a larger pattern, is the Swede Sven Delblanc's magnificent tetralogy, based on his own family history, the third volume of which has the illustrative title *Kanaans land* (1984).[6] Like Laxness's novel, it has a documentary basis, as well as a strong tone of resignation. And it shares with most of the emigrant narratives the aspect of using the emigration motif in the thematic context of searching for a meaning in life.

The novels considered here differ greatly in terms of their use of emigration material and the extent to which emigration is a central issue in each work. But it should be underlined that elements of an existential quest can be found in all these books, and, thus, such a quest seems to be an integral part of the theme of emigration.

## Notes

[1] The present writer, in Kongslien, *Draumen om fridom og jord* (1989), has studied the works of these four writers from the point of view of "emigrant novels," i.e., as portrayals of the emigration process. Cf. also a short article summing up some of the main points of the dissertation, namely, Kongslien, "Fiction as Interpretation."

² A note of a more personal character must be added at this point. In the summer of 1978, when spending a couple of months in the U.S. to do research for my upcoming dissertation on the Scandinavian emigrant novels, I was so lucky as to be included in Harald's summer class at the University of Wisconsin. In 1984, I was invited back to Madison to a conference on Scandinavian Immigration, Settlement, and Acculturation that was cochaired by Harald. I cherished the talks on emigration and emigrant literature we had on both occasions, and I believe Harald helped direct my attention towards the psychological and the existential aspects of these works of fiction, when — as the mode of the time, especially in Scandinavia, required — I was mainly interested in their historical and social references.

³ Holmes, in *Vilhelm Moberg* (1980), deals with this book in a subchapter under the main chapter title "The Emigrant Novels," together with the tetralogy.

⁴ Hallberg, in *Halldór Laxness* (1970), sees Laxness's attitude around the time of his publishing *Paradísarheimt* as one of repudiation of all doctrinal systems. This comes from the author's own experience, according to Hallberg. Having been at earlier points in his life a true believer of both Catholicism and socialism, Laxness had subsequently "adopted a skeptical attitude of noninvolvement as his guiding star" (186).

⁵ Laxness himself comments on the creation of *Paradísarheimt* in his essay "Tildrög Paradísarheimtar," which was printed as a preface, "The Origins of Paradise Reclaimed," in the English translation of his book in 1962.

⁶ The other volumes of Sven Delblanc's tetralogy are *Samuels bok* (1981), *Samuels döttrar* (1982), and *Maria ensam* (1985).

## Works Cited

Bojer, Johan. *Vor egen stamme*. Oslo: Gyldendal, 1924. Trans. as *The Emigrants* (1925).

Delblanc, Sven. *Kanaans land*. Stockholm: Bonniers, 1984.

Hallberg, Peter. *Halldór Laxness*. Twayne's World Authors Series 89. Boston: Twayne Publishers, 1971.

Hauge, Alfred. *Cleng Peerson. Hundevakt; Cleng Peerson. Landkjenning; Cleng Peerson. Ankerfeste*. Oslo: Gyldendal, 1961; 1964; 1965. Trans. as *Cleng Peerson I-II* (1975).

Holmes, Philip. *Vilhelm Moberg*. Twayne's World Authors Series 584. Boston: Twayne Publishers, 1980.

Kongslien, Ingeborg. *Draumen om fridom og jord. Ein studie i skandinaviske emigrantromanar*. Oslo: Det Norske Samlaget, 1989.

——. "Fiction as Interpretation of the Emigrant Experience: The Novels of Johan Bojer, O. E. Rølvaag, Vilhelm Moberg and Alfred Hauge." *American Studies in Scandinavia* 18 (1986): 83-92.

Laxness, Halldór Kiljan. "The Origins of Paradise Reclaimed." Preface for *Paradise Reclaimed*. Trans. Magnus Magnusson. New York: Crowell, [1962].

——. *Paradísarheimt*. Reykjavik: Helgafell, 1960.

Moberg, Vilhelm. *Utvandrarna; Invandrarna; Nybyggarna; Sista brevet till Sverige*. Stockholm:

Bonniers, 1949; 1952; 1956; 1959. Trans. respectively as *The Emigrants* (1951); *Unto a Good Land* (1957); *The Settlers* (1956); *Last Letter Home* (1961).

——. *Din stund på jorden*. Stockholm: Bonniers, 1963. Trans. as *A Time on Earth* (1965).

Rølvaag, Ole Edvart. *I de dage; Riket grundlægges; Peder Seier; Den signede dag*. Oslo: Aschehoug, 1924; 1925; 1928; 1931. Trans. as *Giants in the Earth* (1927, vols. 1 & 2); *Peder Victorious* (1929); *Their Fathers' God* (1931).

V. *Fin de Siècle*: The 1900s

We project our existential anxieties on to history; there is a real correlation between the ends of centuries and the peculiarity of our imagination, that it chooses always to be at the end of an era.

Frank Kermode, *The Sense of an Ending*, 1967

# Premodernism and Postmodernism: "Decadence" Before and Now

## Otto Hageberg

ONE OF THE MOST important contributions to Norwegian literary studies in recent years is Per Thomas Andersen's doctoral dissertation, submitted to the University of Tromsø in 1990. The dissertation offers an interesting critique of the concept "decadence," discussing the term from the points of view of both intellectual and literary history; but primarily the dissertation offers an analysis of four Scandinavian novels: Herman Bang, *Haabløse Slægter* (1880); Ola Hansson, *Sensitiva amorosa* (1887); Arne Garborg, *Trætte Mænd* (1891); and Tryggve Andersen, *Mot kvæld* (1900). The final chapter suggests perspectives pointing forward to modernism and postmodernism.

Andersen demonstrates that these four novels from the end of the last century, the *fin-de-siècle* period, have a common important basic structure. The portrayal of decadence is founded on an opposition between, on the one hand, a value-laden referential world and, on the other, an existential space devoid of value. The protagonists of the novels belong to a world in which all values have been punctured; in the novels of decadence this opposition can, however, find expression in two different ways. In the portrayal, the protagonist may go through a development that takes him from a value-potent point of reference to a universe empty of meaning; alternatively, he may already find himself in a state of decadence; thus, the point of departure for the action of the novel lies in a period after the fall from value has occurred. In the last case, too, the world of values from which the fall has taken place will be a structuring element that can easily be identified. In all the novels in question important contemporary values are done away with or devalued.

At the same time the novels show that this value-deflated world is tantamount to a state of chaos in which, in the final analysis, it is impossible to survive. The texts reveal that it is necessary for man to have a core of values capable of sustaining a sense of authenticity. Per Thomas Andersen characterizes the thematic centre of the literature of decadence as a problem of myth's Chaos vs. Cosmos.

Dekadansebevegelsen er en bevegelse fra kosmos til kaos, og dekadanse-verket viser at i kaos, i det forskjellsløse rom, der det ikke finnes noen verdier som gir grunnlag for orientering, i dette homogene rom kan mennesket ikke leve. (Andersen 370)

## Arne Garborg: *Trætte Mænd*

The example from the 1890s that first comes to mind is Arne Garborg's *Trætte Mænd*, the diary entries of the deeply divided modern city-dweller Gabriel Gram. Thoughtfully and sentimentally he surveys his own life in Oslo — or Christiania — where he often walks the streets, preferably in the company of young women. He summarizes conversations about marriage and love, about science and scholarship, and about life and death. He dreams, philosophizes, and indulges in idle speculations. He goes to cafés and brothels. From the very beginning it is clear that he lives in an empty universe. He is no doubt aware of traditional values, which may function as elements of order for others, for example love, friendship, and religion. But he has himself left this world of values. He is condemned to a life of unhappy reflection that tears apart all feelings, and to a scepticism which makes all acts of cognition empty. He completely lacks the ability to act. He is the prototype of what Andersen calls "the intransitive personality." For him social life, too, is devoid of any content. In the final analysis he relates only to himself; life therefore becomes something like a solipsistic hell. True, Gram is a man of refined sensibility with erotic and religious longings, but he is unable to commit himself. For him emotions are something to experiment with. Caressing the fine flowers of his soul provokes sensations. They are the only guarantee that he still is alive, but he knows full well that these vibrations are without lasting value. He vacillates between the role of being a sentimental spectator to his own inner life and his other role as a cynic, bored and tired of life, somebody who can demolish every gentle sentiment by demonic irony.

It becomes increasingly clear to Gram that it is impossible for him to live in this value-deflated space:

Ak, Herre, hvor længe?
Naar skal jeg overvinde denne evige Uro, denne nagende Utilfredshed og Utilfredsstillethed, denne Tørhed og Tørst gjennem alt mit Væsen. . . Jeg er som et Dyr i en Ørken hvor der ikke findes Vand; som en fanget Løve der løber om bag Burets Stænger søgende Friheden. Alt hvad der er uroligt og higende og speidende og længselsfuldt og fredløst har samlet sin Kval i mig, ligger mig i Brystet som en slidende Vaande. (Garborg 203)

The text of the novel, with its many jumps, gaps, and inconsistent trains of thought, shows that Gabriel Gram is looking desperately for a way out.

And the text is his own, consisting of entries in his diary covering several years and some attempts at combining the scattered materials into a unifying interpretation of them. Gram dreams about writing a novel and, through it, creating an ordered structure of meaning. But nothing comes of it. Fragments, scattered impressions, and reflections: these are the results that the text offers the reader. Gram's own comments on the act of writing clearly reveal his realization that his is not art that transcends and redeems; it can only dissolve the world into new fragments. Gradually suicide becomes an insistent alternative. At any rate the idea of suicide plays an important role for him. However, in this case madness or a disintegration of personality seems a more likely "solution" to his dilemma.

In the end the solution is a different one. Gabriel Gram apparently achieves contact with one of those values of existence which before has been confidently deflated, that is, Christianity. The novel ends with Gram's conversion, and in terms that emphatically diagnose his problem as a crisis of value in a world that has lost the centre that alone can constitute its meaning:

> Han indsætter Værdier for mig; hvad der laa spredt og henslængt og meningsløst for mit Blik, blir sammenhængende, sjælfuldt. Han reconstruerer Tilværelsen for mig ved at give den et Centrum. (Garborg 221)

However, if the diagnosis is clear, the cure is more problematic. The passage just cited has two possible subject referents. "Han" may refer to Christ, but is more likely to refer to a certain Doctor Thisted, who becomes a therapist of sorts for Gabriel Gram. But he is also the doctor of Fanny Holmsen, the woman who has been and continues to be the object of Gram's fantasies of love. At the same time he has neurotically rejected her, and she has wounded him by entering into a marriage into which he — in essence — had frightened her. She is unhappy in her marriage, but according to Dr. Thisted the Church has brought her peace and calmed her nerves. Gabriel Gram may well be dreaming of achieving a secret and compensatory contact with her if he chooses to follow the course she has chosen. This becomes the new centre of his existence. "Vi skal træffes, hun og jeg, paa en bedre Maade end vi engang tænkte" (Garborg 221).

There were cultural critics in the 1890s who wished that Garborg would endorse his protagonist's conversion and bring him safely to an edifying conclusion. Yet there can be little doubt that the novel views its protagonist in an ironic light. His conversion is in fact an escape and a regression, rather than an exemplary solution to the existential problems confronting him. What Gram experiences is a crisis of values or an existential crisis of a general kind that is an integral part of "modernity" and not something from which one can escape.

*Trætte Mænd* is a representation of what Per Thomas Andersen calls "dekadansens problem": A man whose world has become decentred is impelled towards a new centre and a new system of values that may reconstruct Cosmos for the decadent personality. What is modern about

*Trætte Mænd* is not the "solution," but the fact that the novel makes a theme of a profound crisis of values, a crisis that in terms of intellectual history has its roots in, for example, Nietzsche and that has become a key element in twentieth-century modernism.

## From 1890 to 1990

*Trætte Mænd* is a novel characteristic of the 1890s. We may refer to its thematics as "neoromantic" or, in Garborg's own words, "neoidealist" — or we may describe it as a *fin-de-siècle* thematics typical of the transition period between the nineteenth and twentieth centuries. When the novel first appeared, it was felt to be both modern and topical, and today it is easy to see that central features of twentieth-century modernism are anticipated by its thematic foregrounding of existential crises and of the alienation from life experienced in the modern world to which man is condemned, yet from which he longs to escape. We are fully justified in describing *Trætte Mænd* as a premodernist novel.

Living in a world that is totally different from the 1890s, we are today on the threshold of another century. The science-fiction-like fantasies about "television" at the end of *Trætte Mænd*, which nobody at that time could have found believable, have long ago been overtaken by the course of technological developments, in a century that is at the same time the most bloody and the most fertile in human history. Superb technological triumphs, marvels of communication, and well-organized mass killings: these are all part of the twentieth century. The deflating of values, too, has continued. This has in various ways been made a theme in modernist art — and no less so in that later phase which we sometimes refer to as postmodernism. It is commonly said that postmodernism represents not only the definitive collapse of traditional values as a basis for ethical validation but also an acceptance of an existence in which all contact with a unifying mythology has become an impossibility. Per Thomas Andersen quotes the Danish critic Helmut Friis, who makes use of the term "homo decorans" to designate postmodern man:

> Postmoderniteten kendetegnes af, at de sidste rester af trosgenstande, de sidste store helheder, og fortællinger, der gav retning og mening til historien, har mistet deres troværdighed. (Andersen 378)

The dissolution of the great "totalities" that gave direction and meaning to history began in a way in the 1890s, with early modernism. Per Thomas Andersen writes briefly, but interestingly, about the connections that exist between postmodernist fiction and the structural features he has discovered in the novels of the decadent period. He stresses, however, that the *fin-de-siècle* "decadent" and postmodern man may solve the crisis of value in different ways. The "decadent," like Gabriel Gram, may choose passivity or regressive escape, while the postmodernist tends to choose an anarchistic solution. Andersen quotes Brian McHale, who in his book *Postmodernist*

*Fiction* (1987) maintains that the postmodernist tends to meet the collapse of values with a form of anarchism: "This is precisely the postmodern condition: an anarchic landscape of worlds in the plural" (Andersen 384).

## Jan Kjærstad: *Rand*

This postmodern perspective invites a comparison between the literature of decadence from the end of the last century and recent works of fiction. Among modern novels I select Jan Kjærstad's *Rand* (1990), which in my view clearly thematizes a postmodern crisis of value. There are connections and similarities between *Trætte Mænd* and *Rand*. But the difference between the two novels is more striking. Whereas in *Trætte Mænd* we have to do with a crisis of values that is evident from the very beginning of the book, the crisis in *Rand* is at first only latent, and it is moreover a crisis that hardly ever becomes conscious to the protagonist himself. Nevertheless, the crisis is real enough here, too, and of such a kind that the text anticipates and foregrounds important features of postmodern culture, even if they are seen as if in a distorting mirror.

This novel cannot without difficulty be said to be representative. *Rand* is a book that fills the reader with repugnance. It has a terrifying course of action, mediated amorally and unfeelingly through the protagonist, who writes his own story and who on the surface is a successful, modern human being. He is a data specialist, who is equally at home with programmes and networks, works flexible hours, and enjoys a comfortable income. He is happily married to an air hostess. The couple have two children, who are both at school abroad. In a few months at the end of the 1980s this man, whose name we never learn, kills six people in the streets of Oslo, without any specific motive. He subsequently applies for a job as a data specialist in the police force in order to help solve the case of the mysterious and terrible murders. There are good reasons for classifying such a novel as a pathological study of a mentally deranged person. But such a classification does not dispose of the text. *Rand* is a novel of powerful fascination, carefully worked out in every detail, and with a gripping sub-text.

## A "Known" Sub-Text

To me, hidden patterns have become clear through comparison with the premodern, decadent novels analyzed by Per Thomas Andersen. Andersen's formulations also help us to describe *Rand*.[1] Its structure, too, is based on a fundamental opposition between a world devoid of value and an ordered, coherent, and meaningful universe. Again the thematic core lies in a mythic Chaos-Cosmos problematic. On the other hand, in this modern novel there is no real fall into a state of decadence. There is no traditional world of values initially, to which the protagonist is either positively tied or in opposition. The only cosmos he knows is the electronic network, which enables communication but entails no risk of human closeness. The protagonist is his own centre, and up to a point that is enough. He lives his life "i det forskjellsløse rom, der det ikke finnes noen verdier som gir grunnlag for orientering." Even so, on the basis of the text it is possible to reconstruct fragments of a world with other parameters, and it is the need for meaning that drives forward both the action and the writing.

"Arne Garborgs plass" is the very first street name to be mentioned in *Rand*: "Akkurat her inntraff det første forbausende — jeg kunne si: det første signalet om at jeg uventet sto i ferd med å erverve meg nye kunnskaper," we are informed (10). This may or may not suggest a conscious use of intertextuality on Kjærstad's part. However that may be, there is a definite formal kinship between the two novels. Also *Rand* is a first-person novel, consisting of undated diary entries covering a period of less than a year. The entries contain both detailed reports of what happens and meticulous reflections on it. As in *Trætte Mænd*, the process of writing is "thematized" in *Rand*, and here too as noncommunicative action. The writer alone is the addressee of the text, and he knows this: "Jeg må skrive det ned fordi jeg aldri vil kunne fortelle det til noen" (51). Even so, the very act of writing is an important process:

> Dette bekrefter noe jeg har ant hele tiden: at dødsfallene umulig kan være meningsløse, at noe. . . om du kunne. . . hvis bare. . . at en sammenheng. . . Dette styrker meg også i bevisstheten om å skrive disse hendelsene ned, i vissheten om at de fortjener å bli fortalt, i seg selv, tross at de ikke kan fortelles høyt og langt mindre publiseres. Her jeg sitter, som en kaptein ved skatollet, føler jeg meg — uten å få stormannsnykker (allikevel litt skremt?) — som Darwin. Jeg så engang et TV-program om ham (fra BBC?), om hvordan han skrev dagbok eller noterte om bord på "Beagle," disse opptegnelsene som da virket kaotiske og som den unge Darwin selv neppe visste hva han skulle bruke til eller iallfall følgene av, men som gjemte kimen til det som en gang skulle bli en ny og revolusjonerende erkjennelse. (125)

Because it creates order, this act of writing makes a paradoxical contrast to the dominant aspects of the protagonist and his way of life. He is a modern city dweller who feels no loyalty to any centre outside himself. He exists in the changeable moment and accepts it. He is, as it were, totally without any awareness of the past, and to such a striking extent that it becomes thematically relevant. The only thing he appears to remember from his childhood is the fact that his father had difficulties in finding parking space for his car. His mother or other close relatives are strikingly absent. Nor does his cultural heritage have any significance for him. He has read very little. His most important literary references are simple ones: "Som barn leste jeg *Greven av Monte Christo* — den gjorde til gjengjeld inntrykk" (48). Ibsen is a name to him, but it represents something remote and irrelevant:

> Jeg kunne se plakatene for Nationaltheateret, opplyste montre med utydelige fotografier. *Hedda Gabler, Gjengangere*. Passé, tenkte jeg. Fullstendig passé. Som om Jorden fremdeles var solsystemets, ja, Melkeveiens sentrum. (113)

His knowledge of the Bible, too, is of the most cursory and approximate nature: "Står det ikke et sted i Bibelen at mennesket ble skapt av jord?" (90). He has more immediate contact with classical music. Both Monteverdi and Mahler, as well as others, are to be found on his shelves. But he can scarcely identify a single piece of music. His most important spiritual sustenance comes from the mass media, for example, his television set with its sixteen channels, which he can manipulate by remote control. This gives him a certain power, but no great excitement: "Jeg har sett alt før" (21). "Jeg ser mye, men jeg ser lite" (33). He feels most strongly about a morning radio programme, "Nitimen," a popular programme of light music, chitchat, and cosiness: "Jeg mener det virkelig: jeg elsker denne kosestunden, denne pludrende og uhøytidelige atmosfæren — takket være Nitimen er jeg sjelden på jobben før halv elleve" (23).

## Postmodern Landscapes and Postmodern Love

The writer's real domain is the big city landscape, sterile and without traditions. He feels most at home when he sees modern shopping centres growing up around him. Inside them he feels a kind of international atmosphere, without connections to any local culture:

Jeg liker supermarkeder. Jo større, jo bedre. Supermarkeder virker ansporende på fantasien. Der jeg glir med trillevognen mellom høye, fargerike hyller, innbiller jeg meg at jeg er i Venezia, ror med gondol på kanalene, fjetrende blikkfang på alle kanter. (42)

The day when the new supermarket "Oslo City" opens, he experiences a postmodern sense of elation; it reminds him of being a tourist in Notre Dame. But it is the absence of difference in the new complex that fascinates him. It is identical with similar centres in other cities. And it is not newness in itself that moves him most, but rather the fact that the new may be identified through its own changeable nature:

Å komme inn i Oslo City var å komme inn i noe selvfølgelig. Ikke noe nytt. (Jeg tenkte hele tiden på hvor alminnelig og trivielt dette senteret ville virke om fem år, to år, ett år.) Jeg tror attpå til jeg tenkte på dagen da det skulle bli revet. (156)

Glass and concrete, muzak and glowing colours, an intimate absence of contact and a cosmopolitan absence of traditions, variation, and similarity — this is a rich mixture that pleases him:

Jeg nøt, gledet meg over de fremmede navnene: Cookie Man, déjà Vu, Ton Sur Ton, New York Corner, L'émigrant, Tie Rack, Panache, KappAhl. [. . .] Jeg følte meg hjemme, med min jakke fra Manhattan, mitt slips fra Bangkok, min after shave fra Roma. Jeg følte at jeg gled inn i miljøet, var en naturlig del av det, ja, *at dette sydende forretningssenteret var lagd for meg*, et menneske i utvidelse. [. . .] Jeg forsøkte å lytte til. . . nærmest *assimilere* musikken, en ny låt for hver butikk, en ny sound, en ny verden, lag bak lag, jeg gikk rundt i det strålende lyset, solte meg i neonfargene, speilte meg i krom. [. . .] Aller mest nøt jeg menneskene, dette mylderet, dette havet av ukjente historier. [. . .] Jeg var i rus. Jeg var tilbake. Alle disse. . . klisjéene. Jeg hadde trodd de var utbrukt. [. . .] Jeg stod rank i rulletrappen og hørte på dette. . . hva heter det. . . *sorlet* fra tusenvis av stemmer [. . .] ble visdom, ble et metafysisk sus. Jeg visste: Det var nettverket av disse trivielle samtalene (om priser, om utroskap, om matvarer, om utseende, om togtider) som skapte verden, denne verdenen jeg befant meg midt i. (156-57)[2]

He has comparable experiences at "Aker Brygge," a modern shopping centre erected on and around an old industrial site in Oslo. Here his postmodern value system becomes even clearer:

Jeg blir alltid slått av. . . hva jeg våger å kalle livsglede når jeg kommer inn i de omskapte verkstedshallene: de veldige og høye hvite rommene med utenpåliggende glassheiser og åpne gangforbindelser via broer, alle vindusrutene i taket og i kortveggene, terasser av frodige grønne planter, som hengende hager. Alt er så lyst, alt er så strålende, alt er så. . . Jeg tenker umiddelbart på Nitimen. [. . .] Et skipsverft der du nå får kjøpt sjøkart og røket laks, en maskinfabrikk der du nå klipper håret og kjøper compact discs. Jeg liker det. Jeg vet ikke hvorfor, men jeg liker det. Det gjør godt i hele kroppen. [. . .] Å komme inn på Aker Brygge er som å tre inn i en internasjonal sone. Det minner om de store flyplassene. Alt er likt. Det har ingenting med Norge å gjøre. Du kan være hvor som helst. I Milano, Melbourne, Montreal. [. . .] Du befinner deg liksom i transitt. (133-34)

It is an atmosphere that fits in well with Brian McHales's previously quoted precise characterization of the postmodern condition in his *Postmodernist Fiction*: "an anarchic landscape of worlds in plural."

There is a correlation between this multifaceted life experience tied to the changeable physical world and the rather special family life of the *Rand*-character and his wife, the air hostess working for SAS, on international routes. When she is at home, she is, as it were, in transit, and in her guest appearances she feeds him with all kinds of luxuries — delicious, exotic, canned delicacies as well as furnishes him with cultural knickknacks from all corners of the world and sophisticated sexual variations played out on richly coloured sheets. He is overwhelmed by the sexual sensations, happy to have her play the active and normative part. Of course he participates in the sexual act, but he is primarily an observer, with a keen appreciation of the picturesque qualities of all the variations. Sexual experience becomes something like a guided tour for the *Rand*-character, his sex serving, so to say, as a camera that records and registers. He observes in great detail, all the way into his orgasm, and what fascinates most is the unknown and alien:

Jeg forsøker så godt jeg kan å følge med, ser inn i dette ansiktet, dette perfekt sminkede fjeset, en kjent maske foran et menneske jeg ikke kjenner i det hele tatt. (148)

True, he maintains that they talk "about everything" after the love act, but it seems that this "everything" also refers primarily to a life dissolved into mere fragments and surfaces:

> Vi snakker lenge. Hun forteller om et besøk med Henrik i akvariet sør for Los Angeles, om delfiner som hoppet gjennom ringer. Hun mener det var et erotisk syn. Jeg nevner at jeg kunne tenke meg en tur til London. [. . .] Vi snakker om andre ting. Ingeborg snakker om Romerriket. Hvorfor gikk det under? Jeg vet ikke. Vi snakker om Cecilie, om Henrik. Jeg sier: "Mine barn blir kosmopolitter som sin mor." (149)

## Chaos and Cosmos

The *Rand*-character distinguishes between what he likes and does not like. To that extent he has a certain superficial ability to appraise and judge. But moral evaluations are totally alien to his world. There is not a trace of pangs of conscience or regret after the spontaneous murders he commits. Nevertheless the murders may be seen as a perverted form of contact with a world of values that he has fallen from. The people who become his victims arouse a certain interest in him — or at any rate they awaken in him a sense of existential unease that he cannot account for. In conversations in which they insist on connections of which he has no conscious awareness, they take him to the verge of unconscious Chaos lying behind the well-ordered cosmos of everyday life. This contact with Chaos evokes in him an urge towards coherence, order, and meaning, as well as suppressed aggression and fear. The murders are precisely his response to this situation on the verge of the abyss. He experiences a sense of a radical deficiency, which demands to be undone, but in a world completely without any centre of meaning and without values capable of mediating between consciousness and unconscious Chaos, in such a world destructive, demoniac forces take charge. Confronted with this deficiency or absence, the only genuine response he can offer is to exercise a perverse sort of sociality. He kills, and the murders transform the victims into mythic figures in his solipsist universe — or Hell.

Limitations of space make it impossible to analyze this terrifying novel in all its details, but giving a few references to certain points in the text will demonstrate that a Chaos-Cosmos problematic is at the core of the novel. These passages show that the sub-text contains a fundamental theme of decadence, the fall from a value-potent world, which the *Rand*-character is unconsciously aware of, but from which he is fundamentally separated.

The *Rand*-character reports in detail on the conversations he has had with his victims. Everything they have said seems to acquire something like a centripetal force, making every word converge on a centre, where it becomes laden with meaning. This process foregrounds the idea of an unknown coherence, which in a way is still known but has been forgotten or suppressed. This becomes evident for the first time in his conversation

with the first victim, a conversation that has, as one of its themes, decadence and cultural decline, since the two characters talk about the sunken
Atlantis. Later that evening, the *Rand*-character describes it as follows in
his lonely diary:

> Mens han snakket, så jeg hele tiden ned i bakken. Det må ha vært på
> dette tidspunktet jeg øynet det. Eller sanset det. Et svakt lys gjennom en
> sprekk. En sprekk som ikke skulle ha vært der. Eller. . . Jeg makter ikke å
> forklare. Det lignet. . . Som om noen uventet rev bort et teppe og avslørte at
> du i virkeligheten sto på randen av et stup. Det vil si: det var ikke dette med
> stupet som var det fjetrende, men utsikten, den plutselige utsikten mot noe
> du ikke ante om. Denne. . . utvidelsen. (15)

With some variations, this pattern of experience is repeated also in the
notes about the other murders. For instance about murder Number 3, of a
young woman, we are told:

> Jeg får følelsen av å stå på et høyt stup, av å bevege meg mot kanten,
> millimeter for millimeter; en berusende følelse av å kunne miste balansen
> når som helst. [. . .] forsøker intenst å se bak alt dette, prøver å finne ut hva
> det skjuler. (70-71)

When he thinks back on murder Number 4, we are told in a similar manner,
"I et sekund så jeg noe gjennombrytende. En luke ned til et annet rom, et
vindu, en åpning" (117).

It is grotesque, but consistent, that this murderer, who cynically and
with great pleasure follows the uproar that these perplexing atrocities cause
in the media, insists that these murders must have some meaning. It is
consistent, too, and equally grotesque that he becomes more and more
fascinated by his victims. In his imagination he transforms them into
mythical objects that he can worship, and he is both proud of, and happy
about, his secret contact with such interesting people. He establishes an
inner, occult, solipsist community, in which he cultivates an exclusive
intercourse with the dead. They add a mythical dimension to his existence,
and the notion of a secret meaning behind the atrocities keeps at a distance
the disintegration threatening his value-empty existence.

> Jeg sitter stadig [. . .] og tenker på samtalene våre. Jeg har inntrykk av at
> hver replikk [. . .] gjemmer uante invitasjoner til tankeflukt, lik de trange
> sprekkene som fører inn i majestetiske dryppsteinsgrotter; at jeg dermed
> aldri vil bli ferdig med møtene, selv om jeg viet resten av livet til å utforske
> dem. Alene tanken på et "og," et "som" midt i en setning, kan få det til å klø
> i skallebenet. (86)

The effect is particularly powerful when the *Rand*-character discovers
that his victim Number 4, Dan Bergman, had been employed as a waiter at
Theatercaféen. He eats a memorial meal in this café, which assumes something of a ritual quality; it may bring to mind the idea of a sacrament as well
as of cannibalism:

Jeg gjorde meg flid til å yte hver bit, hver slurk rettferdighet. Hvert mikrogram krystet for smak, for lukt, for sansestimulerende muligheter. Samtidig tenkte jeg på Dan Bergmann. Kjøtt, vin, Dan Bergmann. Toner fra et flygel, speil i forgylte rammer, servitører som trancherte hjortestek, Dan Bergmann. (Kan en smak inneholde sannheten?) Jeg var ett med Dan Bergmann. (113)

## The Forgotten World of Values

This peculiar "holy communion" links up with other features in the text. Gradually the entries come to include more and more religious allusions. The *Rand*-character broods over patterns of interpretation, revolving around them like a moth around a candle. This becomes particularly insistent when he tells about a visit to the Jewish synagogue in Oslo, where he suddenly has intimations of being in contact with a mystery:

> Og dette språket — [. . .] er det Guds språk? Denne. . . hva heter det. . . liturgien, representerer den en magisk koreografi, som kan trenge gjennom til den andre siden? Jeg kan ikke la være å undre meg over denne gudens skjulthet. [. . .] På et ubegripelig vis kjenner jeg meg i slekt med disse menneskene som forsøker [. . .] å tvinge fram en. . . annen virkelighet. [. . .] Alt dette taler til meg. Hvorfor? Fordi jeg ikke forstår det! Og likevel lar det meg ane [. . .] noe hellig. (Igjen dette ordet. Går det an å bruke det?) (146, 148)

The religious allusions never go beyond the level of cliché, but even the clichés testify to the character's being aware of other frames of interpretation than the ones he himself recognizes as valid. And the text signals that he in fact has roots in a world of values entirely different from the electronic programmes of his profession and the postmodern city-world in which many of his daily activities are anchored. This basic difference becomes apparent, for example, in the very act of writing, when he writes in a way that is markedly different from the ways in which he conducts his other activities. This data specialist does not write his notes on a computer, but with pen and ink and on the writing lid of an old bureau. The bureau is an heirloom left to him by relatives whom he knows little or nothing about. The drawers of the writing desk are locked, and he does not possess a key. What he appears to know nothing about is nevertheless visible: on the wall above the bureau there are pictures of old family farms and portraits of his ancestors in oval frames. We hear about all this from the very first murder on, and gradually it becomes clearer and clearer. The eyes from the past pursue the *Rand*-character in the act of writing. At the same time he emphatically distances himself from his ancestors; they represent a world utterly different from his own. After murder Number 3 he writes,

> Jeg har sittet her ved skatollet og skrevet ned denne hendelsen så samvittighetsfullt som mulig. Jeg har en god hukommelse. Jeg er oppskaket,

men glad. Jeg føler at jeg står ved en milepæl, selv om steinen har en skrift
jeg ikke kan tyde, heller ikke hvor langt det er igjen. Når jeg ser opp mot
veggen der portrettene av forfedrene våre henger, hundre år gamle, fiskere,
bønder, virker de like fjerne som dinosaurer, en utdødd rase. (74)

But the distant dinosaurs remain in place, and they have a paradoxical
existence. The protagonist himself holds on to them. Screwing up new
hooks for pictures of ancestors and of ancestral farms as he continues to
write: this is part of the process; in fact the murders hasten the process. And
when he is forced to inquire into the backgrounds of the people he has
killed, he is again confronted with his own background, which he cannot get
rid of, even though he consciously disowns it. The fifth murder may in fact
be interpreted as a reflex of moral evaluations that he has inherited from the
past. When the frivolous Magnus Davidsen, a man of many masks, is about
to abandon himself to his animallike sexuality, the protagonist rises up in
protest, and this time he kills in a fury over the "stunted" nature of his
interlocutor. He is himself aware that his reaction this time may not be
entirely arbitrary: "Jeg er ikke fremmed for at besøket på Folkemuseet spilte
inn" (136).

The Folk Museum has given him a special, if you like, "stunted" contact
with the past. He himself lives in a tenement building at Enerhaugen, an old,
but modernized, part of Oslo. In the museum he sees several old houses
from this part of the town, but he strongly rejects the idea that there may be
any kind of connection between him and this past:

> Jeg kjente heller ingen intuitiv sammenheng, dette man kaller "historiske
> røtter." Tvert om. Det var umulig. Jeg ønsket ikke at så mye som en rottrevl
> skulle berøre denne bakevjen. Bare tanken ga meg angstfornemmelser.
> Kjente jeg lukten av. . . lik? (130)

Even so, prowling around and looking in through the windows, he is
magnetically drawn to these old things. Behind a windowpane he sees a
picture that he is able to recognize from his childhood, "den milde, langhårede
Jesus: Se, jeg staar for Døren og banker" (130). And at this point he again
senses that he is in contact with the eyes that watch over the process of
writing at the old bureau:

> Som å se inn av de ovale rammene på veggen hjemme; inn i rommene
> på gamle slektsgårder som klamret seg til en fjellhylle mellom hav og
> himmel.
> Hvor lenge siden. Hvor. . . Det hadde ikke noe med meg å gjøre. Umulig.
> Århundrer imellom.
> Jeg sto ved et hus fra det gamle Enerhaugen, et hus fra det stedet jeg nå
> selv bodde, jeg sto med ansiktet mot vinduet og fornektet. Sa nei til denne
> veggen, denne begrensningen, denne. . . stillstanden. (130)

The pattern is clear. An old world of values is atavistically present, although
it has been abandoned. The fall — his decadence, if we prefer — is also very

clear, both through the conscious renunciation and in the representation of the old, which resists the fall, "clinging to a mountain shelf." In the old world hangs the picture of Jesus. It doubles itself, taking on a contemporary shape and becoming profane as it turns into Theo Zakariassen, the man who is in charge of the investigation of the murders that the *Rand*-character has committed. This doubling is a nodal centre in the text. The identification of Jesus testifies to a latent awareness of a mythical-religious universe that also includes moral dimensions. Seeing the chief investigator "behind" the face of Jesus, the *Rand*-character in a sense establishes a secret, regressive contact with sources of moral authority. But this doubling is at the same time a radical expression of a supreme relativizing of the mythic universe. It becomes possible for the protagonist to hold onto a longing for Cosmos, while at the same time his demonic project, remote from any morality, becomes even more grotesque than before:

> Jeg visste jeg var på vei. Endelig, etter et halvt liv, var jeg på vei mot noe vesentlig, selv om jeg ikke visste hva det var.
> Omsider, etter århundrer var noen på vei.
> Bildet av Jesus hadde minnet meg om noe. Nå så jeg det: Theo Zakariassen. (131)

## The Resolution

The last part of *Rand* deals largely with the contact between the murderer/main protagonist and the chief investigator. A curious situation arises when the murderer becomes employed as a data specialist working with the staff of investigators. He gets perfect opportunities to obscure things, and at the same time he can also cultivate his regressive longing for an unknown order. He becomes the most highly trusted collaborator of his boss, having free access to all the information stored in the data base, the electronic cosmos "uten noe sentrum, bare forbindelser" (223). The database makes no discriminations and never asks about values. The data specialist can go in, checking and cross-checking at will, and call up series of pseudo-connections and thereby keep up a pseudo-contact with a mythical world that he refuses to acknowledge:

> Jeg vet det kan lyde overspent, men idet teksten ruller forbi, kommer jeg til å tenke på skriftrullene i synagogen, at også dette — det jeg ser på skjermen — er en slags hellig skrift, at den rører like mye ved den menneskelige eksistensens gåte, som Bibelens ord. (200)

This electronic cosmos cannot satisfy the urge for order, coherence, and meaning that is a latent "cause" of the murders. Generally it must be right to say that this urge can be satisfied only through a reintegration of those dimensions of existence that have become split off from the consciousness of the *Rand*-character. However, if that is to happen, he will have to face up to the consequences of the acts he has perpetrated and speak about the actual connections, which he alone knows but keeps hidden. This splitting has first and foremost got to do with moral considerations, but it also concerns sociality, that is, the ability to experience other people as independent, autonomous beings. His strategy is in a way to keep up this splitting. The text nevertheless testifies to the latent need to discover meaning; coherence remaining a fact and being strengthened in this process. Theo Zakariassen may function as a figure to whom fantasies of omnipotence can be transferred, but only for a time, since in this world he, too, exists in order to be deluded and manipulated. But when he voices his fear that perhaps there is no meaning whatsoever behind the murders, the possibility is felt to be disturbing and threatening:

> Jeg oppfatter muligheten som. . . umoralsk. Jeg kjenner noe bortimot sinne. "Det er jo fullstendig. . . " Jeg finner ikke uttrykket.
> "Hva om dette er de første meningsløse mord i historien?" sier Zakariassen.
> Jeg vifter i luften med hendene, merker at et helt ukjent raseri arbeider seg opp i meg. (229)

*Rand* is a novel without a resolution. Kjærstad does not bring his protagonist's story to a positive conclusion. It ends in a void, with all the facts available to the protagonist and the reader, but not to the investigators, who are constantly duped by the murderer, who in the final scene pats the chief investigator on the head, saying, "Du kan stole på meg. Det vet du" (259).

## Brief Conclusion

I have characterized *Trætte Mænd* as a novel typical of its time, the 1890s. There were many who resembled both the Gabriel Gram who lived in a state of decadence and the Gabriel Gram who fled from that state into a safer space. It is true that Gabriel Gram is exposed to irony, but it is in a way permissible to feel kinship with him.

Is *Rand*, too, a novel typical of its time? The question is not simply disturbing: we protest against being compared with the murderer. Yet the most disturbing thing is perhaps that there is a still more profound irony in the modern novel. The *Rand*-character is also normal and recognizable, not least in his many banal value choices, which express his inability to evaluate values. Paradoxically he is still governed by his relation to values, above all when he abandons himself to the demonic and kills. The thematics that Per Thomas Andersen discovered the premodern decadent writers had in common may also be found in the postmodern text that the *Rand*-character shapes under the gaze of ancestors in oval frames:

> I det forskjellsløse rom, der det ikke finnes noen verdier som gir grunnlag for orientering, i dette homogene rom kan mennesket ikke leve.

# Notes

[1] In a richly suggestive study emphasizing aesthetic and formal, rather than thematic, aspects of the novel, Knut Brynhildsvoll has drawn attention to the intertextual interplay between *Rand* and Norwegian literature of the 1890s, in particular Knut Hamsun's *Sult* (in Brynhildsvoll).

[2] In the quoted Norwegian text, broken thoughts are represented by unspaced ellipsis points; therefore, deletions of text are made according to the Norwegian usage of ellipsis points within brackets.

# Works Cited

Andersen, Per Thomas. *Dekadanse i nordisk litteratur 1880-1900*. Oslo: Aschehoug, 1992.

Brynhildsvoll, Knut. "Die neo-manieristische *ars combinatoria* des Jan Kjærstad. Am Beispiel des Romanen *Rand*." In *Präsentationen. Norwegische Gegenwortsautoren mit Originalbeiträgen vor Tor Åge Bringsværd, Kjartan Fløgstad, Jan Kjærstad*. Ed. Knut Brynhildsvoll. Artes et Littera Septentrionales. Kölner Studien zur Literatur-, Kunst- und Theaterwissenschaft 10. Leverkusen: Literaturverlag Norden Mark Reinhardt, 1990.

Garborg, Arne. *Trætte Mænd*. 1890. Rpt. in vol. 3 of *Skrifter i samling*. "Jubilæumsutgaava." Kristiania [Oslo]: A. Aschehoug (W. Nygaard), 1922. 7 vols. 1921-22.

Kjærstad, Jan. *Rand*. Oslo: Aschehoug, 1990.

The decadent tone of Western literature, art and society in general was credited to the upset of *fin de siècle* — "the end of the cycle," the close of a century. The decadent style . . . embodied flamboyant moral corruption, fascination with the artificial and a clever but despairing pessimism. With appropriate deceit, the very word "decadent" (from Vulgar Latin *decadere*), could pass as etymologically rooted in "decade" (Late Latin *decas*).

The current, as-yet-unlabeled decade will mark the end of a thousand-year cycle, a big, fat millennium, and there are plenty of signs that the millennial New Year's bash has already begun . . . the mounting craziness.

Travis Charbeneau,
"Apocalypse Soon," *Isthmus*, 1992

# VI. The Naess Bibliography

Fig. VI.1

Harald S. Naess, 1992
Pen-and-ink Portrait
by
Thomasin Ringler

# Professor Harald S. Naess: A Bibliography, 1952-92

A. Gerald Anderson
With Petter Naess

## 1952

"Peter Harboe Frimanns diktning. En studie i stil og metrikk" [Hovedoppgave]. Universitetet i Oslo, 1952.

"Undraðist liti Íslands." *Morgunblaðið* [Reykjavik] 11 July 1952. 7-8.

## 1955

"Bemerkninger om norskstudiet." *Filologen* 15.2 (1955): 8.

"Norwegian Studies." *The Year's Work in Modern Language Studies: 1954* 16 (1955): 364-73.

## 1956

"Norwegian Studies." *The Year's Work in Modern Language Studies: 1955* 17 (1956): 428-42.

## 1957

"Engelsk teater." *Morgenbladet* [Oslo] 52 (1957): 3.

"Fritz Thaulow." *The Norseman* [London] 15 (1957): 98-100.

Introduction. *Ja, vi elsker: The Norwegian National Anthem, Yes We Love with Fond Devotion.* Words by Bjørnstjerne Bjørnson. Music by Rikard Nordraak. Trans. G. M. Gathorne-Hardy. Oslo: Norsk Musikforlag [1957]. [1-2, 5].

"Norwegian Studies." *The Year's Work in Modern Language Studies: 1956* 18 (1957): 415-27.

"Vår tids helt?" *Morgenbladet* [Oslo] 2 Mar. 1957: 3.

## 1958

"Engelsk teater." *Morgenbladet* [Oslo] 82 (1958): 3.

"Modern Norwegian Literature." *Modern Languages* 39 (1958): 11-17.

"Modern Norwegian Poetry." *Modern Languages* 39 (1958): 49-56.

"Modern Norwegian Theatre." *Modern Languages* 39 (1958): 99-101.

"Norwegian Studies." *The Year's Work in Modern Language Studies: 1957* 19 (1958): 462-78.

"Ny engelsk Ibsen." *Morgenbladet* [Oslo] 10 Apr. 1958: 3.

## 1959

"Four Hamsun Letters." *Durham University Journal* 21 (1959): [1]-10.

"Knut Hamsun og verden — En efterkrigsrevy." *Morgenbladet* [Oslo] 31 July 1959: 3.

"Knut Hamsuns brevveksling med postmester Frydenlund." *Edda* 59 (1959): 225-68.

"Tre engelske Ibsenintervjuer i 90-årene." Ed. Harald S. Naess. *Ibsenårbok 1957-59* (1959): 141-60.

## 1960

"Norwegian Studies." *The Year's Work in Modern Language Studies: 1958* 20 (1960): 441-56.

"Norwegian Studies: Literature Since the Reformation." *The Year's Work in Modern Language Studies: 1959* 21 (1960): 396-407.

"The Three Hamsuns: The Changing Attitude in Recent Criticism." *Scandinavian Studies* 32 (1960): 129-39.


## 1961

"Hamsun on Hamsun." *The Norseman* 2 (1961): 12-15.

Rev. of *Ibsen and the Temper of Norwegian Literature*, by James Walter McFarlane. *Journal of English and Germanic Philology* 60 (1961): 356-57.

Rev. of *Ibsen: An Enemy of the People; The Wild Duck; Rosmersholm*, by Henrik Ibsen. Trans. and ed. J. W. McFarlane. *Modern Languages* 41 (1961): 163-64.

Rev. of *En ørn i uvær*, by Sten Sparre Nilson. *Scandinavian Studies* 33 (1961): 113-15.


## 1962

"Et forsøk over Vesaas' prosastil." *Edda* 62 (1962): 148-75.

"Knut Hamsun og Amerika." *Den fjerde internationale studiekonference i nordisk litteratur*. Århus: Aarhus Universitet, 1962. 171-88.

"Norwegian Studies: Literature Since the Reformation." *The Year's Work in Modern Language Studies: 1960* 22 (1962): 444-53.

"Scandinavian Studies in Great Britain and Ireland: An Inventory of People, Places, Publications." *Scandinavian Studies* 34 (1962): 54-64.


## 1963

Rev. of *Fra det moderne Amerikas Aandsliv*, by Knut Hamsun. *Scandinavica* 2 (1963): 148-50.

Rev. of *Knut Hamsuns egen røst*, by Christian Gierløff. *Scandinavian Studies* 35 (1963): 249-52.

## 1964

Rev. of *Hjalmer Hjorth Boyeson*, by Clarence A. Glassrud. *Scandinavian Studies* 36 (1964): 240-42.

"A Strange Meeting with Hamsun's *Mysteries.*" *Scandinavian Studies* 36 (1964): 48-58.

## 1965

"Knut Hamsun and Rasmus Anderson." *Scandinavian Studies: Essays Presented to Henry Goddard Leach.* New York: American-Scandinavian Foundation, 1965. 269-77.

Rev. of *Jonas Lies ungdom*. Vol. 2 of *Dikteren og det primitive*, by Hans Midbøe. *Scandinavian Studies* 37 (1965): 382-83.

## 1966

Introduction. *The Werewolf*. By Aksel Sandemose. Trans. Gustaf Lannestock. Madison: U of Wisconsin P, 1966. [vii]-xvii.

"Norwegian Literature." *1965 MLA International Bibliography of Books and Articles on the Modern Languages and Literatures* (1966): 295-96.

"Peter Harboe Frimann and the *Hornelen* Affair." *Scandinavian Studies* 38 (1966): 26-35.

## 1967

Introduction. *The Great Cycle.* By Tarjei Vesaas. Trans. Elizabeth Rokkan. The Nordic Translation Series. Madison: U of Wisconsin P, 1967. vii-xxvi.

"Knut Hamsun and America." *Scandinavian Studies* 39 (1967): 305-28.

"Norwegian Literature." *1966 MLA International Bibliography of Books and Articles on the Modern Languages and Literatures* 2 (1967): 319-22.

Rev. of *Fra* Den sidste gjest *til* "Mot ballade." Vol. 2 of *Hans E. Kinck. Livsangst og livstro* by Edvard Beyer. *Scandinavica* 6 (1967): 45-47.

Revs. of *Jonas Lies mesterskap* and *Jonas Lies alderdom*. Vols. 3 and 4 of *Dikteren og det primitive*, by Hans Midbøe. *Scandinavian Studies* 39 (1967): 290-92.

"Ukjente Hamsun-tekster." *Aftenposten* [Oslo] 5 Jan. 1967: 3.

## 1968

"Norwegian Literature." *1967 MLA International Bibliography of Books and Articles on the Modern Languages and Literatures* (1968): 324-26.

Rev. of *Bjørnsons skuespill på svensk scene*, by Harald Noreng. *Books Abroad* 42 (1968): 456.

Rev. of *Frå bygda til verda. Studiar i nynorsk 1900-tals dikting*, by Leif Mæhle. *Books Abroad* 42 (1968): 455.

Rev. of *". . . født til kunstner." Et Ibsen-portrett*, by Hans Heiberg. *Books Abroad* 42 (1968): 602-03.

Rev. of *Johanne Dybwad*, by Carla Rae Waal. *Scandinavian Studies* 40 (1968): 260-62.

Rev. of *Norsk litterær årbok 1967*, ed. Leif Mæhle. *Books Abroad* 42 (1968): 454.

Rev. of *Norsk verslære*, by Hallvard Lie. *Books Abroad* 42 (1968): 601-02.

## 1969

"From Hoel to Haavardsholm: Norwegian Literature Since World War II." *Literary Review* 12 (1969): [131]-48.

*Knut Hamsun og Amerika*. Oslo: Gyldendal, 1969.

*Norway Number*. Guest ed. Harald S. Naess. Spec. issue of *The Literary Review* 12.2 (1969).

"Norwegian Literature." *1968 MLA International Bibliography of Books and Articles on the Modern Languages and Literatures* (1969): 363-65.

"Norwegian Poetry Anno 1967." *Books Abroad* 43 (1969) 205-08.

Rev. of *The Birds*, by Tarjei Vesaas. Trans. Torbjørn Støverud and Michael Barnes. *Saturday Review* 27 Dec. 1969: 31.

Rev. of *Blå rytter*, by Finn Havrevold. *Books Abroad* 43 (1969): 432-33.

Rev. of *Henrik Ibsen. Miljø og mennesker*, by Einar Østvedt. *Books Abroad* 43 (1969): 616.

Rev. of *Et speil for oss selv*, by Leif Longum. *Books Abroad* 43 (1969): 431.

Rev. of *Teater i Norge*, by Eli Ansteinsson. *Books Abroad* 43 (1969): 615-16.

## 1970

"From Hoel to Haavardsholm." *Norway: Facts and Fairy Tales.* Oslo: Norwegian Ministry of Foreign Affairs, 1970. 5-15.

"Norwegian Literature." *1969 MLA International Bibliography of Books and Articles on the Modern Languages and Literatures* 2 (1970): 182-85.

Revs. of *Aske, vind og jord,* by Jens Bjørneboe;
*Diabas,* by Peter R. Holm;
*Samlede dikt,* by Gunvor Hofmo;
*Under ordre,* by Astrid Tollefsen; and
*Vårt daglige brød,* by Tor Obrestad. *Books Abroad* 44 (1970): 133-34.

## 1971

"American Attitudes to Knut Hamsun." *Studies in Scandinavian-American Interrelations: Dedicated to Einar Haugen.* Vol. 3 of *Americana-Norvegica.* Eds. Harald Naess and Sigmund Skard. Oslo: Universitetsforlaget, 1971. 339-60.

Introduction. "Our Power and Our Glory," by Nordahl Grieg. *Five Modern Scandinavian Plays.* Ed. Carl Erik Soya [et al.]. The Library of Scandinavian Literature 11. New York: Twayne Publishers and The American-Scandinavian Foundation, 1971. 279-98.

Rev. of *En fortolkning af* "Høit fra Træets grønne top," by Erik M. Christensen. *Books Abroad* 45 (1971): [133].

Rev. of *Garborg-studiar,* by Johannes A. Dale. *Books Abroad* 45 (1971): 140.

Rev. of *Headlines,* by Rolf Jacobsen. *Books Abroad* 45 (1971): 140.

Rev. of *Knut Hamsuns* Mysterier, by Gregory Nybø. *Books Abroad* 45 (1971): 139.

Rev. of *Symbol und Mythos: Studien zum Spätwerk Henrik Ibsens,* by Fritz Paul. *Scandinavian Studies* 43 (1971): 201-05.

Rev. of *"Æsthetisk Lutheraner" og andre studier i norsk senromantikk,* by Sigurd Aa. Aarnes. *Scandinavian Studies* 43 (1971): 199-201.

*Studies in Scandinavian-American Interrelations: Dedicated to Einar Haugen.* Eds. Harald S. Naess and Sigmund Skard. Vol. 3 of *Americana Norvegica.* Publications of the American Institute, University of Oslo. Oslo: Universitetsforlaget, [1971].

## 1972

*Norwegian Literary Bibliography, 1956-1970.* [Madison]: U of Wisconsin, Dept. of Scandinavian Studies, 1972.

"Norwegian Literature." *1970 MLA International Bibliography of Books and Articles on the Modern Languages and Literatures* 2 (1972): 171-74.

Rev. of *Dikt 1970*, by Finn Bjørnseth. *Books Abroad* 46 (1972): 127-28.

Rev. of *Det evige sekund*, by Alfred Hauge. *Books Abroad* 46 (1972): 127.

Rev. of *Life of Ibsen*, by Halvdan Koht. *Monatshefte* 64 (1972): 185-87.

## 1973

"Norwegian Literature." *1971 MLA Bibliography of Books and Articles on the Modern Languages and Literatures* 2 (1973): 177-81.

"Stein Mehren: Dialectic Poet of Light and Dreams." *Books Abroad* 47 (1973): 66-69.

"Ygdrasil Literary Society 1896-1971." *Norwegian Contributions to American Studies: Dedicated to Sigmund Skard.* Vol. 4 of *Americana-Norvegica.* Ed. Brita Seyersted. Oslo: Universitetsforlaget, 1973. 32-46.

## 1974

"Norwegian Literature." *1972 MLA International Bibliography of Books and Articles on the Modern Languages and Literatures* 2 (1974): 194-97.

"The Poetry of Rolf Jacobsen." *American-Scandinavian Review* 62 (1974): 265-69.

Rev. of *Knut Hamsuns* Landstrykere, by Allen Simpson. *Books Abroad* 48 (1974): 382.

## 1975

*Norwegian Literary Bibliography, 1956-1970: Norsk litteraturhistorisk bibliografi, 1956-1970.* Gen. ed. Kaare Haukaas. Norsk bibliografisk bibliotek 50. Oslo: Universitetsforlaget, 1975.

"Norwegian Literature." *1973 International Bibliography of Books and Articles on the Modern Languages and Literatures* 2 (1975): 203-07.

Rev. of *Illusions vej. Knut Hamsuns forfatterskab,* by Jørgen E. Tiemroth. *Books Abroad* 49 (1975): 336.

Rev. of *Norway,* by Ronald Popperwell. *Scandinavian Studies* 47 (1975): 392-94.


# 1976

"The Image of the Nineteenth Century Midwest in Knut Hamsun's Writings." *Norwegian Influence on the Upper Midwest. Proceedings of an International Conference, University of Minnesota, Duluth, Minnesota, May 22-24, 1975.* Ed. Harald S. Naess. Duluth: Continuing Education and Extension, U of Minnesota Extension, 1976. 50-53.

"Mitt møte med amerikansk universitetsliv." *Møte med Amerika. 25 nordmenn oppfatter amerikansk historie og nåtid.* Ed. Bjørn Jensen. Oslo: Aschehoug, 1976. 169-[76].

*Norwegian Influence on the Upper Midwest.* Ed. Harald S. Naess. Duluth: Continuing Education and Extension, U of Minnesota Extension, 1976.

"Norwegian Literature." *1974 MLA International Bibliography on the Modern Languages and Literatures* 2 (1976): 218-21.

"The Presentation of Scandinavia in America." *The Scandinavian Presence.* Ed. Erik J. Friis. New York: Harper's Magazine P, 1976. 179-208.

Rev. of *Fra Hamsun til Falkberget,* by Rolf Nyboe Nettum, Per Amdam, and Bjarte Birkeland. Vol. 4 of *Norges litteraturhistorie.* Ed. Edvard Beyer. *Edda* (1976): 176-78.


# 1977

Rev. of *Å lese skuespill. En innføring i drama-analyse,* by Leif Longum. *World Literature Today* 51 (1977): 634.


# 1978

Revs. of *Olav Duuns soger og forteljingar,* by Bjarte Birkeland, and *Olav Duun. Ei bok til 100-årsjubiléet,* ed. by Olav Dalgard. *Scandinavian Studies* 50 (1978): 339-41.

## 1979

Rev. of *Orda og menneskelivet*, by Magne Eide Møster. *Scandinavian Studies* 51 (1979): 194-96.

Rev. of *Prosessen mot Hamsun*, by Thorkild Hansen. *Scandinavian Studies* 51 (1979): 308-14.

## 1980

"Der Fall Hamsun." *Faschismus und Avantgarde*. Eds. Reinhold Grimm and Jost Hermand. Köningstein: Athenäum Verlag, 1980. 66-82.

Rev. of *Land of the Free: Bjørnstjerne Bjørnson's America Letters, 1880-1881*, by Eva Lund Haugen and Einar Haugen. *Scandinavian Studies* 52 (1980): 87-90.

## 1981

Rev. of *Forfatternes litteraturhistorie*, by Kjell Heggelund, Simen Skjønsberg, and Helge Vold. *Scandinavian Studies* 53 (1981): 491-94.

Rev. of *Makers of an American Immigrant Legacy: Essays in Honor of Kenneth O. Bjork*, ed. by Odd S. Lovell [sic.: Lovoll]. *Scandinavica* 20 (1981): 238-40.

*The Scandinavian Languages*. By Einar Haugen. WITS I, 1-2. Gen. ed. Harald S. Naess. Madison, WI: Dept. of Scandinavian Studies, U of Wis., 1981.

*Short Stories from Norway, 1850-1900*. Comp. and ed. Henning Sehmsdorf. WITS II, 3. Gen. ed. Harald S. Naess. Madison, WI: Dept. of Scandinavian Studies, U of Wis., 1981.

"Strindberg and Hamsun." *Structures of Influence: A Comparative Approach to August Strindberg*. Ed. Marilyn Johns Blackwell. University of North Carolina Studies in the Germanic Languages and Literatures 98. Chapel Hill: U of North Carolina P, 1981. 121-36.

## 1982

"En ukjent Kristiansander i Wisconsin." *Fædrelandsvennen* [Kristiansand, Norway] 7 Apr. 1982: 16.

Rev. of *Ethnicity Challenged: The Upper Midwest Norwegian-American Experience in World War I*, by Carl H. Chrislock. *The American Historical Review* 87 (1982): 868-69.

Rev. of *A History of Scandinavian Literature*, by Sven H. Rossel. *World Literature Today* 56 (1982): 702-03.

Rev. of *Triumph des Irrealismus: Rezeption skandinavischer Literatur im ästhetischen Kontext: Deutschland 1860-1910*, by Walter Baumgartner. *Monatshefte* 74 (1982): 86.

## 1983

Rev. of *Henrik Ibsen. Mennesket og kunstneren*, by Daniel Haakonsen. *Scandinavian Studies* 55 (1983): 75-77.

Rev. of *Ibsen: The Open Vision*, by John S. Chamberlain. *Scandinavian Studies* 55 (1983): 268-69.

## 1984

Hagen, Per. *On Both Sides of the Ocean: A Part of Per Hagen's Journey*. Eds. and trans. Kate Stafford and Harald Naess. Publications of the Norwegian-American Historical Association; Travel and Description Series 10. Northfield, Minnesota: The Norwegian-American Historical Association, 1984.

*Knut Hamsun*. Twayne's World Author Series 715. Boston: Twayne Publishers, 1984.

"Knut Hamsun i Amerika." *Aftenposten* [Oslo] 7 Aug. 1984: 6; 8 Aug. 1984: 6; 9 Aug. 1984: 6; 10 Aug. 1984: 6.

## 1985

"From Memoir to Fiction: Peter Peterson's 'På begge Sider av Havet.'" *Scandinavians in America*. Ed. J. R. Christianson. Decorah, Iowa: Symra Literary Society, 1985. 129-39.

Rev. of vol. 12 of *Norway: Review of National Literatures*, by Sverre Lyngstad. *Scandinavica* 24 (1985): 103-04.

Rev. of *Ole Edvart Rölvaag*, by Einar Haugen. *Scandinavian Studies* 57 (1985): 212-13.

"*Ringen sluttet*: In Defense of Abel Brodersen." *Facets of European Modernism*. Ed. Janet Garton. Norwich: U of East Anglia, 1985. 309-22.

## 1986

"Hamsun — *Victoria* — Victoria." *Scandinavian-Canadian Studies* 2 (1986): 51-58.

"Knut Hamsun and *Growth of the Soil.*" *Scandinavica* 25 (1986): 5-17.

Rev. of *Luft, vind, ingenting. Hamsuns desillusjonsromanar frå* Sult *til* Ringen sluttet, by Atle Kittang. *Scandinavica* 25 (1986): 82-84.

## 1987

"A. M. Iversen and the Scandinavian Moravians in Wisconsin." *From Scandinavia to America.* Eds. Steffen Elmer Jørgensen, Lars Scheving, and Niels Peter Stilling. Odense: Odense UP, 1987. 217-34.

*The History of Scandinavia.* By Stewart Oakley. WITS I, 3. Gen. ed. Harald S. Naess. Madison, WI: Dept. of Scandinavian Studies, U of Wis., 1987.

Introduction to *Fra Dalene,* by Knut Hamsun. *Scandinavica* 26 (1987): 109-10.

Rev. of *Fornnordiskt lexikon,* comp. by Åke Ohlmarks. *Scandinavian Studies* 59 (1987): 125-26.

Rev. of *Von 1860 bis zur Gegenwart,* ed. by Mogens Brøndsted. Vol. 2 of *Nordische Literaturgeschichte. Scandinavian Studies* 59 (1987): [479].

## 1988

*The Geography of Scandinavia.* By Robert Ostergren. WITS I, 4. Gen. ed. Harald S. Naess. Madison, WI: Dept. of Scandinavian Studies, U of Wis., 1988.

"Introduction: Utopias in Scandinavian America." *Scandinavian Studies* 60 (1988): [429]-36. Spec. issue (no. 4); see below.

Rev. of *Enigma: The Life of Knut Hamsun,* by Robert Ferguson. *Scandinavian Studies* 60 (1988): 514-18.

Rev. of *Ibsen's Heroines,* by Lou Salomé. Trans. by Siegfried Mandel. *Scandinavian Studies* 60 (1988): 108.

Rev. of *Norway,* comp. by Leland B. Sather. *Scandinavian Studies* 60 (1988): [107].

*Utopias in Scandinavian America.* Guest ed. Harald S. Naess. Spec. issue (no. 4) of *Scandinavian Studies* 60 (1988).

## 1989

*Erasmus Montanus.* By Ludvig Holberg. Trans. Petter Naess. WITS II, 4. Vol. and series ed. Harald S. Naess. Madison, WI: Dept. of Scandinavian Studies, U of Wis., 1989.

"Georg Brandes and 19th Century Scandinavian Realism." *Neohelicon: Acta Comparationis Litterarum Universarum* 15.2 (1989): 113-34.

"Hamsuns tiggergang." *Aftenposten* [Oslo] 4 Oct. 1989: 41.

"Knut Hamsun." *Sigmund Freud to Paul Valéry.* Vol. 8 of *European Writers: The Twentieth Century.* Ed.-in-Chief George Stade. New York: Scribner's Sons, 1989. 21-43.

"Olav Duun Abroad." *Grenzerfahrung — Grenzüberschreitung: Studien zu den Literaturen Skandinaviens und Deutschlands: Festschrift für P. M. Mitchell.* Eds. Leonie Marx and Herbert Knust. Heidelberg: Carl Winter; Universitätsverlag, 1989. [193]-99.

Rev. of *Bjørnstjerne Bjørnsons Briefwechsel mit Deutschen,* by Aldo Keel. *Journal of English and Germanic Philology* 88 (1989): 55-56.

Rev. of *Livsfragmenter. Ni noveller,* by Knut Hamsun. Comp. and ed. Lars Frode Larsen. *Scandinavica* 28 (1989): 208-11.

## 1990

*Dictionary of Scandinavian Literature.* Ed.-in-Chief Virpi Zuck. Advisory eds. Harald S. Naess and Niels Ingwersen. New York: Greenwood P, 1990.

Hamsun, Knut. *Knut Hamsun: Selected Letters.* Vol. 1: *1879-1898.* Eds. Harald Næss and James McFarlane. Trans. James McFarlane. Norwich: Norvik, 1990.

*Icelandic Libraries & Archives.* By Dennis Hill. WITS I, 5. Gen. ed. Harald S. Naess. Madison, WI: Dept. of Scandinavian Studies, U of Wis., 1990.

Rev. of *Fra Tullin til Sandemose. Studier i norsk litteratur,* by Harald Noreng. *Scandinavica* 29 (1990): 128.

## 1991

"Norwegian Literature on the Prairie: One Week at the University of Wisconsin." *Norwegian Literature 1991.* Ed. Johan Fr. Heyerdahl. Special issues of *The Norseman* 31.4-5 (1991). Oslo: Normanns-Forbundet; NORLA; NFF, 1991. 56-59.

## 1992-

Hamsun, Knut. *Knut Hamsuns brev.* Vol. 1: *1879-1895.* Ed. Harald Naess. Oslo: Gyldendal, 1993. 6 vols. projected.

*The Heroine in Scandinavian Literature.* WITS II, 6. Vol. and series ed. Harald S. Naess. Madison, WI: Dept. of Scandinavian Studies, U of Wis., 1993.

*A History of Norwegian Literature.* Ed. Harald S. Naess. Lincoln, Nebraska: U of Nebraska. Vol. 2 of *A History of Scandinavian Literature.* General ed. Sven Rossel. Lincoln: U of Nebraska P, 1993.

"Introduction to Scandinavia." [A project of video and written lectures supported by the Nordic Council of Ministers.] Harald S. Naess, gen. ed. and coordinator of an initial six-topic "Reader" and "Study Guide for Students" and a "Study Guide for Instructors." Projected for 1994.

Letter to Ron Whitehead, Mar. 28, 1992. In *Thinker Review* [Louisville, KT] 2: 339. Concerning place names used by Knut Hamsun and James Joyce.

There is no heroic poem in the world but is at bottom a biography, the life of a man; also, it may be said, there is no life of a man, faithfully recorded, but is a heroic poem of its sort, rhymed or unrhymed.

Thomas Carlyle,
"Sir Walter Scott," 1838

. . . ours has been the most terrible/most wonderful century, a fitting finale for the last thousand years of what passes for progress . . . Noting the furious momentum of this "progress," who can look forward to the next millennium without a similar or even enhanced sense of dread?

> Travis Charbeneau,
> "Apocalypse Soon," *Isthmus*, 1992

. . . we're not rocks, we can't just wait, even if we go faster than we should, we . . . And wait for what? God . . .

> Tony Kushner,
> *Angels in America: Perestroika*,
> Los Angeles Performance, 1992

Nothing's lost forever. In this world, there is a kind of painful progress. Longing for what we've left behind, and dreaming ahead.

> Tony Kushner,
> *Angels in America: Perestroika*,
> Los Angeles Performance, 1992

I believe everything breathes; even . . . stone must utter a blissful sigh every millenium.

> Glenway Wescott,
> *Continual Lessons*, 1990